EIGHT DECADES

ESSAYS AND EPISODES
BY AGNES REPPLIER

BOSTON

HOUGHTON MIFFLIN COMPANY

The Riverside Press Cambridge

MGE

The Riverside Press
CAMBRIDGE · MASSACHUSETTS
PRINTED IN THE U.S.A.

CONTENTS

EIGHT DECADES

EIGHT
DECADES

1867

I AM ten years old, and I can read. There does not seem
to be anything remarkable about this circumstance, seeing
that most little girls of ten have been reading since they
were seven; but it was not so with me. Three years of in-
tensive teaching have conquered the sluggish mind that
could not be brought to see any connection between the
casual and meaningless things called letters and all the
sweetness and delight that lay between the covers of
books.

And my nursery was rich in sweetness and delight. A
big old-fashioned bookcase crammed with volumes — the
best of them having been left behind by my half-brothers
when they took their flight from home. 'The Arabian
Nights' with double columns of print, and those 'small,
square agitating cuts' so dear to Henley's heart. 'Popular
Tales from the Norse' — wild reading that — and 'Robinson Crusoe' with many woodcuts, and 'Sandford and
Merton.' Then came my own treasures; Miss Edgeworth's
stories which I loved, and Miss Strickland's 'Tales from
History,' which I loved better still, and Hans Andersen's
fairy tales, and 'Undine,' and 'Sintram,' and Tieck's
'Elves,' and 'Paul and Virginia,' and 'The Nutcracker of
Nuremberg,' and two sedate volumes of verse entitled
'The Schoolgirl's Garland.'

This bookcase held all that was lovely to me in life, and when an edict, wise, harsh, and menacing, closed its doors, I was left, a wretched little Peri, standing tear-drenched in an arid wilderness. My mother, pardonably tired of the long years wasted on the first steps in the education of a child who she knew was not a fool, gave strict orders that no one should read me a line. The world of reality closed in upon me, and what did the world of reality mean in 1867 to a little girl whose days were uniformly uneventful? A walk in the dull city streets, a skipping rope on my own pavement, and a patchwork quilt which I was well aware would never reach fulfilment. Amid these depressing surroundings I spent a few days of blank despair. Then I sized up the situation, surrendered at discretion, and quickly, though not easily, learned to read.

And because I was so late learning, I brought a ten-year-old mind to bear upon all I read. Ten is a wonderful age. So, too, is twelve, and possibly fifty; but there is a good deal of wasted time between. The first book I read when I realized that all print was open — though not necessarily intelligible — to me was Hayward's translation of 'Faust.' This was no nursery product, and I raided my mother's shelves in the library to secure it, being moved thereto by pure childish curiosity. A blessed custom of my infancy ordained that every living-room should be dominated by a good-sized centre table, and that on this centre table should repose those ponderous illustrated volumes for which our parents spent vast sums of money, and which we children were never tired of examining. The most attractive and the most bewildering book on my own table was Retzsch's 'Outlines of "Faust,"' 'Fridolin,' and 'The Song of the Bell.' The text was in German. My mother told me the story of 'Fridolin' (it is the kind of story which is sure to be told to little girls); and 'The Song of the Bell' is so transparently simple that even my limited intelligence could grasp its significance. But 'Faust' is of a different order, and in the second part of that deathless, but not facile, poem Retzsch let himself go as far as mortal man has dared. Hayward's translation stopped short with the first part, and I was left to reconstruct the second, with such help as the 'Outlines' could give me — a big job for a child of ten. It took me a long time to get it settled, not satisfactorily, but in working order. Twenty years later I read Goethe's version. It seemed to me to lack coherence and continuity. My own painstaking interpretation remained firmly fixed in my memory.

In this year of grace, 1937, juvenile literature comes tumbling from the press as inexhaustibly as detective fiction. Consequently children, so I am told, read a book once as we read a detective story once (if at all), and turn naturally to something new. But of what earthly good or pleasure is a book which is read only once? It is like an acquaintance whom one never meets again, or a picture never seen a second time. In those joyous months which followed my conquest of print ('Bress de Lawd I'se free!') I read the books I loved best over and over again. A new one had crept in during my period of banishment. It was called 'The Young Crusaders,' and was a tale of the Children's Crusade. I read it from the first word to the last in a passion of pity and pain. When I had finished, I gave a long sigh, turned back to the beginning, and started anew upon its absorbing pages. Thank God I have been able to do the same thing in my old age, notably with Robert

Nathan's 'Road of Ages,' which I re-read instantly while its delicate loveliness was fresh in my mind and heart.

Until I had mastered print, my memory was abnormally retentive. There was nothing to disturb its hold. My mother taught me *viva voce* a quantity of English verse, sometimes simple as befitted my intelligence, sometimes meaningless, but none the less pleasant to the ear. I regret to say that I was permitted and encouraged to repeat these poems to visitors. Why they ever returned to the house I cannot imagine. Perhaps they never did.

One experience, however, remains etched clearly in my memory. A year or so before my tenth birthday, and while I was still steeped — not in ignorance, I protest, but in illiteracy — I was taken to Baltimore, and was privileged to recite 'The Guerillas' before its distinguished author, Severn Teackle Wallis. This gentleman was then at the height of his popularity, having been imprisoned fourteen months for inflammatory language anent the Federal Government. He was destined, like many another malcontent, to become an acquiescent citizen, and also a brilliant leader of the Maryland Bar; but when I was eight his great abilities had yet to be recognized. He was a rebel poet, the delight of rebel hearts. Therefore I stood upon a chair — having the shortness incidental to my years — and one of my grown-up cousins smoothed down my little skirt, and whispered impressively: 'Now do your very best. This is the chance of your life to distinguish yourself.' I wonder if 'The Guerillas' exists anywhere today, save in my faithful memory. I wonder what Mr. Wallis thought of his lurid lines, falling from my infant lips. I wonder if their luridness was ever before so apparent to his intelligence.

And now with my tenth birthday safely past, and the conquest of print safely accomplished, I am going to be sent to boarding school. My mother, reasonably weary of my education, has resolved that it shall be continued as far as possible from her jurisdiction. She knows what depressing items of information it will include. Perhaps she sees in the offing those little imps called numerals, as difficult to master as letters, and leading up to nothing but sums, which are an inadequate compensation. With a sigh of relief she is shipping me off to join the hitherto unknown ranks of childhood, to make war, without being aware that I was making war, against my elders, to bear my part in 'the losing battle against arithmetic, good manners, and polite conversation.'

My own sentiments in the matter are of no interest or concern to anybody. In those serene days adults would have as soon thought of consulting a kitten as of consulting a child when the disposal of either was under consideration. If the kitten or the child were a normal product of its time, it acquiesced inevitably, and the current of its little life was changed. Mine was to be changed beyond recognition or recall. Solitude and story books were about to slide into a dim past. Little girls brimming over with a superfluity of energy would absorb my simplified emotions. To some of them my heart would go out in quick recognition of companionship. A few of them were destined (the Saints be praised!) to be my friends for life. All of them were to seem of infinitely more consequence to me than the immortal children I had left behind between the covers of books. If ever a ten-year-old was fitted for a communal life, I was that happy child.

And what about my education, which was after all the

reason, or the excuse, for sending me from home? What
did the word imply seventy years ago? In my case a
fairly fluent knowledge of French, unloved, but inescap-
able because universal pressure bore down all resistance.
Snippets of history without continuity or the grace of
understanding. Arithmetic — well, the average guinea-
pig would have learned as much of that medley as I did.
And finally, some years later, when I was halfway to another decade, and had begun to understand the possible
pleasures of study, the humorous gods, who had neglected
but not forsaken me, sent to my aid the most fantastic
Latin master who ever jerked a pupil along the paths of
learning. I never saw a Latin grammar, that sure and
strong foundation. I never read Caesar's 'Commentaries,'
about which I had a good deal of curiosity. In their place
I was sent frisking along with Ovid's 'Metamorphoses'
(a modified version), a dictionary, and a teacher whose
pleasure in what he taught far exceeded his interest in the
schoolgirl he was teaching.

To put the 'Metamorphoses' into French prose was my
daily task. It was stiff work, and never done well enough
to merit commendation. My teacher would wrinkle his
brows over my neat pages and bald statements, shorn of
every grace of diction. 'You have made it sound improbable,' he said once discontentedly.

'But it was improbable,' I replied, clinging to what I
felt was security.

He looked at me, and then out of the window at the vast
sky overhead. He shrugged his shoulders gently. 'Not
to Ovid,' he said.

Great is my debt to that remarkable man, for midway
in the first winter he promised me that I should read

Horace the following year. Moreover he pledged his word that no French should enter into the transaction; and by way of sealing the bargain he gave me (being, as I have said, unlike any other teacher in the world) a really beautiful edition of the poet. In those days all schoolbooks were as repulsive as publishers could make them. Their appearance went a long way in discouraging any intimacy with their contents. The costliness of my Horace suggested to me the propriety of covering it with paper muslin, a glazed and rattling substance much used for such fell purposes. This thrifty proposal was imperatively vetoed. The book, I was told, was to be looked at this year, read next year, and loved all my life.

'Suppose I don't love it?' I asked destructively.

There was no reply. A glance at the elderly gentleman sitting on the other side of the table told me plainly what he had in his mind; but as he was a highly paid master in a highly respectable school, he forbore to give it utterance.

1877

I AM twenty years old, and I have begun to write. It is the only thing in the world that I can do, and the urge is strong. Naturally I have nothing to say, but I have spent ten years in learning to say that nothing tolerably well. Every sentence is a matter of supreme importance to me. I need hardly confess that I am writing stories — stories for children, stories for adults. They get themselves published somewhere, somehow, and bring in a little money. Otherwise they would have no excuse for being; a depressing circumstance of which I am well aware. Then one day

— an important day for me — I meet Father Hecker, founder of the Paulist order, and am taken by him around the great Paulist Church in New York. He is old, scholarly, and profoundly democratic, as the word was then understood. When we emerge from the church he asks me suddenly and disconcertingly: 'Why do you write fiction?'

I stare at him aghast. I don't know why. Perhaps it has never occurred to me that I had a choice.

'You are not equipped for it,' he continues. 'You have no knowledge of life and no power of observation. Of course you are too young to have any knowledge of life' (and me twenty!); 'but you are not too young to have some power of observation, and you give no indication of it. Your stories are unconscious reflections of books you have read. You are essentially a bookish person, and you must travel along your appointed path if you are going to get anywhere.'

'But what,' I ask bewildered, 'am I to write?'

'Essays,' is the brief reply.

'I don't know how,' I admit, startled into humility, and forgetting that there had been such things as compositions at school.

Father Hecker ponders for a moment. 'Who is your favourite author?' he asks.

'Ruskin,' I answer promptly. Seven out of ten 'bookish' young women would have made the same reply in 1877.

'Then write me an essay on Ruskin' (my companion had founded that admirable church monthly, *The Catholic World*) 'and I will see that it is published.'

So was I set on the right track, a track I was destined to tread painstakingly for a half century.

In my long life I have had but two words of valuable advice, and I have reason to be grateful for both of them. The first was Father Hecker's; the second came some years later when I was in New York helping Augustus Thomas and Francis Wilson to defend the stage child — a pampered and protected infant — from the assaults of Miss Jane Addams, who was striving with all her might to eliminate it. Perhaps this is the place to acknowledge my debt of gratitude to New York, for its friendly welcome when I was young and struggling, for its generous recognition of my long years of labour. I could not have kept upon the road if I had lacked this keen and kind incentive.

The theatre in which we were going to speak was a large one. I glanced at it despairingly. 'I shall never be heard, never!' I said. The chairman was about to murmur some encouraging fatuity when Augustus Thomas cut him short: 'Look after your consonants,' he said authoritatively; 'and your vowels will look after themselves.'

How simple are the great truths of life! Since that day long past I have been ever mindful of my consonants, and I have been heard.

One more incident of this eventful afternoon I take pleasure in recalling. The luncheon which was to follow the speeches was delayed. I was starving and said so. Francis Wilson, always sympathetic and benevolent, volunteered to forage, slipped into the dining-room, and brought me out a roll, a large and life-giving roll which I was glad to eat. When we went in to luncheon I perceived that he had discovered my place at table, removed my own roll, given it to me as an offering from the gods, and left me breadless and bereft. Moreover, being my next-door neighbour, and knowing my predatory instincts, he had removed his roll to the other side of his plate to be out of reach. 'You cannot eat your bread and have it too,' he said severely. 'This is with me a matter of principle.'

'Since when,' I asked bitterly, 'have you grown principled?'

'Since hearing Miss Addams,' he answered blithely, and I accepted defeat.

Forty years later Mr. Wilson recalled this circumstance to my memory. It pleased him to do so. He seemed to think that we did not need much to make us merry when we were young enough for merriment.

1887

I am thirty years old, and I have been to Boston. I have met men and women who fitted into my school days, who were part and parcel of my education. It was an edifying experience. Doctor Oliver Wendell Holmes, a very old gentleman, smiling and tottering, universally coddled and universally beloved, which was no more than his due. Mrs. Julia Ward Howe, that lady of a single inspiration. Mr. Thomas Bailey Aldrich, most debonair of authors and editors, whom the world — his world — took more seriously than he took himself. As a poet he was a craftsman. He loved delicacy and finesse. As an editor he had superlative courage, and a flair for new writers. They were as welcome to him as they were anathema to most editors of that day. He published Elizabeth Robins Pennell's first essay, and Amélie Rives's first story, and my first ambitious paper. He said that his protégés always made good, and he helped many of them to this happy consummation. In view of which fact it is pleasant to recall the place accorded him in letters, the popularity of the 'Bad Boy,' and 'Marjorie Daw,' and the justice of the gods in giving him a fair and charming wife who could wear strings and strings of amber (always a difficult ornament to assimilate), and who, like all good and helpful wives, firmly believed that her husband was a great man.

Another star in the firmament, and then at the height of her renown, was Mary Wilkins. Her brief and flawless stories of New England life had taken the reading world by storm. It was said of her that she resolutely refused to so much as open other people's books lest the pictures etched so clearly in her mind should grow blurred and confused. I rather think she knew how thin as well as fine was the vein of ore she worked, and that she had resolved none of it should be lost.

She was a small, thin, fair-haired woman. Seen across the room she looked like a girl. Seen close at hand she looked older than her age. She dressed sedately; but, sitting near her one day after luncheon, I noticed three brilliant and beautiful rings on her left hand. They blazed so proudly that my eyes constantly strayed towards them, a circumstance she was quick to observe. 'I can't help it,' I murmured apologetically. 'They will be looked at. They are so lovely.'

Miss Wilkins moved them round and round her thin little fingers. 'They are beautiful,' she said. 'Week before last I was so low in my mind, so dull and dispirited, that I came to Boston and bought these rings to cheer me up.'

Never in my life had I been so staggered by a simple piece of information. In the first place the thought that a book (Miss Wilkins had published but one) might, like Ali Baba's cave, be overflowing with jewels, gave me a new and exalted view of authorship. In the second place, I had never imagined rings as things one bought for oneself like hats and stockings. They were things given, or bequeathed by grand-aunts. Low spirits are common to us all; but who save Mary Wilkins, straightforward, circumscribed, sure of herself, and as unimaginative as a hatrack, would have thought of curing them with rings?

The most impressive figure that dawned upon my Boston horizon was Mr. James Russell Lowell. There was nothing to mar the impression. He looked as he should have looked. He spoke as he should have spoken. Distinction marked him as her own, and he responded without effort to her election. Always the centre of interest and attention, no one lost anything by granting precedence to a man so flawlessly urbane. His interest in me centred solely in the fact that I was a townswoman, or as good as a townswoman, of Walt Whitman, and fairly well acquainted with that unclassified genius. 'Why,' he asked, 'do you Philadelphians call him the Good Gray Poet?'

I explained that the name had been given to him by a fiery New York journalist, and that he, Mr. Whitman, liked it. He called himself the Good Gray Poet whenever he had the opportunity.

'I dare say,' grumbled Mr. Lowell. 'But nobody calls me the Good Gray Poet, though I am as gray as Whitman, and quite as good — perhaps a trifle better.'

He paused, and for an instant I was on the point of saying, 'Then there is only the poet to consider,' but I forebore. A half century ago how many Americans would have ventured to put the Camden storm-centre alongside of the finished Boston product, the riotous tosser of words alongside of the man whom 'the dominion of style' held in voluntary subjection. It was left for a few enthusiasts and an onrushing generation to understand the vital force which was vivifying the nation at the expense of an occasional lapse from good taste. In 1887 vital force was supposed to be the quality of statesmen and financiers, and taste to be the quality of authors, and artists, and college presidents. Lincoln had no need of taste, and Whitman considered that he had no need of it either. The world has agreed with both; and what critics there were have long been silenced. Yet we discern a restraining force in the belief (now extinct) that this neglected quality of taste was in its way an asset.

1897

I AM forty years old, and I have acquired a literary friend. Not that my life has been hitherto devoid of such indulgences, for Doctor Horace Howard Furness and Doctor Weir Mitchell have been friends and kind friends for years. Doctor Furness accepted me as a legacy from his father, Doctor William Henry Furness, to have known whom was a benefaction; and Doctor Mitchell was well disposed towards writers, and did his best to like them when he could. These two men gave to Philadelphia a distinction akin to that which Mr. Lowell and Mr. Aldrich gave to Boston; but Boston accorded a glad reception to anything good that came its way. It liked being enriched intellectually by its citizens, and was more prone to worship with undue warmth than to shiver and withdraw.

No men could have been more unlike than Doctor Fur-

ness and Doctor Mitchell, but they were firm and understanding friends. I know of but one approach to discord
in their relations, and of one mutual disagreement which
was rather amusing than otherwise. Doctor Mitchell had
written a particularly charming little book called 'The
Madeira Habit,' in which the dignified conviviality of
former Philadelphians was duly celebrated. He was also
accustomed to wining as well as dining his friends with
well-chosen liberality. Naturally he considered himself to
be a judge of wine. Doctor Furness possessed, as it
chanced, some old and rare Madeira, how acquired I have
forgotten, and he told me with deep conviction that 'Weir'
had failed to recognize its quality. He had just drunk it
down as if it were the ordinary Madeira of commerce.
'I watched him closely,' said Doctor Furness, 'and he
never responded for an instant. He did not know what he
was drinking.'

I tried to look shocked and sympathetic, but in my soul
of souls I did not believe that either of these men had ever
had the training and devotion necessary to a perfected
palate. I had been early taught by wine-drinking forbears (who bequeathed to me nothing but gout) that the
one thing never to be trusted in the most honest and up-
right of men was their boasted knowledge of wine.

The second discordant note, though it did no lasting
harm, was of a more serious character. Doctor Mitchell
had written a poem on Agincourt, a very spirited poem,
as good as anything in 'Drake.' He brought it out to
Wallingford, and read it to us after dinner. He always
read his own work well, and on this occasion — though
it was difficult to speak into his host's ear-trumpet — he
threw fire and force into every line. Doctor Furness looked

and expressed the admiration that he felt. Doctor Mitchell threw the poem on the great desk, littered with many papers, and said with a laugh: 'Well, all I ask is that the next time you give a reading of "Henry V," you will preface it with "Agincourt."'

A silence fell upon the room. I looked steadily at the wall, reflecting as I did so on the comfort of having a wall in every room to look at. Casual conversation was renewed, and Doctor Mitchell soon after took his leave. Doctor Furness saw him off, and returned to the library. 'Agnes,' he asked in a stricken sort of voice, 'did you hear what Weir asked me to do?'

I said I had heard, and I forbore to add that Doctor Mitchell was as far as any man in Christendom from ranking himself with Shakespeare. Doctor Furness knew this as well as I did. But there is a difference between admiring a poet and worshipping at a shrine. Doctor Mitchell spoke thoughtlessly and gleefully. Doctor Furness felt as Saint Jerome might have felt had he been asked to preface his 'Vulgate' with the charming story of Saint Christopher.

The third friend who whirled into my orbit like a comet, and whirled out again with a comet's splendid inconstancy, was Andrew Lang. He began the friendship (I never began anything) with a letter written because he had seen in one of my essays an allusion to Guibert de Nogent. I felt from the first the inadequacy of this alliance, inasmuch as Guibert de Nogent was little to me but a name. I knew him only as the schoolboy who said: 'If I die of my whippings, I mean to be whipped,' so highly did he savour the knowledge which most schoolboys can readily relinquish; and as the chronicler of the first Crusade. To Lang he was one of the most appealing of medieval figures, schooled in the classics, keen for a higher standard of scholarship in the monasteries, and delicately precise when he put his pen to paper. The British writer, pleased to see Guibert's name mentioned anywhere in print, conceived mistakenly that he had found a kindred spirit, and held out the hand of recognition.

What followed was a storm of letters, written anywhere and everywhere. Lang had no need of especial surroundings or appurtenances for writing. When he told me that he had composed the greater part of 'Helen of Troy' in cabs, I believed him. A cab was as good as a desk to him any day in the week. The ease and speed with which he wrote were to me in the nature of a miracle. I did not answer all of his letters, nor a third of them. That would have been impossible. Nor did he seem to care. His writing was abominably illegible, but he did not think so. A manuscript on 'Love's Labour's Lost,' sent to *Harper's Magazine* to be published with a drawing of Abbey's for illustration, made good its title by disappearing from the mail. It was before the happy advent of typewriters, or at least before their common use, and I suggested that the lost screed might be found parading as a Coptic manuscript in one of the adjacent colleges. To my amazement the jest was taken in bad part, not because it was heartless, but because it implied that my friend's writing was not of the copy-book variety.

Certain of Mr. Lang's books are so self-revealing that no letters could give us a better understanding of the sad heart and gay temper which is the most charming combination in the world; or of the frivolous style backed by scholarship. When a man can read Homer, his slang will never degenerate into vulgarity. When a scholar loves Homer with his whole heart as well as with all his mind, he can afford to amuse himself with Thomas Haynes Bayley.

Mr. Lang's letters were as a rule ill natured, full of bitter and diverting little jibes. He illustrated them occasionally with pen-and-ink drawings of unabashed rudeness. Now and then he dropped into verse, always in French, and always in praise of his cats. In point of fact, cats constituted a stronger bond between us than did the shadowy Guibert de Nogent. When the one I loved best died, I wrote to him, sure of sympathy, and declaring after the foolish fashion of grief that I would never take another kitten under my roof.

'Don't say that,' he wrote back. 'It is in human nature to replace what is lost. Why, look at Henry the Eighth.'

About this time the University of Pennsylvania was meditating a course of lectures on the religions of the world, or on the history of religions, or on something equally expansive; and greatly desired Mr. Lang (as one who could make the subject popular) to open the series. Doctor William Pepper, then provost of the University, asked me to write to my friend, and persuade him to accept the invitation. He wrote back promptly: 'If your good people of Philadelphia have not lost their letters, tell them to read my book, "Myth, Ritual and Religion." They will then know all that I knew when I wrote it, and far more than I know now, as I have forgotten most of it since.'

One secret jest Mr. Lang and I shared between us, and it afforded some entertainment. His 'Blue Poetry Book' and my 'Book of Famous Verse' were published within a year of each other, and we had a good deal to say concerning the choice of material. The 'Blue Poetry Book' is a more desirable volume than the 'Book of Famous

Verse.' That much I granted freely. In the first place it
is bigger, and therefore has room in it for more beauty
than I could accommodate. In the second place it is
illustrated, not skimpingly but profusely, after the fashion
that children love. In the third place Mr. Lang had a
perfectly free hand. He put into his collection just what
he wanted and nothing more. I had undisturbed freedom
of selection, but my publishers considered that their copy-
righted American poets should be adequately represented;
a justifiable point of view when the volume was intended
for reading in the public schools. Unfortunately Mr.
Lowell is distinctly a writer for adults; William Cullen
Bryant, except for 'Robert of Lincoln,' is hopeless; and
Whittier is nearly as bad, though he wrote 'The Barefoot
Boy,' patronizing beyond the endurance of most boys, and
that charming poem, 'My Playmate.' I searched and
scraped and finally produced my selections, feeling tolerably sure that no child would willingly read them.

These difficulties I confided to Mr. Lang, and he wrote
back promptly: 'Never mind! Just wait and see the puff
I am going to give you as a good American.'

I did wait through some uneasy weeks, and sure enough
there appeared among the *Cornhill* reviews an emphatic
paragraph, praising the book, but regretting the excess of
patriotism which included in its contents such verse as
Mr. Bryant's 'Song of Marion's Men.' This jest, understood only by myself, and amusing only to me, would have
passed unnoticed had it not been so unfortunate as to
catch the eye of Mr. Henry Cuyler Bunner, the brilliant
editor of *Puck*. Naturally he took it as serious comment;
and, being in an ill-natured mood, he wrote a few words,
affecting to sympathize with me at seeing myself praised

for a quality I did not possess. 'Miss Repplier,' he said, 'seems to be forever echoing the words of Sydney Smith: "Who reads an American book?"'

I sent this comment to Mr. Lang, who was delighted with it, and with himself for having called it into being. But I was not so well pleased. I was growing tired of being told what books to read and what authors to quote. Mr. Brander Matthews had reproached me, more in sorrow than in anger, for having written a whole volume without a single quotation from Lowell, 'than whom a more quotable writer never lived.' Augustine Birrell had come to my defence with a firm denial that it was anybody's duty to quote anyone. An author's birthplace, he said, concerned himself alone. The world was wide, and the whereabouts of his cradle could not be considered as an incentive or a deterrent to quotation.

By this time I had learned the joy that Europe gives, and had become as much of a wanderer as the circumstances of life permitted. Consequently I wandered into London just when Mr. Lang's letters were most tumultuously gay. He was very hospitable. I dined and lunched and drank tea with him, and went with him to a cricket match at Lord's (which he at least enjoyed), and to an exhibition of fans and miniatures. He did all that a reasonable man could do for my entertainment. He bade me a cheerful farewell when I left London, and he never wrote to me again. The inference was tolerably plain. There are not many things in this world that we absolutely know. The borderland between knowledge and ignorance is hazy with uncertainties. But on one point we are sure. We know when we have had enough of a friend, and we know when a friend has had enough of us. The first truth is no more palatable than the second.

1907

I AM fifty years old, and it has been my good fortune to
see something of foreign lands. I am the worst of travellers, detesting all modes of transportation (I detest them
still, and motors most of all); but I am the happiest of
tourists, loving each spot that I visit so ardently that I
never want to leave it. I grieve that there are many
languages in the world, and that I am acquainted with
so few. When I have striven to shop in Buda-Pesth, and
have asked in flawless German for a gauze veil, it is disheartening to be met with a polite entreaty: 'Bitte
sprechen-sie Hungarian?' As if a lifelong dweller in Philadelphia would be likely to know that remote vocabulary.

The real trouble in Europe is the necessity of choosing
between the known and the unknown, between the delight of seeing a place for the first time and the joy of seeing
it for the second. It is not well to ponder too long on this
problem, for if we do, we are apt to find ourselves in Rome.
Why, after all, go anywhere else when Rome sits on her
seven imperceptible hills, and awaits our coming? She
has beauty beyond compare, and the secrets of life and
death, and a message for every receptive soul. She has
an admirable climate for people who do not ask the impossible. I have tried her for eleven months out of the
twelve, and have never found her wanting. I once met an
Englishwoman who had not left Rome for a night in
twenty-four years. She was in excellent health. Rome
had nurtured her. And look at the vigorous old age of
Leo XIII, who pottered around the tiny Vatican garden,
compared to the ailments of his successors whose doctors
insisted upon a more invigorating air. I am not, so far

as I am aware, an orphan of the heart; but if I were, I should follow Byron's admirable advice, and seek an orphanage in Rome.

There are other enchanted spots in an enchanting, if unsatisfactory, world. I hope their beauty is thrilling eyes as keen as mine. The old seraglio in Stamboul was, I felt sure, the loveliest spot on earth until the nobler glory of the Acropolis dimmed its memory. The first glimpse of the pyramids, seen from the opposite side of the Nile in the long level light which precedes dusk, is an arresting moment. It can never be forgotten while anything on earth is remembered.

Perhaps Constantinople provided more small shocks and surprises than any other spot encountered by ordinary tourists like ourselves. I enjoyed them, and thanked Heaven repeatedly for having given me companions of a humorous turn of mind who forgave me my sins as a traveller for the sake of the moments in which I was not sinning. We were in a state of perpetual wonderment. Why was the first Turk whom we came to know (a very distinguished gentleman) as fair as a Norseman, with white hair, and eyes of a deep and burning blue? It was explained to us that his mother had probably been a Circassian, and that the Circassian women were noted for the beauty of their colouring. So far so good. Then this fair-skinned Turk brought his son to call upon us, and the young man was as black as ink in the bottle. It was really a bit bewildering, but again an explanation was in order. The boy's mother must have been a Soudanese, a race compared with whose magnificent and uniform blackness our American negroes seem like a mob of hybrids.

This last solution was proved to be correct when the

old pasha invited us to his harem, and the one and only
inmate whom we encountered was the black mother of
the black boy who had called upon us. Husband and son
deserted us at the door, saying it was against the rule for
them to enter in company with women. Our hostess spoke
a few words of French, but no English; and in her sluggish
movements, her watchful and hostile eyes I read a wish
(which I shared) that we had stayed at home. It was not
in the least like the visits to harems which I had read
about, and we were glad to escape to the men of the family,
who entertained us with dancing dervishes, and gave us
candied fruits too sweet to be eaten, and syrups too sweet
to be drunk. The son, like the father, had a charming
manner and a very agreeable voice; but I should have
liked, on such an occasion, to have encountered something
a trifle more traditional. Later on, in Cairo, I learned
from Mason Bey (son of Mr. James Murray Mason of
Mason and Slidell fame) that there was nothing traditional
or familiar about a Turk's harem. It was his affair and
nobody else's. His intimate friends never knew, or sought
to know, anything about it.

The American representative at Constantinople was
a kind, breezy, hospitable gentleman from the Middle
West. He was uncommonly good to us, and lent us his gor-
geous kavasses if he considered that our undistinguished
little dragoman was an insufficient protection. He always
opened a bottle of champagne when we went to him for
advice or assistance at the unconvivial hour of eleven A.M.
He had a profound admiration for the Sultan Abdul-
Hamid, both as a keen and wary ruler who made capital
of his weakness, which he exaggerated as other rulers exaggerated their strength, and as a private gentleman. The

latter predilection was based upon the Turk's aversion to women's evening dress. Our minister was able to give the sensitive Moslem the assurance that his wife — then absent on a visit to the United States — had never worn a low-cut gown in her life. 'You have the only modest woman for a spouse,' said the approving Sultan. 'You are to be congratulated.'

It seemed to me that this pleasant understanding between the fundamentally simple-minded American and the most secretive ruler in Europe was an interesting thing to contemplate. The American knew himself to be a good sort. The Turk, having a different set of rules to go by, was probably content with his own record. After his deposition he called upon the world to recognize his qualities. 'Did I not permit my own younger brother to live unmolested for thirty years?' he asked, indignant that clemency, so antagonistic to the practical precepts of the Orient, should have won little notice from Christians who were supposed to admire that sort of thing. Was there not in Saint Sophia the tomb of seventeen young princes, sons of Murad III who died in 1594? Their eldest brother ascended the throne as Mahomet III; and the seventeen undesirables were promptly strangled to avert future complications.

It was the wholesale slaughter of Armenians which induced Mr. William Watson to denounce Abdul-Hamid as

'Immortally, beyond all mortals, damned;'

and I can well remember a general conviction that the poet had not assumed the rôle of the Almighty without due provocation. The terms on which the Sultan was permitted to abdicate were deemed far too lenient, and Mr.

Watson was not the only critic who indulged in sulphurous language. The statesmen who had the pacification of Europe on their hands were, however, well content to leave the punishment of sin to God. Therefore Abdul went into exile accompanied by three wives, enough for any reasonable man, four concubines, and twenty servants. It was to his credit that he begged, and received, the companionship of his two youngest sons (dear little boys they were when I saw them riding to the mosque to pray), and of a Persian cat to which he was much attached.

Beside the cities of the world and the loveliness of the world, there were also (for Roman Catholics) the pilgrimages of the world, or of such of them at least as were accessible. The great pilgrimage — that of the Holy Sepulchre — was denied to my enfeebled strength; but as I gained health with every carefree month I made pious excursions galore. They have the great and abiding charm of association. The hopes and fears of humanity press upon us at their doors. The prayers of the devout hang like incense in the air. Moreover they are sure to be spots of exceptional beauty, and this circumstance seems natural and fitting. When we descended from our carriage at the gates of Genezzano, beside the great fountain where the oxen were drinking and the women were filling their jars, and when we started to climb the streets, too steep and narrow for our horses, we recognized at a glance the supreme perfection of this tiny hill town.

Once it had been of value to men who were forever fighting their neighbours. It had changed masters so often that its fortress and its castle were as wrecked as was the Roman aqueduct towering superbly over our heads. Only the church of Santa Maria di Buon Consiglio, completed in 1356, and served ever since by the Augustinians, had survived, even in part, such repeated devastations. On its altar stands the beloved picture, incalculably old, but perfectly distinct, and the friendliest painting in the world. The divine Child whispers in His mother's ear the advice she is to give. He lays His little hand upon her neck to command attention. Her expression is one of serious and profound concern. The priest who accompanies us tells us that two popes, Urban VIII and Pius IX, have made this pilgrimage. He nods at Our Lady, as much as to say: 'You remember, don't you?' and the meditative, unelated Virgin looks out from the thin boarding on which she is limned, and listens forever to the words she must hear and say.

We are the only pilgrims, and we have left the artists behind us at Olevano, where they can find a surfeit of beauty and a fair degree of comfort. We carry letters from Rome which will admit us to the shelter built by the Augustinians (there is — or there was — no inn), and to this shelter we are escorted by all the children of Genezzano. There seem to be a great many of them for the size of the town, and their interest in us is profound. One child holds up a little dog that it may see us more readily. They ask for nothing, and they bid us a polite farewell when we reach our destination. Here we are given, as pilgrims, large bare rooms, spotlessly clean beds, harder than marble slabs, and bread, coffee, and red wine, 'the holy simplicities of life.' Those who want more varied fare must bring it with them. This was thirty years ago. Motors may now be standing outside the ancient walls, and citizens of Genezzano may compete with the kind guardians of the shelter, who put no price upon their hospitality, but left it to the pilgrim to pay according to his worldly means.

The same principle prevailed at La Salette, that remote place of pilgrimage amid the tumbled hills of Dauphiné, which seem to have fallen from space with no particular concern as to where they landed. There is a wild beauty in their disorder and in their barrenness. From the top of one of these hills the Blessed Virgin appeared to two young peasants; and the spot became a shrine for pilgrims too humble to object to its inaccessibility. I think a vein of sentiment all my own induced me to take the journey, and to cajole a reluctant friend into accompanying me. When I was a little girl at my convent school the marsh beyond the lake where the white violets grew had been piously christened La Salette. I cared little for white violets which wilted as soon as they were plucked; but I loved the lonely spot where they were found, and where we were invisible, because the hillocks that skirted the lake hid us from the Mistress of Recreation walking soberly to the woods with a bodyguard of children closing about her.

The nuns in charge of La Salette were very kind to us; and we loved the simplicity of our quarters, the plain food, the atmosphere of withdrawal which is the prelude to piety, and the devout behavior of the country people — of the country women at least — who came to Mass. More than any nation in the world, France depends on her women to carry her to Heaven.

The beauty of Lourdes has helped to win it affection. There is nothing hidden or wild or dependent upon association in its loveliness. Nowhere else do the skies look vaster, the earth greener, the hills more harmonious, the little river more friendly in its glancing speed. It is hurried as are most French rivers, but it rounds out the landscape to perfection. Mrs. Meynell in her study of Lourdes confessed to a feeling of disappointment at its first appearance, but I have a distinct recollection of being told by Mrs. Meynell that she did not think the Yosemite Valley beautiful, and of my asking myself for weeks afterwards in a bewildered fashion: 'What, I wonder, has she ever seen on God's earth that she did think beautiful?'

The fortress of Lourdes lends the distinction of the past to the loveliness and holiness of the present. It goes back to a Roman camp — '*Ici, commes partout, nous retrouvons César.*' In Froissart's day it was held to be impregnable; but it changed hands often as the result of surprise or treachery. Here dwelt the noble lady, Pétronille, daughter of a count, ward of a king, and five times married, one husband being the Crusader, Guy de Montford. The Black Prince committed the care of the castle to Arnaud de Béarn, as brave a soldier and as true a knight as any in Christendom. It was long besieged by the French, and Froissart tells us joyously, '*Il y eut de beaux combats sous les murs.*' That was as it should have been; but when repeated attempts were made to seduce Béarn from his allegiance, he repelled all bribes with scorn. In consequence of this simple attitude he was stabbed to death by Gaston de Foix (at least so says Froissart), whose hospitality he had accepted in the spirit of good faith with which Christian gentlemen met one another. He fell sobbing out: '*Monseigneur, vous ne faites pas gentillesse!*' and the nobly spoken words echo from the ruins today. What restraint even in a reproach that can never die!

In sharp contrast to the violence of the past is the atmosphere of kindness, of pity, and of service which pervades modern Lourdes. The sick are tended, and every opportunity is afforded visiting physicians to watch the process and examine the results. Those who come to be cured are so few by comparison with those who come to pray (the peasant pilgrims seldom have a patient) that a week went by before my attention concentrated itself upon three sufferers whom I saw daily at the shrine. One was a German priest, apparently in early middle age, but wasted by illness to the shadow of a man. He was accompanied by an elderly couple, his father and mother doubtless, who waited on him devotedly, but fussily, after the fashion of families. He looked so weary, so utterly weary, not of pain only, but of life, that I felt sure the peace of death would have been as welcome to him as a cure.

The second patient in whom I grew deeply interested was a young English girl, always in a rolling chair accompanied by two nursing sisters. She was silent, composed, watchful, and acquiescent. Her seriousness was never broken, and whatever thoughts absorbed her were mysterious because she seemed to be shut up with them. In a place where words were freely spoken, she had none, not even for her companions, or for the occasional English pilgrims who proffered a friendly greeting.

The third petitioner was a Japanese blind boy who knelt most of the day close to the grotto, erect and motionless as stone. He seemed an embodiment of that age-old cry: 'Lord, that I may see!' On the feast of Corpus Christi the procession was so long that I found myself on one of the little heights overlooking the basilica while the priest who was carrying the host crossed the open square. He stopped halfway, and two attendants brought forward

the young Japanese. I saw him kneel with statue-like immobility in the path of the priest, who leaned forward
and touched his eyes with the monstrance. And as I
gazed I said suddenly to myself: 'It is raining — raining
from a sunlit sky.' But they were not raindrops that I
felt. They were my own tears falling fast on the parapet
over which I leant.

1917

I AM sixty years old, and this is the third year of the
World War. It is useless to suppose that we Americans
of the Atlantic seaboard, or close to it, think or talk of
anything but the war. We have lived under its dominion
so long that it absorbs us utterly. The suddenness with
which it darkened the sky was like the speed of nature
hurrying to destroy. 'Fifty years had made Europe in-
flammable, and a few days were enough to detonate it.'
The rape of Belgium, the loss of life along the western
front, the avertible tragedy of the Dardanelles, the collapse of Russia, and finally the submarine warfare have
inured us to horror, and destroyed every vestige of pleasure
in life.

This on the Atlantic seaboard; but was it possible to go
a few miles inland, and pick up the threads of ordinary
everyday existence? Dorothy Canfield, who is apt to know
whereof she writes, has told us a story of the Middle
West which covers the period of the World War. In its
pages an elderly woman of intelligence and her supremely
unintelligent son are discussing their domestic affairs on
the street. It is the crucial and tragic year, 1916. 'A
newsboy passed them, damp fresh papers under his arm.'

"Great Allied Victory on the Russian Front," he shouted.
Neither Mrs. Bascomb nor Ralph paid the least attention
to his cry. The war had been going on for more than a
year, and none of its cries had reached their ears. They
had quite other and more pressing things to think about.'

'None of its cries had reached their ears!' We have
been often told that geography is the key to man's disposition, and that we must turn to maps if we would
understand the wide divergences of human nature. But
is it possible that a mere matter of miles — miles of corn-
field, miles of wheat, or miles of desert — can change the
characteristics of a nation? Did Mrs. Fisher intend us to
believe that this callous unconcern was normal in one
section of the country and abnormal in another? The
'pressing things' that Mrs. Bascomb and Ralph had to
think about were ordinary discords, depressing, but not
necessarily deadening, and certainly far from unusual.
Dwellers on the Pacific coast were not free from domestic
trials while they feverishly watched Japan and waited
for New York. Seaboard called to seaboard as mountain
calls to mountain. They listened and understood.

What Germany did not understand was the peace-loving,
industry-loving country known as the United States. It
seems incredible that any nation in the world should have
flouted another nation so contemptuously as Prussia flouted
us when we tried the unaccustomed rôle of conciliation.
There is an adage old enough to be worth considering
about the worm that turns, and when the worm is as long
and as thick as a boa constrictor it is well not to inflame
it needlessly. By 1917 the submarine warfare overshad-
owed all other tragedies. It was sheer murder, and it
had reached appalling figures. Day after day came the

long lists of the drowned, and night after night the ocean bed gave up its ghosts to haunt us. The intrepidity of the little cargo-boats, 'England's pride,' was like no other intrepidity shown by the war; for the men who went out in them were not combatants but tradesmen carrying what was needful to British ports, and taking their chances of survival. After a time American ships shared their peril and their unconcern. Even our tankers puffed scornfully out to sea, believing in sailors' luck, and laughing at destiny. And when that happened, America's entrance into the war was a sure thing. No people can see a little black tanker as stout-hearted as a man of war, and not be fired by a desire to protect it.

It was characteristic of the United States that one of our first actions as a combatant (we had a navy) was the laying of the barrage across the two hundred and fifty miles wide passage between Norway and Scotland. England gasped at this infringement of neutral rights; but we finished the work and discussed it afterwards. We had learned all about neutral rights during the years in which we had been a neutral nation, and we were prepared to do as we had been done by.

The last weeks of our neutrality were lived at high pressure. Germany made a final effort at terrorization which failed of its purpose. Because Mr. Wilson had kept his word, and had held us back from war as long as it was humanly possible, he had the nation pushing him into action, which must have been what he anticipated and desired. Men began to talk of their own part in the coming struggle. I sat one night by the side of Theodore Roosevelt in a theatre box at a public meeting. He was silent and preoccupied, turning a troubled glance occasionally in my direction. Suddenly he said; 'You know I'd love to fight, don't you?'

I burst out laughing. In the first place he was so wistful, and in the second place no one who knew him at all could have doubted the simple desire of his heart. He laughed too, but ruefully: 'Yes, I should love to fight,' he said; 'but I shall never be allowed to do so. I am the type of man who ages rapidly. I have sons, and they will go; but I shall be left at home.'

He was left at home, and so was I. When my chance came to work in Milan, I was pronounced physically unfit. I had not aged rapidly, but I was nevertheless old, and liable to be more of a hindrance than a help. 'Europe is full of American women who have broken under the strain,' wrote my Milanese correspondent to me a few months later. 'They are being eliminated as rapidly as possible. Thank Heaven, you did not add to the number.'

But after all, what difference did it make, who went and who stayed at home? The nation had responded. The nation was arming itself with incredible slowness but to some purpose. A weight heavier than lead had been lifted from our hearts. We no longer awoke to the bitterness of inaction, but to play our part in the drama of life and death. We knew the cost when we accepted the conditions. There have been many impressive scenes in our national record, but none to surpass that in which President Wilson asked Congress to declare a state of war. His speech was simple and clear, eloquent and restrained. He was a past master of words. When he concluded with the echo of Luther's familiar phrase, there was a breathless silence in the house. Then Chief Justice White raised his steady hands: 'God in Heaven be thanked!' he said.

1927

I AM seventy years old, a gray age weighted with uncompromising biblical allusions. It ought to have a gray outlook, but it hasn't, because a glint of dazzling sunshine is dancing merrily ahead of me. Spain is meditating an exposition — not an international exposition, but one which is to be strictly Spanish Iberian, and the United States, in honour of Columbus, has been invited to join. The invitation has been accepted (if Spain can forget Cuba so can we), and Mr. Coolidge has appointed me one of six commissioners to go to Seville. How this ever came to pass, Heaven alone knows. Sometimes I dimly surmise that the suggestion came from Mr. Hoover who was indebted for it to Mrs. Hoover; but all I know is the miraculous fact that I am going for four months to the loveliest of cities, which I had thought never to see again.

For a year the commission did nothing but meet in Washington to discuss its future duties. By the end of the winter I at least understood that my duty would be to follow closely the lead of the commissioner general whose scrupulous politeness did little to conceal his contempt for our opinions when we had any. He was, however, extraordinarily kind to us in Seville, determined that we should be as comfortable as that steady-going old hotel, the Inglaterra, could make us, and visibly anxious that his wife should be on easy terms with us all. He need not have been concerned. Everybody was on easy terms with everybody else. The American group was for a time a large one. Secretaries, a commandant to represent the navy, architects who had designed the admirable exposition buildings so perfectly in keeping with their surroundings, and a host of other workers. Some one made the futile remark that we were like one big family, which was precisely what we were not. The essence of a family is permanence; the essence of our Seville adventure was impermanence, the certainty that in a few months our easy intimate life would be dissolved into a mist of memories.

Of course there were episodes too manifestly imperfect for praise. The commissioner general in his expansive generosity had saddled his women commissioners with an assistant. She was a resident of Seville, a past master of Spanish, and a woman of real intelligence. She was also an unwearied talker, and so determined to be useful that she drained us dry in a week. Had we been overworked and underpaid, she would have been a treasure. As it chanced, we were overpaid and underworked; and we honestly desired — at least we women did — to be worth our salt. We had no task to share with our assistant because we needed all we had to do for the preservation of our own self-respect. It was impossible to yield to her clamorous demands and insistent presence. Only those who have read Mr. Anstey's flawless story, 'Accompanied by a Flute,' can perhaps understand what we suffered. Mr. Anstey's Roman general murders his flute-player because it is the only practical way of getting rid of him; but we could not murder our assistant. I would creep warily out in the morning, and see her sitting in the lobby erect and vigilant, her eyes fixed upon the staircase down which she knew we must descend. I didn't descend. I crept safely back to the room of my fellow commissioner: 'Miss W. is waiting in the lobby,' I said.

'I know it,' was the composed answer. 'I saw the top of her hat from the gallery.'

The hardest thing to bear was the spiritual ruin of our day at La Rábida, that convent by the sea where Columbus found shelter and understanding friends. Here is his cell, here are numerous relics of his residence. The place in its loneliness, its austerity, its poverty, and its unquenchable distinction is the proper guardian of his memories. Then what was the matter with us? In the first place a new road was being made, and we had motored for hours through ditches and over piles of stones. In the second place our indomitable assistant had talked brightly and manfully the whole way. My mind was a pulp. In the third place it was Friday, and the convent rice cooked with fish and oil wrought strange havoc within me. Columbus had no doubt eaten that same combination Friday after Friday, and had triumphantly crossed the sea. What a weakling I was, and how completely my nobler and finer feelings lay at the mercy of things too base for consideration. We got back to Seville in a state of collapse, and the commissioner general asked us promptly if we had seen two places of interest near La Rábida. We answered unregretfully that we had not. 'I must say,' he observed, 'that for women with a whole day and a motor at their disposal you did uncommonly little.'

Meantime the opening of the exposition was close at hand. All the exhibitors were ready and waiting except Cuba, which was unconcernedly hammering at its walls, while its exhibits lay close packed in boxes. Cuba, I was told, was never nearer than that to being ready for anybody or anything. '*Mañana*' (tomorrow) is its motto. The king arrived twenty-four hours before the opening, and worked like a beaver from morn to even, his hat tilted at the back of his head, his face flushed with heat

and determination. I am disposed to think he worked to
some purpose, for the next day in the clearest sunshine,
and in cool sweet air that might have blown from Heaven,
the exposition was opened brilliantly and beautifully. The
speeches were few and short. The king, resplendent in
his uniform was vastly different from the king with tilted
hat and his stick swinging from his arm. The Spanish
crowd looked, as a Spanish crowd always looks, in perfect
harmony with its setting. The flowing mantillas of white
or black lace composed themselves into the landscape.
There was but one discordant note. The queen and the
royal princesses had refused the smallest concession to
Spain. Their dresses and hats were as English as London
could make them. I heard bitter comments upon this
later. It was hard to think that so insignificant a bêtise
could have affronted so many people.

When the king opened the American exhibition, he
lingered long over the handsome new consulate which was
the exhibitors' pride; and the rooms from which he refused to be driven were the kitchen, the cellar, the bath-
rooms, and the toilets. Never had I dreamed that plumbing, good up-to-date but ordinary American plumbing,
could be so interesting to anyone but a plumber. For
three quarters of an hour his Majesty asked rational
questions, and for three quarters of an hour anybody who
knew anything was called upon to answer him. When we
emerged into the sunlight he stood near me for a minute,
and spoke a few words. 'I trust,' he said in a beautifully
modulated voice, 'that you like Seville.'

'I love it dearly,' was my sincere reply.

'But not so well as Madrid?' he asked with a hint of
warning in his voice.

'Infinitely better,' I insisted stoutly.

'So do I,' said the king.

I may add that the commissioner general conceived an ardent admiration for Primo de Rivera, with whom he had conversed most of the time. 'A very intelligent man,' he kept on repeating through the evening, 'a vastly intelligent man.'

'The king was intelligent about the plumbing,' I hinted.

'I dare say,' said the chief dryly. 'Plumbing has not chanced to come my way. But for a grasp on affairs, for a complete knowledge of the political situation! I don't see how Spain could ever get along without Primo!'

And it hasn't.

The opening of the exposition let loose a flood of entertainments; receptions which involved hours of standing, and huge dinners which began at bedtime and ended at the sacred hour of breakfast. We had also a number of distinguished visitors to receive and entertain. The most impressive was the Cardinal of Tangiers, who, being pressed for time, arrived at night. The grounds were brilliantly lit up in his honour. His clerical train was handsome, his presence and manner were superb. He spoke French by preference, looked patiently at our government exhibits (we had no others), and declined the cinema theatre, thereby earning my lifelong gratitude. It was a handsome little theatre with educational films. A great deal of his time was taken up blessing the crowd which followed him from building to building, and sank on its knees every time he appeared in a doorway. He showed no impatience at these repeated manifestations of piety, but maintained a sacerdotal solemnity which must have been deeply gratifying. The poor understand such things and value them.

A very different visitor was Queen Marie of Roumania, who was always circling round Europe, and who took us in her stride. She sent word that she was travelling privately, and wished no attention to be paid her. The commissioner general, who did not know the lady, and whose duties had grown very onerous, was delighted to take her at her word. He provided some handsome flowers (flowers are a drug in Spain), a tastefully draped Roumanian flag (his collection of flags was complete), summoned his weary but faithful followers, and awaited the royal visitor. She arrived with a longer line of motors than we had yet seen, made a stately entrance into our building, and evaded looking at the exhibits. The commissioner, however, succeeded in getting her shut up in the cinema theatre, and we sank into our seats, hoping for a half-hour's respite. We did not get it. In twenty minutes the queen had seen as much as she could bear, and made a break for the door, followed joyously by her ladies. As she emerged into the dazzling sunlight, she was received in respectful silence by a large circle of our employees, and a much larger circle outside — the crowd which gathers in Spain on the smallest possible provocation. The royal photographer was waiting to chronicle every move. In our front row stood the commissioner general's chauffeur, wearing his new khaki uniform. He was a young Cuban of much skill, but so ill-mannered that petitions for his dismissal were of daily occurrence. The queen caught sight of the khaki, drew a swift but erroneous conclusion, walked nimbly across the open space, and shook hands cordially with the smiling young man while the photographer recorded her urbanity. Then she and her ladies stepped into their motors and disappeared from our sight.

'I think,' I observed, 'that she was disappointed in her reception.'

The chief wrinkled his brows. 'I dare say she was,' he said unconcernedly, 'but that is not the worst of it. I shall have to get rid of that young man now. It will be impossible to keep him. And he is the only good chauffeur in Seville.'

On the twenty-first of April Mrs. Harry Payne Whitney unveiled her statue of Columbus at Huelva. There had been a deal of discussion over the site; the Spaniards, who are fussy about facts, insisting that as Columbus had not sailed from Huelva, it was not the proper place for a memorial; the Americans, who had given this work of art, being wholly indifferent to such considerations. The statue itself, as seen from its base, was a trifle bewildering, looking more like an old woman than the great adventurer; but we were told that it was meant to be glimpsed by mariners far out at sea, and that to them it was noble and imposing. There were several large boats waiting to carry us to a possible viewpoint; but to our shame be it recorded not one of us was willing to embark. It rained dismally, and we preferred taking shelter in a comfortable little room cut in the foundation of the monument, where a life-sized marble Isabella was laying down the law to an acquiescent Ferdinand. On the walls of this room were cut the names of the crew who had crossed the sea with Columbus, and who certainly deserved this much consideration from the world. That they ever received it was due to the indefatigable antiquarian, Miss Alice Gould.

All spring the ordinary features of a Seville season succeeded one another in rhythmical order. The processions of Holy Week were more beautiful than when I had last seen them. The strange snatches of song in the streets were more frequent. The Miserere was superb. With Easter came the bull fights which I attended every Sunday afternoon without enjoyment and without enthusiasm save when an American lad from Brooklyn was admitted into the ring, being qualified for that august privilege. He was received with generous enthusiasm by the toreadors, who manifested their delight when he killed his two bulls swiftly and cleanly. As for the few Americans present, they were so swept by pride and pleasure that one might have imagined our national ambition was no other than to breed bull fighters for Spain.

The reason for my faithful attendance on Sunday afternoons was simple enough. I went always to the box of an old Spanish lady who was good to me, and to whom I had grown oddly attached. She could not understand my distaste for anything so natural as a bull fight; but she was too philosophic to expect, or even desire, the concurrence of friends. What she liked was to feed them. I went home with her every Sunday, and found some twenty or thirty casual acquaintances who had dropped in for tea. The preparations were on a suitable scale. I have counted sixteen kinds of cake on her overburdened tables. On Easter Sunday, when we were surfeited and supine, the doors were thrown open, and two footmen entered bearing plates and forks and apple fritters, hot and fragrant. Never shall I forget my despair as I realized my impotence to deal competently with those fritters. The smell of them hurled me back to the days of my youth when I could have met them with the intrepidity they deserved, and when they were of infrequent occurrence. What a farce life is, anyway!

The Feria is always a little disappointing after the supreme beauty of Holy Week, but the display of horsemanship is admirable. It has a picturesque quality unknown to horsemanship elsewhere. The Feria is not a matter-of-course event like an Englishman riding to hounds. It is a yearly meet at which men, women, and beasts appear to their utmost advantage. Foreigners may not always appreciate this circumstance; but Spaniards are alike critical and enthusiastic. To them it is a show, and they are well aware of its quality and distinction.

As for the four days pious picnic known as the Romero, it is a charming sight for half an hour, but for no longer. A hundred decorated ox wagons looking uncommonly alike spell weariness to American eyes. Unluckily I had gone with Spanish friends, and for six hours, six long unbroken hours, they gazed without fatigue at wagons, and brightly dressed country girls. I had learned in Rome the marvellous tenacity with which Latins 'stay on.' I learned it afresh in Seville.

And now the time was coming all too fast when the mounting heat of June warned us that the exposition would close its doors, and that our departure was imminent. Every morning I rose early and looked from my balcony at the beauty that lay on every side of me. I had been faithful since childhood to my love for Spain; and even in my infantile ignorance I dimly surmised what that consummate scholar, Helen Waddell, has so well expressed: 'For austere and gracious allegory, for much of its mysticism and its chivalry, its ardours and its endurances, the world is indebted to Spain.' Perhaps I thought that everyone who had to go away would feel as sorrowful as I did — an illusion amusingly dispelled.

Washington had sent us for a month a good military band. It played with spirit and understanding. Under its touch the national airs became vibrant with emotion. That of Spain, so triumphant and so heart-breaking, has haunted me ever since, as well it might with the heart-break always uppermost. Two days before this band departed it gave a farewell concert in the public gardens that fronted the Inglaterra. I joined the crowd, and in the first intermission talked with one of the musicians. He was young, good-looking, and distrait. 'You are sailing soon for home,' I said.

'We are that,' was the cheerful reply.

'Are you sorry to go?' I asked.

'I am not. I am glad.'

His manifest exultation hurt me. 'But surely,' I said, 'you must have liked it here. The weather has been perfect, you have been made comfortable, I trust, and the town is beautiful.'

My companion looked about him with some interest. Evidently this view of his surroundings had not hitherto suggested itself. 'Yes,' he admitted, 'it is a handsome city. But' (he became suddenly confidential) 'how would you like to be sent for a whole month to a place as big as this which hasn't a bandstand or a peanut?'

So was Seville tried and found wanting.

1937

Temps s'en va
Et rien n'ai fait,
Temps s'en vient
Et ne fais rien.

It is the last of my decades, and I am eighty years old. There seems to be nothing to add to this statement. I have reached the age of undecorated facts — facts that refuse to be softened by sentiment, or confused by nobility of phrase. I have always mistrusted emotional praises of old age. They are as a rule self-praise, a habit of speech to which septuagenarians, to say nothing of octogenarians, are much addicted. They call attention to the spirit and courage with which their writers are facing the impenetrable future; and they seem unaware that men and women all over the world are doing the same thing because they have no choice in the matter. I never read one of these well-expressed adjustments to fate without thinking of Margaret Fuller's magniloquent aphorism, 'I accept the universe,' and Carlyle's grim comment, 'Gad, she'd better!'

Walt Whitman was perfectly simple and sincere in his self-appreciation. When he ceased drawing attention to his lusty manhood, he passed by a natural transition to drawing attention to his serene old age. When he ceased to sing,

'O my brave soul!
O farther, farther sail!'

he sang instead a hymn of thanks for the long years (they were only seventy-three) which set him on a 'lambent peak,' and enabled him

'to know the mighty ones,
Job, Homer, Eschylus, Dante, Shakespeare, Tennyson, Emerson.'

His final summing-up is familiar to us all:

'For I do not see one imperfection in the universe,
And I do not see one cause or result lamentable at last.'

We know little about the universe; but with the run of events on our own planet we are tolerably well acquainted. They may turn out to be satisfactory 'at last'; but it is hard to see them moving jauntily in that direction. It was just as hard in Whitman's day. His bouncing optimism was not the result of observation. When he looked about him, he saw things clearly and irrevocably; but when he looked at himself he was dazzled by the picture that he drew.

Henley's attitude was no less an attitude than Whitman's. Being a poet, he could give it adequate expression, but he could not give it vitality. We are only in part the captains of our souls; and the nearer we grow to captaincy, the less do we shout defiance to the winds. Tennyson was thirty-three, the age of perfect manhood, when he wrote the perfect lines which strip longevity of its profits. He knew that Ulysses should have rested tranquil and content by the side of his hard-won hearth; but he knew also the impelling power of memory. Penelope is 'aged.' There is no denying this fact, nor that she has grown aged in defending her husband's rights. Telemachus is dull. His dulness is glossed over with decent words of praise which make it the more glaringly apparent. Ithaca is also dull, its boors (who are lucky boors) being content to feed and sleep and hoard. Ulysses, instead of drawing a radiant picture of himself in this tranquil setting, confesses to a deep disquietude. He recalls the days when his comrades were valiant and wise:

'Myself not least, but honour'd of them all,'

and he tries to believe that

'Some work of noble note may yet be done,
Not unbecoming men that strove with gods.'

His plans are vague with the vagueness of old age, but one thing is sure — he will get away from Ithaca, and from all his duties as father, husband, and king. Because Tennyson was a poet it was given him to so read the mind of this great old man that a vision is transformed into reality. We believe, though we know better, that Ulysses did set sail, and did bravely meet whatever fate the sportive gods assigned him.

Wisdom is said to be the funded experience which man has gathered by living; but for so many harvests the crop is still a light one. Knowledge he has gained and power, but not goodness and understanding. As for things alien to civilization, like violence and cruelty, where shall we turn to escape them! One might be tempted to moralize over this disheartening circumstance had not William James — who must have read George Eliot too insistently — asked with a show of temper: 'Why does it make women feel good to moralize?' If it does (and we have only his word for it), who will condemn so harmless a path to complacency? It is often said that Americans — men as well as women — plead a moral preoccupation as an excuse for intellectual sins. If a moral preoccupation means morality, we are nearer the goal than is apparent. If it means moralizing, we are a little like the wheel of Buddha which forever moves around but never forward. Perhaps this is the especial predicament of old age, in which case let me follow the wise example of Oliver Herford's cat, and 'let others talk.'

'*On arrive novice à tous les ages,*' said the wisest of men,

La Rochefoucauld. The illusion of progress clings to us so tightly that we are ready to part with our civic liberty (that true and tried friend), in exchange for unsubstantial visions. Other nations have been compelled to make this bargain, and are still compelled to say they like it; but we have been beguiled by promises. We want and we need to be let alone, yet we are more directed and controlled every year. Business is shackled into incompetence. Boys are turned into bandits and thugs and house-breakers because they are not allowed to work and earn money. Most of them would rather work than steal; but that fatal word, child-labour, blocks their path. They may be six feet tall, but in the eyes of the law they are still wearing pinafores. They ought to go to school, but they won't. They ought to spend improving evenings in club rooms, but they don't. They ought to cultivate little gardens, and be moved to gentle thoughts by a delphinium, but they one and all prefer cigarettes.

Yet, although boys like to annoy — a purpose they easily achieve — they do not like, as a rule, to break the law and risk jail. They know that it is organized labour which, fearing competition, keeps them idle, and we know that idleness is a disintegrating thing. It does more harm to a boy's mind than work does to his body. Like all Americans, he wants money — wants it as a rule for harmless, needless things, but wants it imperatively and insistently. He will work hard for it if he be given the chance. He is ready, as a last resource, to steal it.

Goethe in his extreme old age undertook to add up and estimate the good hours of his life. He found that in the course of eighty years he had enjoyed four months of happiness, which seems to most of us a fairly generous allowance. There are not many men to whose words on such a theme we should pay any attention; but Goethe was a truth-teller. The whole episode of living (save as it disquieted a day) seemed to him a matter for adjustment. To him, as to Santayana, 'experience led to conclusions.' And what serenity in the soul of a man who could keep his public waiting twenty-four years for the completion of his masterpiece! The public also was serene. It folded its hands and waited without a murmur. But it takes a very great man to be assured of this soothing circumstance.

William the Silent, who could speak to some purpose when he spoke at all, gave to his world a line of counsel so wise and so hard that we should never heed it were we not aware that it was the rule by which the founder of the Dutch Republic ordered his life: 'It is not necessary to hope in order to undertake, nor to succeed in order to persevere.' This seems too much to ask of Adam's sons; but in an age of sentimental twaddle the words stand out with noble distinctness. They would have been understood and accepted by the ancients better than we can understand and accept them today. Pindar, who might reasonably have asked to be exempt from every duty save the writing of triumphant odes, assigned himself a more austere rule of life. Being loved of the gods, he died young; but the stage of pure enjoyment had been passed when he wrote with that lovely combination of sense and piety which is our best inheritance from an undefeated past:

'With God's help may I still love what is good, and strive for what is attainable.'

Amen

HORACE

HORACE

THAT a poet should survive two thousand years is not remarkable. Whatever changes two thousand more may bring about, they will not affect the standing of Homer or of Virgil. '*Ce n'est que le premier pas qui coûte.*' If you survive your first thousand, the others will fall into line. But that a poet writing two thousand years ago should today be the helpmate and spokesman of humanity is in the nature of a miracle. It can be accounted for only by the fact that Horace was a man wholly disillusioned, and wholly good-tempered.

No word in our language has been so misused in the past nineteen years as the word 'disillusionment.' It has come to mean the perpetual grouch of men still deeply resentful that the World War was not in the nature of a garden party, and that the World Peace was not a highway to Utopia. Every crime and every folly have been excused on this ground. Even the kaleidoscopic divorces of Reno, the suspension of privacy, the repeal of reticence, have been accounted for by the disillusionment of youth at the way the world was run when it was too young to run it, as the natural result of a war which saw greater acts of heroism and of supreme self-sacrifice than had ever before purified the souls of men.

The disillusionment of Horace was not of this order. It meant that he had awakened from the noble dreams of youth to the equally noble realities of manhood. He saw

life as a whole, and this educational process taught him
that it is not easy to find happiness in ourselves, and that
it is not possible to find it elsewhere. Reason, moderation,
content, a wide mental horizon, a firm foundation of principle — these were the gifts of the gods (and Horace
reverenced his gods) to men of good purpose and sobriety.

His upbringing was of the best. His father, though but
a freedman who had received his name, Horatius, either
because he had been the property of some member of the
patrician family of Horatii, or because his birthplace,
Venusia, was part of their vast estates in Apulia, was
sanely ambitious for his promising young son. He took
him to Rome to be educated — an extravagance he could
ill afford — provided for him liberally, and watched over
him with care. We hear nothing of the mother, so presumably she was dead. Rome was more concerned with
the functions of motherhood than was Greece. She could
not have endowed the world with her two great gifts, the
sanctity of the family and the majesty of the law, she
could not have given to it, as she did, a life morally worth
the living, if she had not looked sharply after her women,
emphasizing their duties rather than their privileges. But
she was far from being a matriarchy like the United States.
She was not a nation of husbands, but a nation of men.
The foundation of the family was the father. He had un-
disputed authority, unshared responsibility, and often un-
limited devotion.

Certain it is that Horace pays a tribute of gratitude to
the father who begrudged him nothing that it was in his
power to give. He permitted the boy to be freely flogged
by his severe master, Orbilius, having the male parent's
insensitiveness in this regard; but he protected him alike

from folly and from misdoing. 'He kept me chaste,'
wrote Horace in after years, 'free from shameful deeds,
and from the breath of dishonour.'

His Roman schooling over, young Horace was sent to
Athens, still the thrice superb teacher of the world; and
there, free from his father's restraining hand, he did what
all young men of spirit have done since the beginning of
time — he went to the wars. The profitless murder of
Julius Caesar had brought Brutus to Greece. Horace, being twenty-two, an age singularly sensitive to oratory,
joined the republican army, and was given the post of
military tribune — a circumstance usually mentioned as
proof of his talent, but which seems rather to indicate a
shortage of trained soldiers. If we may trust to his recollections, as embodied in his lines to Pompeius Varus, his
military experiences were not altogether unpleasant. There
were hours of relaxation to compensate for hours of peril:

'Full oft we sped the lingering day,
Quaffing bright wine as in our tents we lay,
With Syrian spikenard on our glistening hair.'

It is an agreeable picture of campaigning; but the curtain
fell on the desolate field of Philippi. Brutus and Cassius
died by their own hands; and Horace, convinced that his
was not a military genius, profited by the general amnesty
to return to Rome.

It was a hard home-coming. His father was dead, his
small estate in Venusia had been confiscated — which was
to have been expected — and he himself was under suspicion as a pardoned enemy of the state. He had much to
live down, and he had much to build up. He secured his
daily bread by working as a scribe in the quaestor's office,
and he began his career as poet. Naturally he began it

by writing satires. What else should a brilliant and bitterly disappointed young man have written? And just as naturally he regretted many of these satires when time had brought him reason.

We all remember how Byron strove to blot out of existence his outbreak of ill-temper, 'English Bards and Scotch Reviewers,' and how he found out that as soon as English readers discovered they could no longer get that particular poem they were all possessed by a desire to have it. Horace would have liked to blot out his early satires. They were not his métier. The concentrated anger of Juvenal or of Swift was utterly foreign to his nature. Swift was a great and powerful humorist, and Juvenal was esteemed a wit; but in their two souls 'rage accumulated like water behind a dam,' and burst into devastating floods. Horace had not even the tenacity of wrath which made an indifferent poet like Lucilius a fairly great satirist; but in its place he had a gift which was slowly maturing — a balanced and delicate irony, playful but with a rapier's point. The charming picture of country life, simple, serene and self-respecting, which the moneylender, Alfius, contemplates with unction but decides not to live, is a perfect example of the ironical, of the laughter that is so low-pitched it seems — for one mistaken moment — to be kindly. As admirable in its more worldly way is his epistle to the young Tiberius, heir to the throne, introducing a persistent acquaintance who will not be set aside. This is the ninth epistle of the first book. As there are few of us who have not suffered a somewhat similar experience, its study cannot fail to be of service.

In the fifth epode we find the first direful picture of the witch, Canidia, a singularly disgusting person. It is at once

the most tragic and the most dramatic poem that Horace
ever wrote. Curiously dramatic, for it opens with the outbreak of terrified anger from the patrician child who has been
trapped into the witches' den, there to die in slow torment
for the better making of a love philtre; and it closes with
the curse which the doomed boy hurls at his destroyers.
Fear has left him, and fury has taken its place. He bids
the hags remember that no magic can alter right and
wrong, or avert retribution. He, dying at their hands, will
pursue them to their shameful deaths. The rabble will
pelt them with heavy stones, and fling their unblessed
bodies to the wolves:

'This shall my parents see,
Alas! surviving me.'

Horace was always concerned with witches and sorcerers;
but the trend of his mind was sceptical. He reached the
sane conclusion that they were malignant but impotent.

All this time he was making friends of an agreeable order. The reign of the great Augustus, even the consulship
of the great Octavius, was singularly favourable to brilliant
young men. Rome was extravagant and immoral; but it
was full of artistic and intellectual fervour. Horace's per-
sonality was charming, his attainments were remarkable.
Virgil, whose own estate had been confiscated and restored,
was his intimate companion; and it was Virgil who presented him to Maecenas, the minister and confidential
adviser of Octavius. From this introduction and the friendship that followed sprang one of the most perfect inter-
changes of gifts the world has ever known. Maecenas gave
Horace a farm in the Sabine hills, and the very modest
independence he desired. Horace gave Maecenas an im-
mortality that can never be disassociated from his own.

The more we think about it, the more sure we are that the fates — kindly for once — put these two men in the same place at the same time for the perfecting of their lives.

Augustus would have taken the accomplished young poet for one of his own secretaries, and would in all likelihood have treated him with the generosity he lavished upon Virgil; but Horace, lacking ambition, was not of the stuff out of which good courtiers are made. His political views had undergone a sobering change. He began to understand the mighty mission of Rome; the need of her to hold the western world together; her policy of conciliating and amalgamating conquered nations; her 'thrice-hammered hardihood' which nothing human could resist. No pride of citizenship ever equalled hers; and even her politicians still retained some measure of disinterested patriotism. Her monumental achievement, her lasting gift to the world she ruled, was law.

In the strengthening of imperial Rome, Maecenas played an important rôle. He was of Etruscan descent and a very great gentleman, scholarly, hospitable, public-minded. Where the superb basilica of Santa Maria Maggiore now stands, there stood his villa. Thither Augustus when ill had himself carried, to recover in purer air and more spacious quarters than his own palace, simple and plain, afforded him. The self-indulgence of the Roman emperors had no example in him. Since the lamentable Ides of March which saw the murder of Caesar, Maecenas had guided, supported, and restrained Caesar's nephew and heir. Many are the stories told of him, the most characteristic being that of his prompt action in the Forum when Octavius in an unrelenting mood was sentencing one po-

litical offender after another to death. Unable to approach
the tribune on account of the crowd that surged about it,
Maecenas wrote on his tablets, *Surge tandem Carnifex!*
('Butcher, break off!') and flung them straight into the
ruler's lap. Octavius read the words, rose silently, and
quitted the judgment seat which he had been pronounced
unworthy to fill.

Under the protection of Maecenas, Horace lived his
life serenely, and his talents ripened to perfection. His
lovely odes gave the same delight then that they give now;
his Roman soul venerated what was admirable, and strove
for what was attainable. He spent the best months of
the year in the country, where, unhurried by engagements
and unharassed by acquaintances, he wrote with delight
and deliberation. Like Marcus Aurelius, he was able to
be alone; but he was far too wise to make of himself that
lopsided thing called a recluse. He felt with Montaigne
the rare delight of dividing his life between the solace
afforded him by nature and the stimulus afforded him by
men.

It must be admitted that he had uncommon luck in
his dealings with both. Most of us could live in stable
harmony with nature if our meeting place were a beautiful and fertile corner of Italy. What did Horace know of
the malignant nature that rules supreme over wilderness
and jungle, desert and swamp? What of disastrous nature
hurling tornadoes and dust storms at her helpless children?
What of relentless nature that hates a farmer, and sends
sodden floods, or blighting droughts, or armies of pestif-
erous insects, to ruin him? The casual fashion in which
the poet alludes to unfavourable weather conditions proves
how small a part they played in his life. Not for nothing

has Italy been called the sweetheart of the world. Horace's farm was small, thirteen hundred feet above the sea, and surrounded by beautiful woods. It produced corn, olives and vines, though he thought poorly of the wine made from its grapes. It was managed by a bailiff, and cultivated by five families of freedmen. All its owner had to do was to eat and drink its products. He had also eight slaves to wait upon him, and, like most Roman slaves, they had uncommonly little to do. Even his modest meals of pancakes, lentils, and peas were served to him by three young slaves, smiling boys with whom he occasionally conversed. It was what was then called the simple life; but, as compared with the crude and elemental thing which goes by that name in this our land today, it is recognizable as the austere luxury of a very cultivated poet.

Rome, too, had its simplicities as well as its grandeurs. The citizen who stepped from his silken litter into a Roman street might be tripped into the gutter by one of the pigs that, like the happy Plantagenet pigs of London (at a later date), enjoyed unmolested the freedom of the city. Horace preferred on the whole the free and roving pig to the free and roving dog. The pig was at least sane. The dog might be rabid, and snap at him as it ran by. His satires, which grew at once keener and kinder as he approached his thirty-sixth birthday (they were given to the world collectively in 29 B.C.), describe for us the follies and extravagances of Rome; and, as unmitigated seriousness is always out of place in human affairs, these follies and extravagances amuse us as they amused the satirist two thousand years ago, as they must always amuse as well as instruct the student of human nature. It was from Horace that Thackeray learned how to people the canvas

of 'Vanity Fair.' 'To Thackeray,' says Sir Theodore
Martin, 'Horace was a breviary.'

'Out of Plato,' says Emerson, 'come all things that are
still written or debated among men of thought.' And if
this be true, we may add one word more. Out of Horace
come most things that are still enjoyed and respected by
men of feeling. The clear-sighted do not rule the world,
but they sustain and console it. It is not in human nature
to be led by intelligence. An intelligent world would not
be what it is today; it would never have been what it has
been in every epoch of which we have any knowledge.
Horace had no illusions on this score. He did not pass his
life in ignorance of the ills about him. Men lived on their
elemental instincts then as now. They wanted to keep
what they had, or they wanted to get what their neighbours had, just as they do today. Horace knew this, and
he invented no fancy phrases to decorate a bald fact. To
understand life was, indeed, a classic form of consolation,
a mental austerity which Pope failed to take into account
when he wrote:

> 'Horace still charms with graceful negligence,
>   And, without method, talks us into sense.'

Yet the little Queen Anne man had a deep admiration
for the poet who distilled philosophy from life, and whose
counsel of perfection is based upon the feasibility of performance. There was none of Goethe's 'negative and sceptical neutrality' about Horace. He knew that Rome was
the best possible means for ordering a large fraction of
humanity. He knew that discipline at home and invul-
nerability abroad were necessary for this end. He loved
with a passionate intensity of devotion the greatness of
Roman traditions, and the memory of the mighty dead.

Two notes of admonition he struck. One is in the tenth
ode of the second book, where he warns Licinius, and
through him all Romans, of the unwisdom of plotting
against the state: 'Reef your sails while there is yet time.'
The other is the third ode of the third book, one of the
great Alcaics on which the fame of the poet securely rests.
In it Juno herself sings the praises and the triumphs of
Rome — Rome destined to unite the severed countries of
the world, provided only that she paid no heed to her
own rabble (Horace and Shakespeare held the same opinion as to the intelligence of mobs), and curbed her own
cupidity:

> 'Riches the hardy soldiers must despise,
> And look on gold with undesiring eyes.'

It is not clear why this ode is held by most commentators
to refer to the hidden treasure of Darius (which, by the
way, still awaits discovery). It seems to allude merely to
the gold which all men knew to be buried deep in mines,
and which wise men believed had much better be left
there.

'The understanding sadness of Horace,' says Edith
Hamilton, 'tempers the gaiety of his verse into something
infinitely endearing.' The sobering truth which he bore
ever in mind he expressed with customary terseness:

> 'We may be wise, or rich, or great,
> But never can be blest.'

Therefore he sang unceasingly the praises of sweet content which springs from 'those deep regions of self where
the issues of character are decided.' This tenderness combined with disillusion has made him a helpmate for two
thousand years. Cheerfulness and melancholy can be, and
usually are, equally odious; but a sad heart and a gay

temper hold us in thrall. Even the amatory odes, which are so perfect and so unweighted by passion, have in them an undertone of regret. Commentators, always immersed in sentiment, have concluded that Cinara was to Horace what Lucy was to Wordsworth — a lost love and a lasting memory. But all we know is that she died young, and that Horace regretted with tempered sadness her early loss:

'I am not the man I was under the reign of Cinara.'

Lucy has no rival in the field. Cinara shares the canvas with shy Chloe, and false Neaera, and forward Glycera, and heartless Barine, and that accomplished flirt, Pyrrha,

'Plain in her neatness'

and Lydia, the lady of an ode as fragile and as flawless as a butterfly, which has been entitled in English 'The Reconciliation.' It has been translated by many lovers of Horace, never better perhaps than by Ben Jonson, though its sentiment is far from the direct and powerful emotions of the Elizabethans and of their immediate successors. It accords with the grace of the cavaliers, the playtime of the Restoration. Sir Charles Sedley should have translated it. Lovelace might have written it. Horace opens the dialogue. He is reproachful, but far from downcast, as he reminds Lydia that once he was her chosen lover. Lydia replies with spirit that when she reigned in his heart and in his song she asked no happier fate; but that she is not prepared to play second fiddle to Chloe. Horace admits the impelling power of Chloe, her sweetness, and her skill with the lyre. Of course his heart is hers. Lydia, not to be outdone in inconstancy, avows her love for Calais, Calais the son of Ornytus, a youth so engaging she would

gladly die for him. Horace, an old hand at the game of
love, asks what would happen should he discard bright
Chloe, and return a suppliant to his earlier love. Lydia,
in a suspiciously sudden surrender, responds with a cry of
joy: though Calais be fairer than a star, and Horace inconstant and rough as the sea,

'Yet should I wish to love, live, die with thee.'

Horace, like Virgil, remained contentedly unmarried.
He had the uneasy married lives of Augustus and of Maecenas by way of warning. His interest in women was an
undertone. The stifling problem (it is called a problem)
of sex which excites half the world to frenzy, and bores
the other half to extinction, resolves itself in his hands
into its simplest elements. His great emotions lay elsewhere, and he held even his great emotions in control.
The supreme Roman virtue was patriotism — to serve the
state and to die for it. Yet in what temperate language
Horace clothes his maxims, the very triteness of which
proves them immortal. *Dulce et decorum est pro patria
mori*. Not a flourish! Not a gesture! Yet life becomes a
thing of value and of sweetness because men can renounce
it with dignity. And there is nothing in the written history of the world to outstrip Horace's description, in the
fifth ode of the third book, of Regulus returning to Carthage: "'Tis said he put away his chaste wife's kisses and
his little children, as one bereft of civil rights, and bent his
gaze upon the ground till he should strengthen the Senate's
wavering purpose by advice never before given, and turn
his steps to exile.'

Next to the unswerving loyalty to Rome came the love
which Horace bore his friends, and, above and beyond all

other friends, to Maecenas, whose bread he ate, and whose
heart he held in his keeping. 'Remember,' said the dying
Maecenas to the Emperor Augustus, who stood sorrowing
by his bedside, 'remember Flaccus as you would remember
me.'

There was no need for this entreaty. In three weeks
Horace followed his friend, and was buried by his side on
the Esquiline Hill. This was as he had always foretold.
'When the blow falls it will crush us both; and to whatever
bourne you lead the way, I shall follow.' Fifty-seven
years the poet had lived, enjoying the ripeness of middle
age, and escaping the frosts that ensue. He had achieved
the utmost renown that Rome could give. A great lyric
poet; a philosopher whose epistles embody all pagan wisdom and a perfect understanding of humanity. The writer
of the Secular Hymn had become the arbiter of taste, the
spokesman of the Emperor, the persuasive exponent of a
reasonable life, the clear, sad thinker who led no man
astray. His death was so sudden that he had no time to
summon a scribe and dictate a will. Therefore he made
it orally, bequeathing his modest estate to the Emperor.
Such wills held good in Roman law, where many simplicities survived; but, in view of the uncertainties attendant upon men's recollections, it was wise to leave all to
the throne. If ever an oral will was sure to be remembered
rightly, it was when Augustus was the heir.

Horace not only reverenced his gods, but he believed
that he had been kindly treated by them. He was disposed to see something above and beyond nature in the
protection afforded him. When he was a little lost child
in the forest, and the leaves drifted upon him as he slept,
he felt sure that the birds had covered him, as in later

years they covered the hapless Babes in the Wood. The
falling tree that grazed but did not harm him, the wolf
that turned from his path when he was wandering in the
Sabine hills, composing an ode to Lalage — these things
did not happen by chance. Maecenas, too, had in his day
been snatched from danger; but mighty Jove conceived it
his duty to look after Maecenas; whereas

> 'Pan, who keeps watch
> O'er easy souls like mine,'

had turned smiling to the aid of Horace. Therefore it
behooves Maecenas to build a shrine and offer tribute;
but Horace will sacrifice a young lamb to the sylvan god.

The poet was the most hospitable of men. He dearly
loved the companionship of friends; and, having a perfectly
correct sense of values, he saw no reason why Maecenas
should not leave his stately home, which so far exceeded in
splendour the Emperor's palace, and spend his birthday
by the Sabine fireside, where Virgil had been content to
sit. The preparations for his coming were of a joyous
rusticity. Horace does not appear to have had the furni-
ture polished, as when the advocate, Torquatus, came to
visit him; but the silver vessels were burnished brightly,
garlands were gathered, the altar wreathed with sacred
leafage, the kitchen fires roared hospitably, and a jar of
Alban wine, nine years old, was waiting to be unsealed.
Horace had the poorest possible opinion of water drinkers,
and was convinced that not one of them ever wrote a
song that lived.

It behooved the poet to be out of the way a goodly
portion of his time, because he was too much wanted in
Rome. Maecenas wanted him and the Emperor wanted
him; and these two august and powerful men thought it

right that they should have what they desired. Horace thought otherwise. He clung tenaciously to his liberty, and he achieved it because he stood ready to sacrifice, if need be, all luxuries, comforts, and pleasures for its sake. He would not write his verse and he would not live his life to order. In a very determined and very delicate fashion he makes this known to Maecenas in the seventh epistle of the first book. He has left Rome for a week and he has stayed away a month — greatly to his friend's displeasure. After all, the month was August, and August is a season when anyone would be well advised to stay away from Rome. Horace says so plainly. It is the season, he writes, when the first figs and the mounting sun keep the undertaker busy. His health requires the cooler air, and, what is more important, his soul requires the freedom to make its own choice. 'Every man must measure himself by his own rule and standard.'

With Augustus the task was more difficult. The Emperor wanted to be sung, and he wanted to be sung in an intimate and homely strain. Horace wrote his most noble odes to celebrate the triumphs of Rome. He wrote charming songs to celebrate the peace and plenty which Augustus ensured to the Romans: 'The ox roams the pastures in safety, Ceres makes plentiful the crops, the sea is calm, the shrines are sacred, the home is unpolluted.' He also wrote the Secular Hymn at the instigation of the ruler. But that was as far as he would go. He never lessened the distance between the Emperor and the subject. He never affected an easy intimacy with the throne, though Augustus had asked him mockingly if he were ashamed of such a friendship. We cannot conceive him addressing the Caesar as the courtiers of Charles the Second addressed their easygoing monarch. And in all this he was more than worldly-wise. He was safeguarding his own self-respect, and preserving a fine and delicate standard of personal honour.

Of the poet's second home at Tibur we know little save that he loved it, and that it was surpassingly beautiful. The villa probably belonged to Maecenas, who slept more sweetly to the sound of falling waters, and Horace lived in it, off and on, for nineteen years. The Franciscan monks, with that unerring eye for beauty which all the religious orders have displayed, built the monastery of San Antonio on the site of his villa. It stood on the borderland between the Sabine country and the Campagna. Catullus, who lived near by, was wont to say that if his friends wished to mock at him as a rustic, they called him a Sabine. If they wished to imply that he was a gentleman, they called him a Tiburtine.

For Tibur, now Tivoli, is an older city than Rome, and was once its equal. In its earlier phase it was a city of smiths who fashioned and sharpened swords for the perpetual warfare of the day. The surrounding soil is more fertile than in the hill country. It grows better vines and more abundant crops. If Horace missed the Fountain of Bandusia, that leaping cascade which he was wont to climb so far to see, and to whose guardian deity he sacrificed a flower-decked kid, he had in its stead the falling waters of the Anio; the Cascata Grande, not then the torrent it is now, and the lovely Cascatelle streaming down the hillside in broken threads of silver. The orchards of Tibur were wet with spray, and the Tiburtine Sibyl delivered her oracles to the sound of many waters. Even Italy had nothing better to give. Small wonder that Horace wrote with a sigh of content, 'May Tibur, founded by Argive wanderers, be the home of my old age and my final goal.'

The scholars of the last century believed firmly that the classics offer us both a training for life and a help in living it. This is the hold that Horace has had on humanity, and his fashion of speech is such that educated youth gladly accepts his spokesmanship. We are told that a hundred years ago most public-school boys in England, and almost all Etonians, knew their Horace if they knew nothing else. It was not unusual for a lad of intelligence to have most of the odes by heart. The twentieth century has many new voices (some of them very insistent), but no one of them speaks to us with the accent of Horace. Hugh Macnaghten, for many years a master at Eton, and a translator of the classics, tells us a pleasant story in this regard. In the second year of the World War he had a letter from a former student, Henry Evelyn Platt, then fighting in France. It requested — of all things in the world — a copy of Horace, a small book, 'with perhaps a crib for the hard words,' and it gave the reason why. Young Platt was one of three Etonians in that line of trenches, and they had recently been joined by a Harrovian who was always quoting Horace. The Etonians were not so preoccupied with the deadly details of their lives as to be indifferent to this challenge. Come what might, they would reread their Horace for their own satisfaction, and for the honour of Eton.

Surely the soul of Horace, wherever it is located, was made glad by that letter. It was just what he had fore-told. Death for the pagan was a dismal thing. The bright gods dwelt on Olympus; but they shared their bliss with

none, and the realm of Pluto was but a poor exchange for
Athens or for Rome. But Horace knew that he would
triumph over death. *Non omnis moriar* ('Not all of me
shall die'). He spoke as prophets speak, piercing the future. While Rome lived, he would live. 'As long as the
Pontiff climbs the Capitol with the silent Vestal by his
side, I shall be famed, and beyond the boundaries of Rome
I shall travel far.'

> 'Barbarians unborn my name shall know.'

We know it and are glad.

THE MASTERFUL PURITAN

THE
MASTERFUL
PURITAN

WHEN William Chillingworth, preaching at Oxford in the first year of England's Civil War, defined the Cavaliers as publicans and sinners, and the Puritans as Scribes and Pharisees, he expressed the reasonable irritation of a scholar who had no taste or aptitude for polemics, yet who had been blown about all his life by every wind of doctrine. Those were uneasy years for men who loved moderation in everything, and who found it in nothing. It is not from such that we can hope for insight into emotions from which they were exempt, and purposes to which they held no clue.

In our day it is generously conceded that the Puritans made admirable ancestors. We pay them this handsome compliment in after dinner speeches at all commemorative meetings. Just what they would have thought of their descendants is an unprofitable speculation. Three hundred years divide us from those stern enthusiasts who, coveting lofty things, found no price too high to pay for them. 'It is not with us as with men whom small matters can discourage, or small discontentments cause to wish themselves at home again,' wrote William Brewster, when one half of the Mayflower Pilgrims had died in the first

terrible year, and no gleam of hope shone on the survivors.
To perish of hunger and cold is not what we should now
call a 'small discontentment.' To most of us it would
seem good and sufficient reason for abandoning any enterprise whatsoever. Perhaps if we would fix our attention
upon a single detail — the fact that for four years the
Plymouth colonists did not own a cow — we should better
understand what life was like in that harsh wilderness,
where children who could not get along without milk had
but one alternative — to die.

Men as strong as were the Puritan pioneers ask for no
apologies at our hands. Their conduct was shaped by
principles and convictions which would be insupportable
to us, but which are none the less worthy of regard.
Matthew Arnold summed up our modern disparagement
of their standards when he pictured Virgil and Shakespeare crossing on the Mayflower, and finding the Pilgrim fathers 'intolerable company.' I am not sure that
this would have been the case. Neither Virgil nor Shakespeare could have survived Plymouth. That much is
plain. But three months on the Mayflower might not have
been so 'intolerable' as Mr. Arnold fancied. The Roman
and the Elizabethan were strong-stomached observers of
humanity. They knew a man when they saw one, and
they measured his qualities largely.

Even if we make haste to admit that two great human-
izers of society, art and letters, played but a sorry part in
the Puritan colonies, we know they were less missed than
if these colonies had been worldly ventures, established
solely in the interest of agriculture or of trade. Sir Andrew Macphail tersely reminds us that the colonists possessed ideals of their own, 'which so far transcended the

things of this world that art and literature were not worth
bothering about in comparison with them.' Men who believe that, through some exceptional grace or good fortune, they have found God, feel little need of culture. If
they believe that they share God with all races, all nations,
and all ages, culture comes in the wake of religion. But
the Puritan's God was a somewhat exclusive possession.
'Christ died for a select company that was known to Him,
by name, from eternity,' wrote the Reverend Samuel
Willard, pastor of the South Church, Boston, and author
of that famous theological folio, 'A Compleat Body of
Divinity.' 'The bulk of mankind is reserved for burning,'
said Jonathan Edwards genially; and his Northampton
congregation took his word for it. That these gentlemen
knew no more about Hell and its inmates than did Dante
is a circumstance which does not seem to have occurred
to anyone. A preacher has some advantages over a poet.

If the Puritans never succeeded in welding together
Church and State, which was the desire of their hearts,
they had human nature to thank for their failure. There
is nothing so abhorrent — or so perilous — to the soul of
man as to be ruled in temporal things by clerical authority.
Yet inasmuch as the colony of Massachusetts Bay had
for its purpose the establishment of a state in which all
citizens should be of the same faith, and church member-
ship should be essential to freemen, it was inevitable that
the preacher and the elder should for a time dominate
public counsels. 'Are you, sir, the person who serves
here?' asked a stranger of a minister whom he met in the
streets of Rowley. 'I am, sir, the person who rules here,'
was the swift and apt response.

Men whose position was thus firmly established resented

the unauthorized intrusion of malcontents. Being re-
formers themselves, they naturally did not want to be re-
formed. Alone among New England colonists, the Pilgrims
of Plymouth, who were Separatists or Independents,
mistrusted the blending of civil and religious functions,
and this mistrust had deepened during the sojourn of their
leaders in Holland. Moreover, unlike their Boston neighbours, the Pilgrims were plain, simple people; 'not acquainted,' wrote Governor Bradford, 'with trades nor
traffique, but used to a countrie life, and the innocente
trade of husbandry.' They even tried the experiment of
farming their land on a communal system, and, as a result,
came perilously close to starvation. Only when each man
cultivated his own lot, that is, when individualism sup-
planted socialism, did they wring from the reluctant soil
food enough to keep them alive.

To the courage and intelligence of the Pilgrim and
Puritan leaders, Governor Bradford and Governor Winthrop, the settlers owed their safety and survival. The
instinct of self-government was strong in these men, their
measures were practical measures, their wisdom the wisdom of the world. If Bradford had not made friends with
the great sachem, Massasoit, and clinched the friendship
by sending Edward Winslow to doctor him with 'a con-
fection of many comfortable conserves' when he was ill,
the Plymouth colonists would have lost the trade with
the Indians which tided them over the first crucial years.
If Winthrop had not by force of argument and persuasion
obtained the lifting of duties from goods sent to England,
and induced the British creditors to grant favourable
terms, the Boston colony would have been bankrupt. The
keen desire of both Plymouth and Boston to pay their

debts is pleasant to record, and contrasts curiously with the reluctance of wealthy States to accept the Constitution in 1789, lest it should involve a similar course of integrity.

It is hardly worth while to censure communities which were establishing, or seeking to establish 'a strong religious state' because they were intolerant. Tolerance is not, and never has been, compatible with strong religious states. The Puritans of New England did not endeavour to force their convictions upon unwilling Christendom. They asked only to be left in peaceful possession of a singularly unprolific corner of the earth, which they were civilizing after a formula of their own. Settlers to whom this formula was antipathetic were asked to go elsewhere. If they did not go, they were sent, and sometimes whipped into the bargain — which was harsh, but not unreasonable.

Moreover, the 'persecution' of Quakers and Antinomians was not primarily religious. Few persecutions recorded in history have been. For most of them theology has merely afforded a pious excuse. Whatever motives may have underlain the persistent persecution of the Jews, hostility to their ancient creed has had little or nothing to do with it. To us it seems well-nigh incredible that Puritan Boston should have vexed its soul because Anne Hutchinson maintained that those who were in the covenant of grace were freed from the covenant of works — which sounds like a cinch. But when we remember that she preached against the preachers, affirming on her own authority that they had not the 'seal of the Spirit'; and that she 'gave vent to revelations,' prophesying evil for the harassed and anxious colonists, we can understand their eagerness to be rid of her. She was an able and intelligent woman, and her opponents were not always able and intelligent men. When the turmoil which followed in her wake destroyed the peace of the community, Governor Winthrop banished her from Boston. 'It was,' says John Fiske, 'an odious act of persecution.'

A vast deal of sympathy has been lavished upon the Puritan settlers because of the rigours of their religion, the austerity of their lives, their lack of intellectual stimulus, the comprehensive absence of anything like amusement. It has been even said that their sexual infirmities were due to the dearth of pastimes; a point of view which is in entire accord with modern sentiment, even if it falls short of the facts. Impartial historians might be disposed to think that the vices of the Puritans are apparent to us because they were so industriously dragged to light. When all moral offences are civil offences, and when every man is under the close scrutiny of his neighbours, the 'find' in sin is bound to be heavy. Captain Kemble, a Boston citizen of some weight and fortune, sat two hours in the stocks on a wintry afternoon, 1656, doing penance for 'lewd and unseemly behaviour'; which behaviour consisted in kissing his wife 'publiquely' at his own front door on the Lord's day. The fact that he had just returned from a long voyage, and was moved to the deed by some excess of emotion, failed to win him pardon. Neighbours were not lightly flouted in a virtuous community.

That there were souls unfit to bear the weight of Puritanism, and unable to escape from it, is a tragic truth. People have been born out of time and out of place since the Garden of Eden ceased to be a human habitation. When Judge Sewall read to his household a sermon on the text, 'Ye shall seek me and shall not find me,' the household doubtless protected itself by inattention, that refuge from admonition which is Nature's kindliest gift. But there was one listener, a terrified child of ten, who had no such bulwark, and who brooded over her unforgiven sins until her heart was bursting. Then suddenly, when the rest of the family had forgotten all about the sermon, she broke into 'an amazing cry,' sobbing out her agonized dread of Hell. And the pitiful part of the tale is that neither father nor mother could comfort her, having themselves no assurance of her safety. 'I answered her Fears as well as I could,' wrote Judge Sewall in his diary, 'and prayed with many Tears on either part. Hope God heard us.'

The incident was not altogether uncommon. A woman of Boston, driven to desperation by the uncertainty of salvation, settled the point for herself by drowning her baby in a well, thus ensuring damnation, and freeing her mind of doubts. Methodism, though gentler than Calvinism, accomplished similar results. In Wesley's journal there is an account of William Taverner, a boy of fourteen, who was a fellow passenger on the voyage to Georgia; and who, between heavy weather and continuous exhortation, went mad with fear, and saw an indescribable horror at the foot of his bed, 'which looked at him all the time unless he was saying his prayers.'

Our sympathy for a suffering minority need not, however, blind us to the fact that the vast majority of men hold on to a creed because it suits them, and because their souls are strengthened by its ministrations. 'It is sweet to believe even in Hell,' says that arch-mocker, Anatole France; and to no article of faith have believers clung more tenaciously. Frederick Locker tells us the engaging story of a dignitary of the Greek Church who ventured, in the early years of faith, to question this popular tenet; whereupon 'his congregation, justly incensed, tore their bishop to pieces.'

No Puritan divine stood in danger of suffering this particular form of martyrdom. The religion preached in New England was a cruel religion, from which the figure of Christ, living mercifully with men, was eliminated. John Evelyn noted down in his diary that he heard the Puritan magistrates of London 'speak spiteful things of our Lord's Nativity.' William Brewster was proud to record that in Plymouth 'no man rested' on the first Christmas day. As with Bethlehem, so with Calvary. Governor Endicott slashed with his sword the red cross of Saint George from the banner of England. The emblem of Christianity was anathema to these Christians, as was the Mother who bore Christ, and who saw Him die. The children whom He blessed became to Jonathan Edwards 'young vipers, and infinitely more hateful than vipers.' The sweetness of religion, which had solaced a suffering world, was wiped out. 'The Puritans,' wrote Henry Adams pithily, 'abandoned the New Testament and the Virgin in order to go back to the beginning, and renew the quarrel with Eve.'

It took strong men to live and thrive under such a ministration, wrestling with a sullen earth for subsistence, and with an angry Heaven for salvation. Braced to endurance by the long frozen winters, plainly fed and plainly clad, in peril, like Saint Paul, of sea and wilderness, narrow of vision but steadfast to principles, they fronted life resolutely, honouring and illustrating the supreme worth of freedom.

That they had compensations, other than religious, is apparent to all but the most superficial observer. The languid indifference to our neighbour's moral and spiritual welfare, which we dignify by the name of tolerance, has curtailed our interest in life. There must have been something invigorating in the iron determination that neighbours should walk a straight path, that they should be watched at every step, and punished for every fall. The Puritan who said, 'I will not. Thou shalt not!' enjoyed his authority to the uttermost. The prohibitionist who for ten years repeated his words was perhaps the only man who had a thoroughly good time during that fretful decade. It is hard, I know, to reconcile 'I will not. Thou shalt not!' with freedom. But the early settlers of New England were controlled by the weight of popular opinion. A strong majority forced a wavering minority along the road of rectitude. Standards were then as clearly defined as were boundaries, and the uncompromising individualism of the day permitted no juggling with responsibility.

It is not possible to read the second chapter of 'The Scarlet Letter,' and fail to perceive one animating principle of the Puritan's life. The townspeople who watch Hester Prynne stand in the pillory are moved by no common emotions. They savour the spectacle, as church-goers of an earlier age savoured the spectacle of a penitent in sackcloth at the portal; but they have also a sense of personal participation in the dragging of frailty to light. Hawthorne endeavours to make this clear when, in answer to Roger Chillingworth's questions, a bystander congratulates him upon the timeliness of his arrival on the scene. 'It must gladden your heart, after your troubles and sojourn in the wilderness, to find yourself at length in a land

where iniquity is searched out, and punished in the sight
of rulers and people.' An unfortunate speech to make to
the husband of the culprit (Hawthorne is seldom so ironic),
but a cordial admission of content.

There was a picturesque quality about the laws of New
England, and a nicety of administration, which made them
a source of genuine pleasure to all who were not being
judged. A lie, like an oath, was an offence to be punished;
but all lies were not equally punishable. Alice Morse
Earle quotes three penalties, imposed for three falsehoods,
which show how much pains a magistrate took to discriminate. George Crispe's wife who 'told a lie, not a
pernicious lie, but unadvisedly,' was simply admonished.
Will Randall who told a 'plain lie' was fined ten shillings.
Ralph Smith who 'lied about seeing a whale,' was fined
twenty shillings and excommunicated — which must have
rejoiced his suffering neighbours' souls.

The rank of a gentleman, being a recognized attribute
in those days, was liable to be forfeited for a disgraceful
deed. In 1631, Josias Plastowe of Boston was fined five
pounds for stealing corn from the Indians; and it was like-
wise ordered by the Court that he should be called in the
future plain Josias, and not Mr. Plastowe as formerly.
Here was a chance for the community to take a hand in
punishing a somewhat contemptible malefactor. It would
have been more or less than human if it had not enjoyed
the privilege.

By far the neatest instance of making the punishment
fit the crime is recorded in Governor Bradford's 'Diary of
Occurrences.' The carpenter employed to construct the
stocks for the Plymouth colonists thought fit to charge an
excessive rate for the job; whereupon he was speedily

clapped into his own instrument, 'being the first to suffer this penalty.' And we profess to pity the Puritans for the hardness and dulness of their lives! Why, if we could but see a single profiteer sitting in the stocks, one man out of the thousands who impudently oppress the public punished in this admirable and satisfactory manner, we should be willing to listen to sermons two hours long for the rest of our earthly days.

And the Puritans relished their sermons, which were masterful like themselves. Dogma and denunciation were dear to their souls, and they could bear an intolerable deal of both. An hour-glass stood on the preacher's desk, and youthful eyes strayed wistfully to the slender thread of sand. But if the discourse continued after the last grain had run out, a tithingman who sat by the desk turned the glass, and the congregation settled down for a fresh hearing. A three-hour sermon was a possibility in those iron days, while an eloquent parson, like Samuel Torrey of Weymouth, could and did pray for two hours at a stretch. The Reverend John Cotton, grandfather of the redoubtable Cotton Mather, and the only minister in Boston who was acknowledged by Anne Hutchinson to possess the mysterious 'seal of the Spirit,' had a reprehensible habit of preaching for two hours on Sunday in the meetinghouse (his family and servants of course attending), and at night, after supper, repeating this sermon to the sleepy household who had heard it in the morning.

For a hundred and fifty years the New England churches were unheated, and every effort to erect stoves was vigorously opposed. This at least could not have been a reaction against Popery, inasmuch as the churches of Catholic Christendom were at that time equally cold. That the

descendants of men who tore the noble old organs out of
English cathedrals, and sold them for scrap metal, should
have been chary of accepting even a 'pitch-pipe' to start
their unmelodious singing was natural enough; but stoves
played no part in the service. The congregations must have
been either impervious to discomfort, or very much afraid
of fires. The South Church of Boston was first heated in
the winter of 1783. There was much criticism of such
indulgence, and the *Evening Post* of January 25 burst into
denunciatory verse:

> 'Extinct the sacred fires of love,
> Our zeal grown cold and dead;
> In the house of God we fix a stove
> To warm us in their stead.'

Three blots on the Puritans' escutcheon (they were men,
not seraphs) have been dealt with waveringly by historians.
Witchcraft, slavery, and Indian warfare gloom darkly
against a shining background of righteousness. Much has
been made of the fleeting phase, and little of the more
permanent conditions — which proves the historic value
of the picturesque. That Salem should today sell witch
spoons and trinkets, trafficking upon memories she might
be reasonably supposed to regret, is a triumph of com-
mercialism. The brief and dire obsession of witchcraft was
in strict accord with times and circumstances. It bred fear,
horror, and a tense excitement which lifted from Massachusetts all reproach of dulness. The walls between the
known and the unknown world were battered savagely,
and the men and women who thronged from house to
house to see the 'Afflicted Children' writhe in convulsions
had a fearful appreciation of the spectacle. That terrible
child, Ann Putnam, who at twelve years of age was in-

strumental in bringing to the scaffold some of the most
respected citizens of Salem, is a unique figure in history.
The apprehensive interest she inspired in her townspeople
may be readily conceived. It brought her to ignominy in
the end.

The Plymouth colonists kept on good terms with their
Indian neighbours for half a century. The Bay colonists
had more aggressive neighbours, and dealt with them ac-
cordingly. It was an unequal combat. The malignancy of
the red men lacked concentration and thoroughness. They
were only savages, and accustomed to episodic warfare.
The white men knew the value of finality. When Massachusetts planned with Connecticut to exterminate the
Pequots, less than a dozen men escaped extermination.
It was a very complete killing, and no settler slept less
soundly for having had a hand in it. Mr. Fiske says that
the measures employed in King Philip's War 'did not lack
harshness,' which is a euphemism. The flinging of the
child Astyanax over the walls of Troy was less barbarous
than the selling of King Philip's little son into slavery.
Hundreds of adult captives were sent at the same time to
Barbados. It would have been more merciful, though less
profitable, to have butchered them at home.

The New England settlers were not indifferent to the
Indians' souls. They forbade them, when they could, to
hunt or fish on the Lord's day. John Eliot, Jonathan
Edwards, and other famous divines preached to them ear-
nestly, and gave them a fair chance of salvation. But, like
all savages, they had a trick of melting into the forest
just when their conversion seemed at hand. Cotton
Mather, in his 'Magnalia,' speculates ruthlessly upon their
condition and prospects. 'We know not,' he writes, 'when

or how these Indians first became inhabitants of this mighty continent; yet we may guess that probably the Devil decoyed these miserable savages hither, in hopes that the Gospel of the Lord would never come to destroy or disturb his absolute Empire over them.'

Naturally, no one felt well disposed towards a race which was under the dominion of Satan. Just as the Celt and the Latin have small compunction in ill-treating animals, because they have no souls, so the Puritan had small compunction in ill-treating heathens, because their souls were lost.

Slavery struck no deep roots in New England soil, perhaps because the nobler half of the New England conscience never condoned it, perhaps because circumstances were unfavourable to its development. The negroes died of the climate, the Indians of bondage. But traders, in whom conscience was not uppermost, trafficked in slaves as in any other class of merchandise, and stoutly refused to abandon a profitable line of business. Moreover, the deep discordance between slavery as an institution and Puritanism as an institution made such slave-holding more than ordinarily odious. Agnes Edwards, in an engaging little volume on Cape Cod, quotes a clause from the will of John Bacon of Barnstable, who bequeathed to his wife for her lifetime the 'use and improvement' of a slave-woman, Dinah. 'If, at the death of my wife, Dinah be still living, I desire my executors to sell her, and to use and improve the money for which she is sold in the purchase of Bibles, and distribute them equally among my said wife's and my grandchildren.'

There are fashions in goodness and badness as in all things else; but the selling of a worn-out woman for Bibles goes a step beyond Mrs. Stowe's most vivid imaginings.

These are heavy indictments to bring against the stern forbears whom we are wont to praise and patronize. But Pilgrim and Puritan can bear the weight of their misdeeds as well as the glory of their achievements. Of their good old English birthright, 'truth, pitie, freedom, and hardiness,' they cherished all but pitie. No price was too high for them to pay for the dignity of their manhood, or for the supreme privilege of dwelling on their own soil. They scorned the line of least resistance. Their religion was never a cloak for avarice, and labour was not with them another name for idleness and greed. Eight hours a day they held to be long enough for an artisan to work; but the principle of giving little and getting much, which rules our industrial world today, they deemed unworthy of freemen. No swollen fortunes corrupted their communities; no base envy of wealth turned them into prowling wolves. If they slew hostile Indians without compunction, they permitted none to rob those who were friendly and weak. If they endeavoured to exclude immigrants of alien creeds, they would have thought shame to bar them out because they were harder workers or better farmers than themselves. On the whole, a comparison between their methods and our own leaves us little room for self-congratulation.

From that great mother country which sends her roving sons over land and sea, the settlers of New England brought undimmed the sacred fire of liberty. If they were not akin to Shakespeare, they shared the inspiration of Milton. 'No nobler heroism than theirs,' says Carlyle, 'ever transacted itself on this earth.' Their laws were made for the strong, and commanded respect and obedience. In Plymouth few public employments carried any salary; but no man might refuse office when it was tendered to him. The Pilgrim, like the Roman, was expected to serve the state, not batten on it. What wonder that a few drops of his blood carries with it even now some measure of devotion and restraint. These were men who understood that life is neither a pleasure nor a calamity. 'It is a grave affair with which we are charged, and which we must conduct and terminate with honour.'

THE PERILS OF IMMORTALITY

THE PERILS
OF
IMMORTALITY

Peu de génie, point de grâce.

THERE is no harder fate than to be immortalized as a fool; to have one's name — which merits nothing sterner than obliteration — handed down to generations as an example of silliness, or stupidity, or presumption; to be enshrined pitilessly in the amber of the 'Dunciad'; to be laughed at forever because of Charles Lamb's impatient and inextinguishable raillery. When an industrious young authoress named Elizabeth Ogilvy Benger — a model of painstaking insignificance — invited Charles and Mary Lamb to drink tea with her one cold December night, she little dreamed she was achieving a deathless and unenviable fame; and that, when her half dozen books should have lapsed into comfortable oblivion, she herself should never be fortunate enough to be forgotten. It is a cruel chance which crystallizes the folly of an hour, and makes it outlive our most serious endeavours. Perhaps we should do well to consider this painful possibility before hazarding an acquaintance with the Immortals.

Miss Benger did more than hazard. She pursued the Immortals with insensate zeal. She bribed Mrs. Inchbald's servant-maid into lending her cap, and apron, and

tea-tray; and, so equipped, penetrated into the inmost
sanctuary of that literary lady, who seems to have taken
the intrusion in good part. She was equally adroit in
seducing Mary Lamb — as the Serpent seduced Eve —
when Charles Lamb was the ultimate object of her designs. Coming home to dinner one day, 'hungry as a
hunter,' he found to his dismay the two women closeted
together, and trusted he was in time to prevent their
exchanging vows of eternal friendship; though not — as
he discovered later — in time to save himself from an
engagement to drink tea with the stranger ('I had never
seen her before, and could not tell who the devil it was
that was so familiar'), the following night.

What happened is told in a letter to Coleridge; one of
the best-known and one of the longest letters Lamb ever
wrote — he is so brimful of his grievance. Miss Benger's
lodgings were up two flights of stairs in East Street. She
entertained her guests with tea, coffee, macaroons, and
'much love.' She talked to them, or rather *at* them, upon
purely literary topics, as, for example, Miss Hannah
More's 'Strictures on Female Education,' which they had
never read. She addressed Mary Lamb in French — 'possibly having heard that neither Mary nor I understood
French' — and she favoured them with Miss Seward's
opinion of Pope. She asked Lamb, who was growing more
miserable every minute, if he agreed with D'Israeli as to
the influence of organism upon intellect; and when he tried
to parry the question with a pun upon organ — 'which
went off very flat' — she despised him for his feeble flip-
pancy. She advised Mary to carry home two translations
of 'Pizarro,' so that she might compare them *verbatim* (an
offer hastily declined), and she made them both promise

to return the following week — which they never did —
to meet Miss Jane Porter and her sister, 'who, it seems,
have heard much of Mr. Coleridge, and wish to meet *us*
because we are *his* friends.' It is a *comédie larmoyante*.
We sympathize hotly with Lamb when we read his letter;
but there is something piteous in the thought of the poor
little hostess going complacently to bed that night, and
never realizing that she had made her one unhappy flight
to fame.

There were people, strange as it may seem, who liked
Miss Benger's evenings. Miss Aikin assures us that 'her
circle of acquaintances extended with her reputation, and
with the knowledge of her excellent qualities, and she was
often enabled to assemble as guests at her humble tea-
table names whose celebrity would have insured attention
in the proudest salons of the metropolis.' Crabb Robinson,
who was a frequent visitor, used to encounter large parties
of sentimental ladies; among them, Miss Porter, Miss
Landon, and the 'eccentric but amiable' Miss Wesley —
John Wesley's niece — who prided herself upon being
broad-minded enough to have friends of varying religions,
and who, having written two unread novels, remarked
complacently to Miss Edgeworth: 'We sisters of the quill
ought to know one another.'

The formidable Lady de Crespigny of Campion Lodge
was also Miss Benger's condescending friend and patroness;
and this august matron — of insipid mind and imperious
temper — was held to sanctify in some mysterious manner all whom she honoured with her notice. The praises
lavished upon Lady de Crespigny by her contemporaries
would have made Hypatia blush, and Sappho hang her
head. Like Mrs. Jarley, she was the delight of the nobility

and gentry. She corresponded, so we are told, with the *literati* of England; she published, like a British Cornelia, her letters of counsel to her son; she was 'courted by the gay and admired by the clever'; and she mingled at Campion Lodge 'the festivity of fashionable parties with the pleasures of intellectual society, and the comforts of domestic peace.'

To this array of feminine virtue and feminine authorship, Lamb was singularly unresponsive. He was not one of the *literati* honoured by Lady de Crespigny's correspondence. He eluded the society of Miss Porter, though she was held to be handsome — for a novelist. ('The only literary lady I ever knew,' wrote Miss Mitford, 'who didn't look like a scarecrow to keep birds from cherries.') He said unkindly of Miss Landon that, if she belonged to him, he would lock her up and feed her on bread and water until she left off writing poetry. And for Miss Wesley he entertained a cordial animosity, only one degree less lively than his sentiments towards Miss Benger. Miss Wesley had a lamentable habit of sending her effusions to be read by reluctant men of letters. She asked Lamb for Coleridge's address, which he, to divert the evil from his own head, cheerfully gave. Coleridge, very angry, reproached his friend for this disloyal baseness; but Lamb, with the desperate instinct of self-preservation, refused all promise of amendment. 'You encouraged that mopsey, Miss Wesley, to dance after you,' he wrote tartly, 'in the hope of having her nonsense put into a nonsensical Anthology. We have pretty well shaken her off by that simple expedient of referring her to you; but there are more burs in the wind.' . . . 'Of all God's creatures,' he cries again, in an excess of ill-humour, 'I detest letters-affecting, authors-hunting ladies.' Alas for Miss Benger when she hunted hard, and the quarry turned at bay!

An atmosphere of inexpressible dreariness hangs over the little coterie of respectable, unilluminated writers, who, to use Lamb's priceless phrase, encouraged one another in mediocrity. A vapid propriety, a mawkish sensibility were their substitutes for real distinction of character or mind. They read Mary Wollstonecraft's books, but would not know the author; and when, years later, Mrs. Gaskell presented the widowed Mrs. Shelley to Miss Lucy Aikin, that outraged spinster turned her back upon the erring one, to the profound embarrassment of her hostess. Of Mrs. Inchbald, we read in 'Public Characters' for 1811: 'Her moral qualities constitute her principal excellence; and though useful talents and personal accomplishments, of themselves, form materials for an agreeable picture, moral character gives the polish which fascinates the heart.' The conception of goodness then in vogue is pleasingly illustrated by a passage from one of Miss Elizabeth Hamilton's books, which Miss Benger in her biography of that lady (now lost to fame) quotes appreciatively:

'It was past twelve o'clock. Already had the active and judicious Harriet performed every domestic task; and, having completely regulated the family economy for the day, was quietly seated at work with her aunt and sister, listening to Hume's "History of England," as it was read to her by some orphan girl whom she had herself instructed.'

So truly ladylike had the feminine mind grown by this time that the very language it used was refined to the point of ambiguity. Mrs. Barbauld writes genteelly of the behaviour of young girls 'to the other half of their species,' as though she could not bear to say, simply and coarsely, men. So full of content were the little circles who listened to the 'elegant lyric poetess,' Mrs. Hemans, or to 'the female Shakespeare of her age,' Miss Joanna Baillie (we owe both these phrases to the poet Campbell), that when Crabb Robinson was asked by Miss Wakefield whether he would like to know Mrs. Barbauld, he cried enthusiastically: 'You might as well ask me whether I should like to know the Angel Gabriel!'

In the midst of these sentimentalities and raptures, we catch now and then forlorn glimpses of the Immortals, of Wordsworth at a literary entertainment in the house of Mr. Hoare of Hampstead, sitting mute and miserable all the evening in a corner, which, as Miss Aikin truly remarked, was 'disappointing and provoking'; of Lamb carried by the indefatigable Crabb Robinson to call on Mrs. Barbauld. This visit appears to have been a distinct failure. Lamb's one recorded observation was that Gilbert Wakefield had a peevish face — an awkward remark, as Wakefield's daughter sat close at hand and listening. 'Lamb,' writes Mr. Robinson, 'was vexed, but got out of the scrape tolerably well' — having had, indeed, plenty of former experiences to help him on the way.

There is a delightful passage in Miss Jane Porter's diary which describes at length an evening spent at the house of Mrs. Fenwick, 'the amiable authoress of "Secrecy." ' (Everybody was the amiable authoress of something. It was a day, like our own, given over to the worship of ink.) The company consisted of Miss Porter and her sister Maria, Miss Benger and her brother, the poet Campbell and his nephew, a young man barely twenty years of age. The lion of the little party was of course the poet, who endeared himself to Mrs. Fenwick's heart by his attentions to her son, 'a beautiful boy of six.'

'This child's innocence and caresses,' writes Miss Porter gushingly, 'seemed to unbend the lovely feelings of Campbell's heart. Every restraint but those which the guardian angels of tender infancy acknowledge was thrown aside. I never saw Man in a more interesting point of view. I felt how much I esteemed the author of the "Pleasures of Hope." When we returned home, we walked. It was a charming summer night. The moon shone brightly. Maria leaned on Campbell's arm. I did the same by Benger's. Campbell made some observations on *pedantic* women. I did not like it, being anxious for the respect of this man. I was jealous about how nearly he might think *we* resembled that character. When the Bengers parted from us, Campbell observed my abstraction, and with sincerity I confessed the cause. I know not what were his replies; but they were so gratifying, so endearing, so marked with truth, that when we arrived at the door, and he shook us by the hand, as a sign of adieu immediately prior to his next day's journey to Scotland, we parted with evident marks of being all in tears.'

It is rather disappointing, after this outburst of emotion, to find Campbell, in a letter to his sister, describing Miss Porter in language of chilling moderation: 'Among the company was Miss Jane Porter, whose talents my *nephew* adores. She is a pleasing woman, and made quite a conquest of him.'

Miss Benger was only one of the many aspirants to literary honours whose futile endeavours vexed and affronted Charles Lamb. In reality she burdened him far less than others who, like Miss Betham and Miss Stoddart, succeeded in sending him their verses for criticism, or who begged him to forward the effusions to Southey — an office he gladly fulfilled. Perhaps Miss Benger's vivacity jarred upon his taste. He was fastidious about the gaiety of women. Madame de Staël considered her one of the most interesting persons she had met in England; but the approval of this 'impudent clever' Frenchwoman would have been the least possible recommendation to Lamb. If he had known how hard had been Miss Benger's struggles, and how scanty her rewards, he might have forgiven her that sad perversity which kept her toiling in the field of letters. She had had the misfortune to be a precocious child, and had written at the age of thirteen a poem called 'The Female Geniad,' which was dedicated to Lady de Crespigny, and published under the patronage of that honoured dame. Youthful prodigies were then much in favour. Miss Mitford comments very sensibly upon them, being filled with pity for one Mary Anne Browne, 'a fine tall girl of fourteen, and a full-fledged authoress,' who was extravagantly courted and caressed one season, and cruelly ignored the next. The 'Female Geniad' sealed Miss Benger's fate. When one has written a poem at thirteen, and that poem has been printed and praised, there is nothing for it but to keep on writing until Death mercifully removes the obligation.

It is needless to say that the drama — which then, as now, was the goal of every author's ambition — first fired Miss Benger's zeal. When we think of Miss Hannah More as a successful playwright, it is hard to understand how any one could fail; yet fail Miss Benger did, although we are assured by her biographer that 'her genius appeared in many ways well adapted to the stage.' She next wrote a mercilessly long poem upon the abolition of the slave trade (which was read only by anti-slavery agitators), and two novels — 'Marian,' and 'Valsinore: or, the Heart and the Fancy.' Of these we are told that 'their excellences were such as genius only can reach'; and if they also missed their mark, it must have been because — as Miss Aikin delicately insinuates — 'no judicious reader could fail to perceive that the artist was superior to the work.' This is always unfortunate. It is the work, and not the artist, which is offered for sale in the market-place. Miss Benger's work is not much worse than a great deal which did sell, and she possessed at least the grace of an unflinching and courageous perseverance. Deliberately, and without aptitude or training, she began to write history, and in this most difficult of all fields won for herself a hearing. Her 'Life of Anne Boleyn,' and her 'Memoirs of Mary, Queen of Scots,' were read in many an English schoolroom; their propriety and Protestantism making them acceptable to the anxious parental mind. A single sentence from 'Anne Boleyn' will suffice to show the ease of Miss Benger's mental attitude, and the comfortable nature of her views:

'It would be ungrateful to forget that the mother of Queen Elizabeth was the early and zealous advocate of the Reformation, and that, by her efforts to dispel the gloom of ignorance and superstition, she conferred on the English people a benefit of which, in the present advanced state of knowledge and civilization, it would be difficult to conceive or to appreciate the real value and importance.'

In *La Belle Assemblée* for April, 1823, there is an engraving of Miss Smirke's portrait of Miss Benger. She is painted in an imposing turban, with tight little curls

and an air of formidable sprightliness. It was this sprightliness which was so much admired. 'Wound up by a cup
of coffee,' she would talk for hours, and her friends really
seem to have liked it. 'Her lively imagination,' writes
Miss Aikin, 'and the flow of eloquence it inspired, aided
by one of the most melodious of voices, lent an inexpressible charm to her conversation, which was heightened by
an intuitive discernment of character, rare in itself, and
still more so in combination with such fertility of fancy
and ardency of feeling.'

This leaves little to be desired. It is not at all like the
Miss Benger of Lamb's letter, with her vapid pretensions
and her stupid insolence. Unhappily, we see through
Lamb's eyes, and we cannot see through Miss Aikin's.
Of one thing only I feel sure. Had Miss Benger, instead
of airing her trivial acquirements, told Lamb that when
she was a little girl, bookless and penniless, at Chatham,
she used to read the open volumes in the booksellers'
windows, and go back again and again, hoping that the
leaves might. be turned, she would have touched a re-
sponsive chord in his heart. Who does not remember his
exquisite sympathy for 'street-readers,' and his unlikely
story of Martin B——, who 'got through two volumes
of "Clarissa"' in this desultory fashion. Had he but
known of the shabby, eager child, staring wistfully at
the coveted books, he would never have written the most
amusing of his letters, and Miss Benger's name would be
today unknown.

TOWN AND SUBURB

TOWN AND SUBURB

I prize civilization, being bred in towns, and liking to hear and see what new things people are up to. — George Santayana.

When I was a child, and people lived in towns and read poetry about the country, American cities had sharply accentuated characteristics, which they sometimes pretended to disparage, but of which they were secretly and inordinately proud. Less rich in tradition and inheritance than the beautiful cities of Europe, they nevertheless possessed historic backgrounds which coloured their communal life, and lent significance to social intercourse. The casual allusion of the Bostonian to his 'Puritan conscience,' the casual allusion of the Philadelphian to his 'Quaker forbears,' did not perhaps imply what they were meant to imply; but they indicated an outlook, and established an understanding. The nearness of friends in those days, the familiar, unchanging streets, the convivial clubs, the constant companionship helped to knit the strands of life into a close and well-defined pattern. Townsmen who made part of this pattern were sometimes complacent without much cause, and combative without any cause at all; but the kind of cynicism which breeds fatigue about human affairs was no part of their robust constitutions.

A vast deal of abuse has been levelled against cities; and the splendour of the parts they have played has been

dimmed by a too persistent contemplation of their sins
and their suffering. Thomas Jefferson said that they were
a sore on the body politic; but then Jefferson appears to
have believed that farming was the only sinless employ-
ment for man. When he found himself loving Paris, because he was an American and could not help it, he
excused his weakness by reflecting that, after all, France
was not England, and by admitting a little ruefully that
in Paris 'a man might pass his life without encountering
a single rudeness.' It was Jefferson's contemporary,
Cobbett, who, more than a hundred years ago, started
the denouncement of towns and town life which has come
rumbling down to us through the century. London was
the object of his supreme detestation. Jews and Quakers
lived in London (so he said), also readers of the *Edin-
burgh Review*; and Jews, Quakers, and readers of the *Edin-
burgh Review* were alike to him anathema. 'Cobbett,'
mused Hazlitt, 'had no comfort in fixed principles'; and
for persistent fixity of principles the *Review* ran a close
third to the followers of Moses and of Fox.

It was pure wrong-headedness on the part of a proletar-
ian fighting the cause of the proletariat to turn aside from
the age-old spectacle of the townsman cradling his liberty,
and rejoicing in his labour. There was not an untidy little
mediaeval city in Europe that did not help to carry humanity on its way. The artisans scorned by Froissart, the
'weavers, fullers, and other ill-intentioned people of the
town,' who gave so much trouble to their betters, battled
unceasingly for communal rights, and very often got them.
The guilds, proud, quarrelsome and defiant, gave to the
world the pride and glory of good work, and the pride
and glory of freedom. As for London, those 'mettlesome

Thames dwellers' held their own for centuries against every form of aggression. The silken cord which halts each king of England at Temple Bar on his way to coronation is a reminder of the ancient liberties of London. There stood the city's gates, which were opened only at the city's will. Charles the First signed his own death warrant when he undertook to coerce that stubborn will. When George the First asked Sir Robert Walpole how much it would cost to enclose Saint James's Park (long the delight of Londoners), and make it the private pleasure-ground of the king, the minister answered in four words, 'Only three crowns, Sire,' and the Hanoverian shrugged his shoulders in silent understanding. What a strange people he had come to rule!

We Americans think that we put up a brave fight against the stupid obstinacy of George the Third, and so we did for seven years. But London fought him all the years of his reign. 'It was not for nothing,' says Trevelyan, 'that Londoners with their compact organization, and their habits of political discipline, proudly regarded themselves as the regular army of freedom.' George, whose conception of kingship was singularly simple and primitive, regarded his hostile city pretty much as Victoria regarded her House of Commons. 'Very unmanageable and troublesome,' was her nursery-governess's comment upon a body of men who were (though she did not like to think so) the law-makers of Britain.

With all history to contradict us, it is hardly worth while to speak of city life as entailing 'spiritual loss,' because it is out of touch with Nature. It is in touch with humanity, and humanity is Nature's heaviest asset. Blake, for some reason which he never made plain (making

things plain was not his long suit), considered Nature —
'the vegetable universe,' he phrased it — to be depraved.
He also considered Wordsworth to be more or less depraved because of his too exclusive worship at her shrine.
'I fear Wordsworth loves Nature,' he wrote (proud of his
penetration) to Crabb Robinson; 'and Nature is the work
of the Devil. The Devil is in us all so far as we are natural.' Yet, when Wordsworth the Nature-lover stood on
Westminster Bridge at dawn, and looked upon the sleeping London, he wrote a noble sonnet to her beauty:

> 'Earth has not anything to show more fair.'

When Blake looked upon London, he saw only her sorrow
and her sin, he heard only 'the youthful harlot's curse'
blighting her chartered streets. She was a trifle more depraved than Nature.

The present quarrel is not even between Nature and
man, between the town and the country. It is between
the town and the suburb, that midway habitation which
fringes every American city, and which is imposing or
squalid according to the incomes of suburbanites. This
semi-rural life, though it has received a tremendous impetus in the present century, is not precisely new. Clerk-
enwell, London's oldest suburb, dates from the Plantag-
enets. John Stow, writing in the days of Elizabeth, says
that rich men who dwelt in London town spent their
money on hospitals for the sick and almshouses for the
poor; but that rich men who dwelt in Shoreditch and other
suburbs spent their money on costly residences to gratify
their vanity. Being an antiquarian, and a freeman of
Merchant Taylors' Company, Stow naturally held by the
town.

It is the all-prevailing motor which stands responsible for the vast increase of suburban life in the United States, just as it was the coming of the locomotive which stood responsible for the increased population of London in Cobbett's last days. 'The facilities which now exist for moving human bodies from place to place,' he wrote in 1827 (being then as much distressed by the excellence of the coaching roads as by the invasion of steam), 'are among the curses of the country, the destroyers of industry, of morals, and of happiness.'

It sounds sour to people who are now being taught that to get about easily and quickly is ever and always a blessing. The motor, we are given to understand, is of inestimable service because it enables men and women to do their work in the city, and escape with ease and comfort to their country homes — pure air, green grass, and so on. Less stress is laid upon the fact that it is also the motor which has driven many of these men and women into the suburbs by rendering the city insupportable; by turning into an open-air Bedlam streets which were once peaceful, comely and secure. Mr. Henry Ford, who has added the trying rôle of prophet to his other avocations, proclaimed twelve years ago that American cities were doomed. They had had their day. They had abused their opportunities. They had become unbearably expensive. They had grown so congested that his cars could make no headway in their streets. Therefore they must go. 'Delenda est Carthago; dum Ford deliberat.'

If Dickens still has readers as well as buyers, they must be grimly diverted by the art with which, in 'A Tale of Two Cities,' he works up the incident of the child run over and killed in the crowded streets of Paris. He makes

this incident the key to all that follows. It justifies the
murder by which it is avenged. It interprets the many
murders that are on their way. It is an indictment of a
class condemned to destruction for its wantonness. And
to emphasize the dreadfulness of the deed, Dickens adds
this damnatory sentence: 'Carriages were often known
to drive on, and leave their wounded behind them.'

All this fire and fury over a child killed in the streets!
Why, we Americans behold a yearly holocaust of children
that would have glutted the bowels of Moloch. When
thirty-odd thousand people are slain by motors in twelve
months, it is inevitable that a fair proportion of the dead
should be little creatures too feeble and foolish to save
themselves. As for driving on and leaving the wounded,
that is a matter of such common occurrence that we have
with our usual ingenuity invented a neat and expressive
phrase for it, thus fitting it into the order of the day.
The too-familiar headlines in the press, 'Hit-and-run
victim found unconscious in the street,' 'Hit-and-run
victim dies in hospital,' tell over and over again their
story of callous cruelty. That such cruelty springs from
fear is no palliation of the crime. Cowardice explains,
but does not excuse, the most appalling brutalities. This
particular form of ruffianism wins out (more's the pity!)
in a majority of cases, and so it is likely to continue. In
a single year, three hundred and sixty-one hit-and-run
drivers remained unidentified, and escaped the penalty
they deserved. Philippe de Comines cynically observed
that he had known very few people who were clever
enough to run away in time. The hit-and-runners of
America could have given him points in this ignoble
game.

The supposed blessedness of country life (see every anthology in the libraries) has been kindly extended to the suburbs. They are open to Whistler's objection that trees grow in them, and to Horace Walpole's objection that neighbours grow in them also. Rich men multiply their trees; poor men put up with the multiplication of neighbours. Rich men can conquer circumstances wherever they are. Poor men (and by this I mean men who are urbanely alluded to as in 'moderate circumstances') do a deal of whistling to keep themselves warm. They talk with serious fervour about Nature, when the whole of their landed estate is less than one of the back yards in which the town dwellers of my youth grew giant rose-bushes that bloomed brilliantly in the mild city air. Mowing a grass-plot is to them equivalent to ploughing the soil. Sometimes they have not even a plot to mow, not even the shelter of a porch, nor the dignity and distinction of their own front door; but live in gigantic sub-urban apartment houses, a whole community under one roof like a Bornean village. Yet this monstrous standardization leaves them happy in the belief that they are country dwellers, lovers of the open, and spiritual descendants of the pioneers.

And the city? The abandoned city whose sons have fled to suburbs, what is it but a chaotic jumble of sky-scrapers, public institutions, and parked cars? A transition stage is an uncomely stage, and cities on the move have a melancholy air of degradation. Shops elbow their uneasy way, business soars up into the air, houses disappear from their familiar settings, tired men and women drop into their clubs on the twentieth story of a neutral building, streets are dug up, paved, and dug up

again, apparently with a view to buried treasure; dirt,
confusion, and piercing noise are permitted by citizens
who find it easier to escape such evils than to control
them. An impression prevails that museums, libraries,
and imposing banks constitute what our American press
delights in calling 'the city beautiful.' That there is no
beauty without distinction, and that distinction is made
or marred by the constant, not the casual, contact of
humanity, is a truth impressed upon our minds by countless towns in Europe, and by a great many towns in the
United States. They tell their tale as plainly as a printed
page, and far more convincingly.

If this tale is at an end; if the city has nothing to give
but dirt, disorder, and inhuman racket, then let its sons
fly to the suburbs and mow their grass-plots in content.
If it has no longer a vehement communal life, if it be not,
as it once was, the centre of pleasure and of purpose, if it
be a thoroughfare and nothing else, then let them pass
through it and escape. One thing is sure. No rural community, no suburban community, can ever possess the
distinctive qualities that city dwellers have for centuries
given to the world. The common interests, the keen and
animated intercourse with its exchange of disputable convictions, the cherished friendships and hostilities — these
things shaped townsmen into a compact, intimate society
which left its impress upon each successive generation.
The home gives character to the city; the man gives character to the home. If, when his day's work is over, he goes
speeding off to a suburb, he breaks the link which binds
him to his kind. He says that he has good and beautiful
and health-giving relations with Nature — a tabloid Nature suited to his circumstances; but his relations with men

are devitalized. Will Rogers indicated delicately this de-
vitalization when he said: 'League of Nations! No, Americans aren't bothering about the League of Nations. What
they want is some place to park their cars.'

Londoners, who have no cause to fear a semi-deserted
London, grieve that even a single thoroughfare should
change its aspect, should lose its old and rich association
with humanity. So Mr. George Street grieved over an
altered Piccadilly, reconstructing the dramas it had wit-
nessed, the history in which it had borne a part; wandering
in fancy from house to house, where dwelt the great, the
gay, and the undaunted. His book, he said, was an epi-
taph. Piccadilly still lived, and gave every day a clamorous demonstration of activity; but her two hundred years
of social prominence were over, and her very distinguished
ghosts would never have any successors.

This is what is known as progress, and from it the great
cities of Europe have little or nothing to fear. London,
Paris, and Rome remain august arbiters of fate. They
may lose one set of associations, but it would take centuries to rob them of all. Only a mental revolution could persuade their inhabitants that they are not good places to
live in; and the eloquence of an archangel would be powerless to convince men bred amid arresting traditions that
they are less fit to control the destinies of a nation than
are their bucolic neighbours.

It would be hard to say when or why the American mind
acquired the conviction that the lonely farmhouse or the
sacrosanct village was the proper breeding-place for great
Americans. It can hardly be due to the fact that Washington was a gentleman farmer, and Lincoln a country boy.
These circumstances are without significance. The youth-

ful Washington would have taken as naturally to fighting, and the youthful Lincoln to politics, if they had been born in Richmond and Louisville. But the notion holds good. It has been upheld by so keen an observer and commentator as Mr. Walter Lippmann, who has admitted that ex-Governor Smith, for whom he cherishes a profound and intelligent admiration, was debarred from the presidency by 'the accident of birth.' The opposition to him was based upon a sentiment 'as authentic and as poignant as his support. It was inspired by the feeling that the clamorous life of the city should not be acknowledged as the American ideal.'

This is, to say the least, bewildering. The qualities which Mr. Lippmann endorses in Mr. Smith, his 'sure instinct for realities,' his 'supremely good-humoured intelligence, and practical imagination about the ordinary run of affairs,' are products of his environment. His name can be written in the book of state as one who knows his fellow men; and he knows them because he has rubbed elbows with them from boyhood. The American people, says Mr. Lippmann, resent this first-hand knowledge. They will not condone or sanction it. 'In spite of the mania for size and the delusions of grandeur which are known as progress, there is still an attachment to village life. The cities exist, but they are felt to be alien; and in this uncertainty men turn to the scenes from which the leaders they have always trusted have come. The farmhouse at Plymouth, with old Colonel Coolidge doing the chores, was an inestimable part of President Coolidge's strength. The older Americans feel that it is in such a place that American virtue is bred; a cool, calm, shrewd virtue, with none of the red sins of the sidewalks of New York.'

There may be Americans who entertain this notion, but
Mr. Lippmann, I am sure, is not of the number. He is well
aware that sin does not belong to sidewalks. It has no pre-
disposition towards pavements or mud roads. It is in-
digenous to man. Our first parents lived in the country,
and they promptly committed the only sin they were given
a chance to commit. Cain was brought up in the heart of
the country, and he killed one of the small group of people
upon whom he could lay his hands. That 'great cities,
with their violent contrasts of riches and poverty, have
produced class hatred all the world over,' is true — but a
half-truth. The *Jacquerie*, most hideous illustration of
well-earned class hatred, was a product of the countryside.
So was the German *Bundschuh.* The French and the Russian Revolutionists lighted up wide landscapes with burning homes, and soaked the innocent soil with blood. The
records of crime prove the universality of crime. Bastards
and morons and paranoiacs and degenerates and the crimi-
nally insane may be found far from the sidewalks of New
York.

To live in stable harmony with Nature should be as easy
for the town dweller as for the countryman. As a matter
of fact, it should be easier, inasmuch as 'the brutal, innocent injustice of Nature' leaves the town dweller little the
worse. Like authorship, Nature is a good stick but a bad
crutch, and they love her best who are not dependent on
her caprices:

> 'Bred in the town am I,
>   So would I wish to be,
> Loving its glimpses of sky,
>   Swayed by its human sea.'

If Browning in his incomparable poem, 'Up at a Villa —

Down in the City,' appears to mock at the street-loving
lady, he nevertheless makes out a strong case in her favour.
I have sympathized with her all my life; and it is worthy
of note that the poet himself preferred to live in towns,
and, like Santayana, see what people were up to. The exceptionally fortunate man was Montaigne who drew a
threefold wisdom from the turbulent city of Bordeaux,
which he ruled as mayor; from the distinction of Paris and
the French court, where he was a gentleman of the king's
chamber; and from the deep solitude of Auvergne, where
stood his ancestral home. He knew the life of the politician, the life of the courtier, the life of the farmer. Therefore, being kindly disposed towards all the vanities of the
world, he was balanced and moderate beyond the men of
his day.

Lovers of the town have been content, for the most
part, to say they loved it. They do not brag about its up-
lifting qualities. They have none of the infernal smugness
which makes the lover of the country insupportable. 'I
gravitate to a capital by a primary law of nature,' said
Henry Adams, and was content to say no more. It did not
seem to occur to him that the circumstance called for
ardour or for apology. But when Mr. John Erskine turned
his ungrateful back upon the city which loved him, he
grew enthusiastic over the joy of regaining 'the feel of
the soil, the smell of earth and rain, the dramatic contact
of the seasons, the companionship of the elements.' It is
a high note to strike; but if for drama we must fall back
upon the seasons, and for companionship upon the elements, ours will be a dreary existence in a world which
we have always deemed both dramatic and companionable.
If, as Mr. Erskine asserts, spring, summer, autumn, and

winter are 'annihilated' in town, we lose their best, but
we escape their worst, features. That harsh old axiom,
'Nature hates a farmer,' has a fund of experience behind
it. A distinguished surgeon, having bought, in a Nature-
loving mood, a really beautiful farm, asked an enlightened
friend and neighbour: 'What had I better do with my
land?' To which the answer came with judicious speed:
'Pave it.'

There is a vast deal of make-believe in the carefully
nurtured sentiment for country life, and the barefoot boy,
and the mountain girl. I saw recently in an illustrated
paper a picture of a particularly sordid slum in New
York's unredeemed East Side, and beneath it the reproachful query: 'Is this a place to breed supermen?' Assuredly not. Neither is a poverty-stricken, fallen-to-pieces
farmhouse, with a hole in its screen door; or a grim little
home in a grim little suburb, destitute of beauty and cheer.
If we want supermen (and to say the truth Germany has
put us out of conceit with the species), we shall have to
breed them under concentrated violet rays. Sunshine and
cloud refuse to sponsor the race.

When Doctor Johnson said, 'The man who is tired of
London is tired of life,' he expressed only his own virile
joy in humanity. When Lamb said, 'That man must have
a rare receipt for melancholy who can be dull in Fleet
Street,' he summed up the brimming delight afforded him
by this epitome of civilization. When Sydney Smith
wrote from the dignified seclusion of his rectory at Combe-
Florey, 'I look forward eagerly to the return of the bad
weather, coal fires, and good society in a crowded city,'
he put the pleasures of the mind above the pleasures of
the senses. All these preferences are temperately and mod-

estly stated. It was only when Lamb was banished from the thronged streets he loved that he grew petulant in his misery. It was only when he dreamed he was in Fleet Market, and woke to the torturing dulness of Enfield, that he cried out: 'Give me old London at fire and plague times rather than this healthy air, these tepid gales, these purposeless exercises.' Yet even then he claimed no moral superiority over the Nature-lovers who were beginning to make themselves heard in England. He knew only that London warmed his sad heart, and that it broke when he lost her.

Generally speaking, and leaving out of consideration the very poor to whom no choice in life is given, men and women who live in cities or in suburbs do so because they want to. Men and women who live in small towns do so because of their avocations, or for other practical reasons. They are right in affirming that they like it. I once said to a New York taxi-driver: 'I want to go to Brooklyn.' To which he made answer: 'You mean you have to.' So with the small-town dwellers. They may or may not 'want to,' but the 'have to' is sure. Professional men, doctors and dentists especially, delight in living in the suburbs, so that those who need their services cannot reach them. The doctor escapes from his patients, who may fall ill on Saturday, and die on Sunday, without troubling him. The dentist is happy in that he can play golf all Saturday and Sunday while his patients agonize in town. Only the undertaker, man's final servitor, stands staunchly by his guns.

It is not because the city is big, but because it draws to its heart all things that are gay and keen, that life in its streets is exhilarating. It is short of birds (even the

friendly little sparrows are being killed off by the drip
of oil into its gutters); but that is a matter of more concern to the city's cats than to the city's inhabitants. It
is needlessly noisy; but the suburb is not without its
sufferings on this score. Motors shriek defiance in the
leafy lanes, dogs bark their refrain through the night,
and the strange blended sounds of the radios, like lost
souls wailing their perdition, float from piazza to piazza.
These are remediable evils; but so are most of the city's
evils, which are not remedied because Americans are born
temporizers, who dislike nothing so much as abating a
public nuisance. They will spend time and money on
programmes to outlaw war, because that is a purely speculative process; but they will not stir themselves to outlaw excessive noise or dangerous speeding, because such
measures mean actual campaigning. 'The city,' says one
clear-eyed and very courageous American, 'is the flower
of civilization. It gives to men the means to make their
lives expressive. It offers a field of battle, and it could
be made a livable place if its sons would stay and fight
for it, instead of running away.'

THE VIRTUOUS VICTORIAN

THE
VIRTUOUS
VICTORIAN

WHEN Miss Amy Lowell, in her essay on Émile Verhaeren, said that the influence of Zola on the younger writers of France and Belgium was necessary 'to down the long set of sentimental hypocrisies known in England as "Victorian,"' she repeated a formula which has been in popular use for many years, and to which we attach no very exact significance. 'Early-Victorian,' 'mid-Victorian,' we use the phrases glibly, and without being aware that the mental attitude to which we refer is sometimes not Victorian at all, but Georgian. Take, for example, that fairly famous sentiment about the British navy being 'if possible, more distinguished in its domestic virtues than in its national importance.' Nothing more oppressively smug was ever uttered in the reign of the virtuous Queen; yet it was written by the most humorous and most pitiless of Georgian novelists, and it expressed the conviction of her soul.

When we permit ourselves to sneer at Victorian hypocrisies, we allude, as a rule, to the superficial observance of religious practices, and to the artificial reticence concerning illicit sexual relations. The former affected life more than it did literature; the latter affected literature more than it did life. A resolute silence is apt to imply or involve an equally resolute denial; and there came a time when certain plain truths were denied because there was no other way of keeping them out of sight. Novelists and poets conformed to a standard which was set by the taste of their day. So profoundly was the great Victorian laureate influenced by this taste that he grew reluctant to accept those simple old English stories, those charming old English traditions, the propriety or impropriety of which had never been a matter for concern. His 'fair Rosamond' believes herself a wedded wife, and so escapes culpability. His 'Maid Marian' wanders through Sherwood Forest under the respectable chaperonage of her father, and will not permit to Robin Hood the harmless liberties common among betrothed lovers.

> 'Robin, I will not kiss thee,
> For that belongs to marriage; but I hold thee
> The husband of my heart; the noblest light
> That ever flashed across my life, and I
> Embrace thee with the kisses of the soul.
> *Robin:* I thank thee.'

It is a bit frigid and a bit stilted for the merry outlaws. 'If love were all,' we might admit that conventionalism had chilled the laureate's pen; but, happily for the great adventures we call life and death, love is not all. The world swings on its way, peopled by other men than lovers; and it is to Tennyson we owe the most splendid denial of domesticity and duty that was ever made deathless by verse. His Ulysses brooks no restraint and heeds no liabilities. He makes plain to us that the Ithacan navy was less distinguished than the British navy for the development of the domestic virtues.

The great Victorian novelists were well aware that, albeit the average man does his share of love-making, he neither lives nor dies for love. Mr. Edmund Gosse, reared in the strictest sect of Plymouth Brethren, and professing religion at ten, was nevertheless permitted by his father to read the novels of Dickens, because they dealt with the passion of love in a humorous manner. More often they deal with it in a purely perfunctory manner, recognizing it as a prelude to marriage, and as something to which the novelist must not forget to make an occasional reference. Nicholas Nickleby is a young man and a hero. Consequently an assortment of female virtues and of female charms is labelled, docketed, provided with ringlets and a capacity for appropriate swooning — and behold, Nicholas has a wife. Kate Nickleby's husband is even more sketchily outlined. He has a name, and — we are told — an impetuous and generous disposition. He makes his appearance when a suitor is needed, stands up to be married when a husband is called for, and that is all there is of him. But what do these puppets matter in a book which gives us Mrs. Nickleby, Vincent Crummles, Fanny Squeers, and the ever-beloved Kenwigses? It took a great genius to enliven the hideous picture of Dotheboys Hall with the appropriate and immortal Fanny, whom we could never have borne to lose. It took a great genius to evolve from nothingness the name 'Morleena Kenwigs.' So perfect a result, achieved from a mere combination of letters, confers distinction on the English alphabet.

The charge of conventionalism brought against Thackeray and Trollope has more substance, because these novelists essayed to portray life soberly and veraciously. 'Trollope,' says Sir Leslie Stephen, 'was in the awkward

position of a realist, bound to ignore realities.' Thackeray
was restrained, partly by the sensitive propriety of British readers who winced at the frank admission of sexual
infirmities, and partly by the quality of his own taste.
In deference to the public, he forbore to make Arthur
Pendennis the lover of Fanny Bolton; and when we remember the gallant part that Fanny plays when safely
settled at Clavering, her loyalty to her old friend, Bows,
and her dexterity in serving him, we are glad she went
unsmirched into that sheltered port.

The restrictions so cheerfully accepted by Thackeray,
and his reticence — which is merely the reticence observed by every gentleman of his day — leave him an
uncrippled spectator and analyst of the complicated business of living. The world is not nearly so simple a place
as the sexualists seem to consider it. To the author of
'Vanity Fair' it was not simple at all. Acting and reacting
upon one another, his characters crowd the canvas, their
desires and ambitions, their successes and failures, inextri-
cably interwoven into one vast social scheme. It is not the
decency of Thackeray's novels which affronts us (we are
seldom unduly aware that they are decent), but the severity
with which he judges his own creations, and his rank and
shameless favouritism. What business has he to coddle
Rawdon Crawley ('honest Rawdon,' forsooth!), to lay siege
to our hearts with all the skill of a great artificer, and compel our liking for this fool and reprobate? What business
has he to pursue Becky Sharp like a prosecuting attorney,
to trip her up at every step, to betray, to our discomfiture,
his cold hostility? He treats Blanche Amory in the same
merciless fashion, and no one cares. But Becky! Becky,
that peerless adventuress who, as Mr. Brownell reminds

us, ran her memorable career before psychology was thought of as an essential element of fiction. Becky, whose scheming has beguiled our weary hours, and recompensed us for the labour of learning to read. How shall we fathom the mental attitude of a novelist who could create such a character, control her fluctuating fortunes, lift her to dizzy heights, topple her to ruin, extricate her from the dust and débris of her downfall — and hate her!

Trollope, working on a lower level, observant rather than creative, was less stern a moralist than Thackeray, but infinitely more cautious of his footsteps. He kept soberly in the appointed path, and never once in thirty years trod on the grass or flower-beds. Lady Glencora Palliser thinks, indeed, of leaving her husband; but she does not do it, and her continency is rewarded after a fashion which is very satisfactory to the reader. Mr. Palliser aspires somewhat stiffly to be the lover of Lady Dumbello; but that wise worldling, ranking love the least of assets, declines to make any sacrifice at its shrine. Trollope unhesitatingly and proudly claimed for himself the quality of harmlessness. 'I do believe,' he said, 'that no girl has risen from the reading of my pages less modest than she was before, and that some girls may have learned from them that modesty is a charm worth possessing.'

This is one of the admirable sentiments which should have been left unspoken. It is a true word as far as it goes; but more suggestive of 'Little Women,' or 'A Summer in Leslie Goldthwaite's Life,' than of those virile, varied, and animated novels which make no appeal to immaturity. In Trollope's teeming world, as in the teeming world about us, a few young people fall in love and are married, but this is an infrequent episode. Most of his men and women, like the men and women whom we know, are engrossed in other activities. Once, indeed, Bishop Proudie wooed and won Mrs. Proudie. Once Archdeacon Grantly wooed and won Mrs. Grantly. But neither of these gentlemen could possibly have belonged to 'the great cruising brotherhood of the Pilgrims of Love.' 'Le culte de la femme' has never been a popular pastime in Britain, and Trollope was the last man on the island to have appreciated its significance. He preferred politics, the hunting-field, and the church.

Yet surely Archdeacon Grantly is worth a brace of lovers. With what sincerity he is drawn, and with what consummate care! A churchman who, as Sir Leslie Stephen somewhat petulantly observes, 'gives no indication of having any religious views whatever, beyond a dislike to dissenters.' A solidly respectable member of provincial clerical society, ambitious, worldly, prizing wealth, honouring rank, unspiritual, unprogressive — but none the less a man who would have proved his worth in the hour of England's trial.

It is a testimony to the power of fiction that, having read with breathless concern and through countless pages Mr. Britling's reflections on the war, my soul suddenly cried out within me for the reflections of Archdeacon Grantly. Mr. Britling is an acute and sensitive thinker. The archdeacon's mental processes are of the simplest. Mr. Britling has winged his triumphant flight from 'the clumsy, crawling, snobbish, comfort-loving caterpillar of Victorian England.' The archdeacon is still confessedly a grub. Mr. Britling has 'truckled to no domesticated god.' The archdeacon's deity is open to such grievous innuendoes. Yet I wish I could have stood on the smooth

lawn of Plumstead, and have heard what the archdeacon
had to say when he learned that an English scholar and
gentleman had smuggled out of England, by the help of
a female 'confidential agent,' a treacherous appeal to the
President of the United States, asking that pressure should
be brought upon fighting Englishmen in the interests of
peace. I wish I could have heard the cawing rooks of
Plumstead echo his mighty wrath. For there is that in
the heart of a man, even a Victorian churchman with a
love of preferment and a distaste for dissenters, which
holds scatheless the sacred thing called honour.

Trollope is as frank about the archdeacon's frailties as
Mr. Wells is frank about Mr. Britling's frailties. In pip-
ing days of peace, the archdeacon's contempt for Mr.
Britling would have been as sincere and hearty as Mr.
Britling's contempt for the archdeacon. But under the
hard, heroic discipline of war there would have come to
the archdeacon, as to Mr. Britling, a white dawn of reve-
lation. Both men have the liberating qualities of manhood.

It is always hard to make an elastic phrase fit with
precision. We know what we mean by Victorian conventions and hypocrisies, but the perpetual intrusion of
blinding truths disturbs our point of view. The new Reform bill and the extension of the suffrage were hardy
denials of convention. 'The Origin of Species' and 'Zoö-
logical Evidences as to Man's Place in Nature' were not
published in the interests of hypocrisy. There was nothing
oppressively respectable about 'The Ring and the Book';
and Swinburne can hardly be said to have needed correc-
tion at Zola's hands. These mid-Victorian products have
a savour of freedom about them, and so has 'The Ordeal
of Richard Feverel.' Even the Homeric eloquence of

Ruskin was essentially the eloquence of the free. If such unpleasant and reiterated truths — as applicable to the United States today as they were to Victoria's England — are 'smug,' then Jeremiah is sugar-coated, and the Baptist an apostle of ease.

The English have at all times lacked the courage of their emotions, but not the emotions themselves. Their reticence has stood for strength as well as for stiffness. The pre-Raphaelites, indeed, surrendered their souls with docility to every wavelet of feeling, and produced something iridescent, like the shining of wet sand. Love, according to their canon, was expressed with transparent ease. It was 'a great but rather sloppy passion,' says Mr. Ford Madox Hueffer, 'which you swooned about on broad general lines.' A pre-Raphaelite corsair languished as visibly as a pre-Raphaelite seraph. He could have been bowled over by a worsted ball; but he was at least more vigorous and more ruddy than a cubist nude. One doubted his seared conscience and his thousand crimes; but not his ability to walk unassisted downstairs.

The Victorian giants were of mighty girth. They trod the earth with proud and heavy steps, and with a strength of conviction which was as vast and tranquil as the plains. We have parted with their convictions and with their tranquillity. We have parted also with their binding prejudices and with their standards of taste. Freedom has come to us, not broadening down

'from precedent to precedent,'

but swiftly and comprehensively. There are no more taboos, no more silent or sentimental hypocrisies. We should now know a great many interesting details concerning the Marquis of Steyne and the Duke of Omnium, if these two imposing figures had not passed forever from our ken. We should have searchlights thrown upon Becky Sharp, if Becky had not escaped into the gloom. Her successors sin exhaustively, and with a lamentable lack of *esprit*. We are bidden to scrutinize their transgressions, but Becky's least peccadillo is more engaging than all their broken commandments. The possibility of profound tediousness accompanying perfect candour dawns slowly on the truth-tellers of fiction. It took a great artist, like Edith Wharton, to recognize and deplore 'the freedom of speech which never arrives at wit, and the freedom of act which never makes for romance.'

LIVING IN HISTORY

LIVING IN HISTORY

WHEN Mr. Bagehot spoke his luminous words about 'a fatigued way of looking at great subjects,' he gave us the key to a mental attitude which perhaps is not the modern thing it seems. There were, no doubt, Greeks and Romans in plenty to whom the 'glory' and the 'grandeur' of Greece and Rome were less exhilarating than they were to Edgar Poe — Greeks and Romans who were spiritually palsied by the great emotions which presumably accompany great events. They may have been philosophers, or humanitarians, or academists. They may have been conscientious objectors, or conscienceless shirkers, or perhaps plain men and women with a natural gift of indecision, a natural taste for compromise and awaiting developments. In the absence of newspapers and pamphlets, these peaceful pagans were compelled to express their sense of fatigue to their neighbours at the games, or in the market-place; and their neighbours — if well chosen — sighed with them over the intensity of life, the formidable happenings of history.

Since August, 1914, the turmoil and anguish incidental to the world's greatest war have accentuated every human type — heroic, base, keen, and evasive. The strain of four years' fighting was borne with astounding fortitude, and Allied statesmen and publicists saw to it that the

clear outline of events should not be blurred by ignorance
or misrepresentation. If history in the making be a fluid
thing, it swiftly crystallizes. Men, 'living between two
eternities, and warring against oblivion,' make their indeli-
ble record on its pages; and other men receive these
pages as their best inheritance, their avenue to understanding, their key to life.

Therefore it is unwise to gibe at history because we do
not chance to know it. It pleases us to gibe at anything
we do not know, but the process is not enlightening. In
the second year of the war, the English *Nation* commented approvingly on the words of an English novelist
who strove to make clear that the only things which
count for any of us, individually or collectively, are the
unrecorded minutiae of our lives. 'History,' said this
purveyor of fiction, 'is concerned with the rather absurd
and theatrical doings of a few people, which, after all,
have never altered the fact that we do all of us live on
from day to day, and only want to be let alone.'

'These words,' observed the *Nation* heavily, 'have a
singular truth and force at the present time. The people
of Europe want to go on living, not to be destroyed. To
live is to pursue the activities proper to one's nature, to
be unhindered and unthwarted in their exercise. It is
not too much to say that the life of Europe is something
which has persisted in spite of the history of Europe.
There is nothing happy or fruitful anywhere but witnesses
to the triumph of life over history.'

Presuming that we are able to disentangle life from
history, to sever the inseverable, is this a true statement,
or merely the expression of mental and spiritual fatigue?
Were the great historic episodes invariably fruitless, and

had they no bearing upon the lives of ordinary men and women? The battles of Marathon and Thermopylae, the signing of the Magna Charta, the Triple Alliance, the Declaration of Independence, the birth of the National Assembly, the first Reform Bill, the recognition in Turin of the United Kingdom of Italy — these things may have been theatrical, inasmuch as they were certainly dramatic, but absurd is not a wise word to apply to them. Neither is it possible to believe that the life of Europe went on in spite of these historic incidents, triumphing over them as over so many obstacles to activity.

When the *Nation* contrasted the beneficent companies of strolling players who 'represented and interpreted the world of life, the one thing which matters and remains,' with the companies of soldiers who merely destroyed life at its roots, we could not but feel that this editorial point of view had its limitations. The strolling players of Elizabeth's day afforded many a merry hour; but Elizabeth's soldiers and sailors did their part in making possible this mirth. The strolling players who came to the old Southwark Theatre in Philadelphia interpreted 'the world of life,' as they understood it; but the soldiers who froze at Valley Forge offered a different interpretation, and one which had considerably more stamina. The magnifying of small things, the belittling of great ones, indicate a mental exhaustion which would be more pardonable if it were less complacent. There are always men and women who prefer the triumph of evil, which is a thing they can forget, to prolonged resistance, which shatters their nerves. But the desire to escape an obligation, while very human, is not generally thought to be humanity's noblest asset.

Many smart things have been written to discredit his-

tory. Mr. Arnold called it 'the vast Mississippi of falsehood,' which was easily said, and has been said in a number of ways since the days of Herodotus, who amply
illustrated the splendours of unreality. Mr. Edward Fitz-
gerald was wont to sigh that only lying histories were
readable, and this point of view has many secret adher-
ents. Mr. Henry Adams, who taught history for seven
years at Harvard, and who built his intellectual dwelling-
place upon its firm foundations, pronounced it to be 'in
essence incoherent and immoral.' Nevertheless, all that
we know of man's unending efforts to adjust and readjust
himself to the world about him we learn from history,
and the tale is an enlightening one. 'Events are wonderful things,' said Lord Beaconsfield. Nothing, for example, can blot out, or obscure, the event of the French
Revolution. We are free to discuss it until the end of time;
but we can never alter it, and never get away from its
consequences.

The lively contempt for history expressed by readers
who would escape its weight, and the neglect of history
practised by educators who would escape its authority,
stand responsible for much mental confusion. American
boys and girls go to school six, eight, or ten years, as the
case may be, and emerge with a misunderstanding of
their own country, and a comprehensive ignorance of all
others. They say, 'I don't know any history,' as casually
and as unconcernedly as they might say, 'I don't know
any chemistry,' or 'I don't know metaphysics.' A smiling young freshman in the most scholarly of women's
colleges told me that she had been conditioned because
she knew nothing about the Reformation.

'You mean ——' I began questioningly.

'I mean just what I say,' she interrupted. 'I didn't know what it was, or where it was, or who had anything to do with it.'

I said I didn't wonder she had come to grief. The Reformation was something of an episode. And I asked myself wistfully how it happened she had ever managed to escape it. When I was a little schoolgirl, a pious Roman Catholic child with a distaste for polemics, it seemed to me I was never done studying about the Reformation. If I escaped briefly from Wycliffe and Cranmer and Knox, it was only to be met by Luther and Calvin and Huss. Everywhere the great struggle confronted me, everywhere I was brought face to face with the inexorable logic of events. That more advanced and more intelligent students find pleasure in every phase of ecclesiastical strife is proved by Lord Broughton's pleasant story about a member of Parliament named Joliffe, who was sitting in his club reading Hume's 'History of England,' a book which well deserves to be called dry. Charles Fox, glancing over his shoulder, observed, 'I see you have come to the imprisonment of the seven bishops'; whereupon Joliffe, like a man engrossed in a thrilling detective story, cried desperately, 'For God's sake, Fox, don't tell me what is coming!'

This was reading for human delight, for the interest and agitation which are inseparable from every human document. Mr. Henry James once told me that the only reading of which he never tired was history. 'The least significant footnote of history,' he said, 'stirs me more than the most thrilling and passionate fiction. Nothing that has ever happened to the world finds me indifferent.' I used to think that ignorance of history meant only a lack of cultivation and a loss of pleasure. Now I am sure that such ignorance impairs our judgment by impairing our understanding, by depriving us of standards, of the power to contrast and the right to estimate. We can know nothing of any nation unless we know its history; and we can know nothing of the history of any nation unless we know something of the history of all nations. The book of the world is full of knowledge we need to acquire, of lessons we need to learn, of wisdom we need to assimilate. Consider only this brief sentence of Polybius, quoted by Plutarch: 'In Carthage no one is blamed, however he may have gained his wealth.' A pleasant place, no doubt, for business enterprise; a place where young men were taught how to get on, and extravagance kept pace with shrewd finance. A self-satisfied, self-confident, money-getting, money-loving people, honouring success and hugging their fancied security, while in far-off Rome Cato pronounced their doom.

There are readers who can tolerate and even enjoy history, provided it is shorn of its high lights and heavy shadows, its heroic elements and strong impelling motives. They turn with relief to such calm commentators as Sir John Seeley, for years professor of modern history at Cambridge, who shrank as sensitively as an eighteenth-century divine from that fell word 'enthusiasm,' and from all the agitation it evoked. He was a firm upholder of the British Empire, hating compromise and guiltless of pacifism; but, having a natural gift for aridity, he saw no reason why the world should not be content to know things without feeling them, should not keep its eyes turned to legal institutions, its mind fixed

upon political economy and international law. The force
that lay back of Parliament annoyed him by the simple
primitive way in which it beat drums, fired guns, and
died to uphold the institutions which he prized; also because by doing these things it evoked in others certain
simple and primitive sensations which he strove always
to keep at bay. 'We are rather disposed to laugh,' he
said, 'when poets and orators try to conjure us with the
name of England.' Had he lived a few years longer, he
would have known that England's salvation lies in the
fact that her name is, to her sons, a thing to conjure by.
We may not wisely ignore the value of emotions, nor
underestimate the power of human impulses which charge
the souls of men.

The long years of neutrality engendered in the minds
of Americans a natural but ignoble weariness. The war
was not our war, yet there was no escaping from it. By
day and night it haunted us, a ghost that would not be
laid. Over and over again we were told that it was not
possible to place the burden of blame on any nation's
shoulders. Once at least we were told that the causes
and objects of the contest, the obscure fountains from
which had burst this stupendous and desolating flood,
were no concern of ours. But this proffered release from
serious thinking brought us scant peace of mind. Every
honest man and woman knew that we had no intellectual
right to be ignorant when information lay at our hand,
and no spiritual right to be unconcerned when great moral
issues were at stake. We could not in either case evade
the duty we owed to reason. The Vatican Library would
not hold the books that have been written about the
war; but the famous five-foot shelf would be too roomy

for the evidence in the case, the documents which are
the foundation of knowledge. They, at least, are neither
too profuse for our patience, nor too complex for our
understanding. 'The inquiry into the truth or falsehood
of a matter of history,' said Huxley, 'is just as much an
affair of pure science as is the inquiry into the truth or
falsehood of a matter of geology; and the value of the
evidence in the two cases must be tested in the same
way.'

The resentment of American pacifists, who, being more
human than they thought themselves, were no better able
than the rest of us to forget the state of Europe, found
expression in petulant complaints. They kept reminding
us at inopportune moments that war is not the important
and heroic thing it is assumed to be. They asked that,
if it is to figure in history at all (which seems, on the
whole, inevitable), the truth should be told, and its brutalities, as well as its heroisms, exposed. They professed a
languid amusement at the 'rainbow of official documents'
which proved every nation in the right. They inveighed
bitterly against the 'false patriotism' taught by American
schoolbooks, with their absurd emphasis on the 'embat-
tled farmers' of the Revolution, and the volunteers of
the Civil War. They assured us, in and out of season,
that a doctor who came to his death looking after poor
patients in an epidemic was as much of a hero as any
soldier whose grave is yearly decorated with flowers.

All this was the clearest possible exposition of the lassi-
tude induced in faint-hearted men by the pressure of great
events. It was the wail of people who wanted, as the
Nation feelingly expressed it, to be let alone, and who
could not shut themselves away from the world's great

tragedy. None of us are prepared to say that a doctor and a nurse who perform their perilous duties in an epidemic are not as heroic as a doctor and a nurse who perform their perilous duties in war. There is glory enough to go around. Only he that loveth his life shall lose it. But to put a flower on a soldier's grave is a not too exuberant recognition of his service, for he, too, in his humble way made the great sacrifice.

As for the brutalities of war, who can charge that history smooths them over? Certain horrors may be withheld from children, whose privilege it is to be spared the knowledge of uttermost depravity; but to the adult no such mercy is shown. Motley, for example, describes cruelties committed three hundred and fifty years ago in the Netherlands, which equal, if they do not surpass, the cruelties committed six years ago in Belgium. Men heard such tales more calmly then than now, and seldom sought the coward's refuge — incredulity. The Dutch, like other nations, did better things than fight. They painted glorious pictures, they bred great statesmen and good doctors. They traded with extraordinary success. They raised the most beautiful tulips in the world. But to do these things peacefully and efficiently, they had been compelled to struggle for their national existence. The East India trade and the freedom of the seas did not drop into their laps. And because their security, and the comeliness of life which they so highly prized, had been bought by stubborn resistance to tyranny, they added to material well-being the 'luxury of self-respect.'

To overestimate the part played by war in a nation's development is as crude as to ignore its alternate menace and support. It is with the help of history that we balance

our mental accounts. Voltaire was disposed to think that
battles and treaties were matters of small moment; and
Mr. John Richard Green pleaded, not unreasonably, that
more space should be given in our chronicles to the mis-
sionary, the poet, the painter, the merchant, and the
philosopher. They are not, and they never have been,
excluded from any narrative comprehensive enough to
admit them; but the scope of their authority is not always
sufficiently defined. Man, as the representative of his age,
and the events in which he plays his vigorous part — these
are the warp and woof of history. We can no more leave
John Wesley or Ignatius Loyola out of the canvas than
we can leave out Marlborough or Pitt. We know now that
the philosophy of Nietzsche is one with Bernhardi's mili-
tarism.

As for the merchant — Froissart was as well aware of
his prestige as was Mr. Green. 'Trade, my lord,' said
Dinde Desponde, the great Lombard banker, to the Duke
of Burgundy, 'finds its way everywhere, and rules the
world.' As for commercial honour — a thing as fine as the
honour of the aristocrat or of the soldier — what can be
better for England than to remember that after the great
fire of 1666 not a single London shopkeeper evaded his
liabilities; and that this fact was long the boast of a city
proud of its shopkeeping? As for jurisprudence — Sully
was infinitely more concerned with it than he was with
combat or controversy. It is with stern satisfaction that
he recounts the statutes passed in his day for the punishment of fraudulent bankrupts, whom we treat so leniently;
for the annulment of their gifts and assignments, which
we guard so zealously; and for the conviction of those to
whom such property had been assigned. It was almost as

dangerous to steal on a large scale as on a small one under the levelling laws of Henry of Navarre.

In this vast and varied chronicle, war plays its appointed part. 'We cannot,' says Walter Savage Landor, 'push valiant men out of history.' We cannot escape from the truths interpreted, and the conditions established by their valour. What has been slightingly called the 'drum-and-trumpet narrative' holds its own with the records of art and science. 'It cost Europe a thousand years of barbarism,' said Macaulay, 'to escape the fate of China.'

The endless endeavour of states to control their own destinies, the ebb and flow of the sea of combat, the 'recurrent liturgy of war,' enabled the old historians to perceive with amazing distinctness the traits of nations, etched as sharply then as now on the imperishable pages of history. We read Froissart for human delight rather than for solid information; yet Froissart's observations — the observations of a keen-eyed student of the world — are worth recording five hundred years after he set them down.

'In England,' he says, 'strangers are well received'; yet are the English 'affable to no other nation than their own.' Ireland, he holds to have had 'too many kings'; and the Scotch, like the English, 'are excellent men-at-arms, nor is there any check to their courage as long as their weapons endure.' France is the pride of his heart, as it is the pride of the world's heart today. 'In France also is found good chivalry, strong of spirit, and in great abundance; for the kingdom of France has never been brought so low as to lack men ready for the combat.' Even Germany does not escape his regard. 'The Germans are a rude, unmannered race, but active and expert where their own personal advantage is concerned.' If history be 'philosophy teaching by example,' we are wise to admit the old historians into our counsels.

To withhold from a child some knowledge — apportioned to his understanding — of the world's sorrows and wrongs is to cheat him of his kinship with humanity. We would not, if we could, bruise his soul as our souls are bruised; but we would save him from a callous content which is alien to his immaturity. The little American, like the little Austrian and the little Serb, is a son of the sorrowing earth. His security — of which no man can forecast the future — is a legacy bequeathed him by predecessors who bought it with sweat and with blood; and with sweat and with blood his descendants may be called on to guard it. Alone among educators, Mr. G. Stanley Hall finds neutrality, a 'high and ideal neutrality,' to be an attribute of youth. He was so gratified by this discovery during the years of the war, so sure that American boys and girls followed 'impartially' the great struggle in Europe, and that this judicial attitude would, in the years to come, enable them to pronounce 'the true verdict of history,' that he 'thrilled and tingled' with patriotic — if premature — pride.

'The true verdict of history' will be pronounced according to the documentary evidence in the case. There is no need to vex our souls over the possible extinction of this evidence, for closer observers than our impartial young Americans have placed it permanently on record. But I doubt if the equanimity which escapes the ordeal of partisanship is to be found in the mind of youth, or in the heart of a child. Can we not remember a time when the Wars of the Roses were not — to us — a matter for neutrality? Our little school histories, those vivacious, anecdotal histories, banished long ago by rigorous educators, were in some measure responsible for our Lancastrian fervour. They fed it with stories of high courage and the sorrows of princes. We wasted our sympathies on 'a mere struggle for power'; but Hume's laconic verdict is not, and never can be, the measure of a child's solicitude. The lost cause fills him with pity, the cause which is saved by man's heroic sacrifice fires him to generous applause. The round world and the tale of those who have lived upon it are his legitimate inheritance.

Mr. Bagehot said, and said wisely after his wont, that if you catch an intelligent, uneducated man of thirty, and tell him about the battle of Marathon, he will calculate the chances, and estimate the results; but he will not really care. You cannot make the word 'Marathon' sound in his ears as it sounded in the ears of Byron, to whom it had been sacred in boyhood. You cannot make the word 'freedom' sound in untutored ears as it sounds in the ears of men who have counted the cost by which it has been preserved through the centuries. Unless children are permitted to know the utmost peril which has threatened, and which still threatens, the freedom of nations, how can they conceive of its value? And what is the worth of teaching which does not rate the gift of freedom above all earthly benefactions? How can justice live save by the will of freemen? Of what avail are civic virtues that are not the virtues of the free? Pericles bade the Athenians to bear reverently in mind the Greeks who had died for Greece. 'Make these men your examples, and be well assured that happiness comes by freedom, and freedom by stoutness of heart.' Perhaps if American boys bear reverently in mind the men who died for America, it will help them too to be stout of heart, and 'worthy patriots, dear to God.'

In the remote years of my childhood, the study of current events, that most interesting and valuable form of tuition, which, nevertheless, is unintelligible without some knowledge of the past, was left out of our limited curriculum. We seldom read the newspapers (which I remember as of an appalling dulness), and we knew little of what was happening in our day. But we did study history, and we knew something of what had happened in other days than ours; we knew and deeply cared. Therefore we reacted with fair intelligence and no lack of fervour when circumstances were forced upon our vision. It was not possible for a child who had lived in spirit with Saint Genevieve to be indifferent to the siege of Paris in 1870. It was not possible for a child who had lived in spirit with Jeanne d'Arc to be indifferent to the destruction of Rheims Cathedral in 1914. If we were often left in ignorance, we were never despoiled of childhood's generous ardour. Nobody told us that 'courage is a sublime form of hypocrisy.' Nobody fed our young minds on stale paradoxes, or taught us to discount the foolish impulsiveness of adults. Our parents, as Mr. Henry James rejoicingly observed, 'had no desire to see us inoculated with importunate virtues.' The Honourable Bertrand Russell had not then proposed that all teaching of history shall be submitted to an 'international commission,' 'which shall produce neutral textbooks, free from patriotic bias.' There was something profoundly fearless in our approach to life, in the exposure of our unarmoured souls to the assaults of enthusiasms and regrets. 'Events are wonderful things,' and we were stimulated by them to believe with Froissart that 'the most profitable thing in the world for the institution of human life is history.'

THE DIVINENESS OF DISCONTENT

THE
DIVINENESS
OF
DISCONTENT

WHEN a distinguished Oxford student told Americans, through the distinguished medium of Harvard College, that they were 'speeding with invincible optimism down the road to destruction,' they paid him the formal compliment of listening to, and commenting upon, his words. They did not go so far as to be disturbed by them, because it is the nature of men to remain unmoved by prophecies. Only the Greek chorus — or its leader — paid any heed to Cassandra; and the folly of Edgar Poe in accepting without demur the reiterated statement of his raven is apparent to all readers of a much-read poem. The world has been speeding through the centuries to destruction, and the end is still remote. Nevertheless, as it is assuredly not speeding to perfection, the word that chills our irrational content may do us some small service. It is never believed, and it is soon forgotten; but for a time it gives us food for thought.

Anyone born as long ago as I was must remember that the virtue most deeply inculcated in our nurseries was content. It had no spiritual basis to lend it dignity and grace, but was inherited from those late Georgian days which were the smuggest known to fame. It was a survival from Hannah More and Jane Taylor, ladies dissimilar in most respects, but with an equal gift for restricting the horizon of youth. I do not remember who wrote the popular story of the 'Discontented Cat' that lived in a cottage on bread and milk and mice, and that made itself unhappy because a wealthy cat of its acquaintance was given buttered crumpets for breakfast; but either Jane Taylor or her sister Ann was responsible for the 'Discontented Pendulum,' which grew tired of ticking in the dark, and, being reminded that it had a window to look through, retorted very sensibly that there was no use having a window, if it could not stop a second to look through it.

The nursery theory of content was built up on the presumption that you were the favoured child of fortune — or of God — while other, and no less worthy, children were objects of no kindly solicitude. Miss Taylor's 'Little Ann' weeps because she sees richly clad ladies stepping into a coach while she has to walk; whereupon her mother points out to her a sick and ragged beggar child, whose

'naked feet bleed on the stones,'

and with enviable hardness of heart bids her take comfort in the sight:

'This poor little beggar is hungry and cold,
    No father nor mother has she;
And while you can daily such objects behold,
    You ought quite contented to be.'

Hannah More amplified this theory of content to fit all classes and circumstances. She really did feel concern for her fellow creatures, for the rural poor upon whom it was not the custom of Church or State to waste sympathy or help. She refused to believe that British labourers were 'predestined to be ignorant and wicked' — which was to her credit; but she did, apparently, believe that they were predestined to be wretchedly poor, and that they should be content with their poverty. She lived on the fat of the land, and left thirty thousand pounds when she died; but she held that bare existence was sufficient for a ploughman. She wrote twenty-four books, which were twenty-four too many; but she told the ever-admiring Wilberforce that she permitted 'no writing for the poor.' She aspired to guide the policies and the morals of England; but she was perturbed by the thought that underpaid artisans should seek to be 'scholars and philosophers,' though they must have stood in more need of philosophy than she did.

It was Ruskin who jolted his English readers, and some Americans, out of the selfish complacency which is degenerate content. It was he who harshly told England, then so prosperous and powerful, that prosperity and power are not virtues, that they do not indicate the sanction of the Almighty, or warrant their possessors in assuming the moral leadership of the world. It was he who assured the prim girlhood of my day that it was not the petted child of Providence, and that it had no business to be contented because it was better off than girlhood elsewhere. 'Joy in nothing that separates you, as by any strange favour, from your fellow creatures, that exalts you through their degradation, exempts you from their toil, or indulges you in times of their distress.'

This was a new voice falling upon the attentive ears of youth — a fresh challenge to its native and impetuous generosity. Perhaps the beggar's bare feet were not a legiti-

mate incentive to enjoyment of our own neat shoes and
stockings. Perhaps it was a sick world we lived in, and the
beggar was a symptom of disease. Perhaps when Emerson
(we read Emerson and Carlyle as well as Ruskin) defined
discontent as an infirmity of the will, he was thinking of
personal and petty discontent, as with one's breakfast or
the weather; not with the discontent which we never dared
to call divine, but which we dimly perceived to have in it
some noble attribute of grace. That the bare existence of a
moral law should so exalt a spirit that neither sin nor
sorrow could subdue its gladness was a profundity which
the immature mind could not be expected to grasp.

Time and circumstance lent themselves with extraordinary graciousness to Emerson's invincible optimism.
It was easier to be a transcendental philosopher, and much
easier to cherish a noble and a sweet content, before the
laying of the Atlantic cable. Emerson was over sixty when
this event took place, and, while he lived, the wires were
used with commendable economy. The morning newspaper did not bring him detailed accounts of war in Ethi-
opia or in Spain. His temperamental composure met with
little to derange it. He abhorred slavery; but until Lincoln
forced the issue, he seldom bent his mind to its consideration. He loved 'potential America'; but he had a happy
faculty of disregarding public affairs. Passionate partisanship, which is the basis of so much satisfaction and discontent, was alien to his soul. He loved mankind, but not
men; and his avoidance of intimacies saved him from wear
and tear. Mr. Brownell says that he did not care enough
about his friends to discriminate between them, which was
the reason he estimated Alcott so highly.

This immense power of withdrawal, this concentration

upon the things of the spirit, made possible Emerson's intellectual life. He may have been, as Santayana says, 'impervious to the evidence of evil'; yet there breaks from his heart an occasional sigh over the low ebb of the world's virtue, or an entirely human admission that the hopes of the morning are followed by the ennui of noon. Sustained by the supremacy of the moral law, and by a profound and majestic belief in the invincible justice, the 'loaded dice' of God, he sums up in careful words his modest faith in man: 'Hours of sanity and consideration are always arriving to communities as to individuals, when the truth is seen, and the martyrs are justified.' Perhaps martyrs foresee the dawning of this day or ever they come to die; but to those who stand by and witness their martyrdom, the night seems dark and long.

There is a species of discontent which is more fervently optimistic than all the cheerfulness the world can boast. It is the discontent of the passionate and unpractical reformer, who believes, as Shelley believed, in the perfectibility of the human species, and who thinks, as Shelley thought, that there is a remedy for every disease of civilization. To the poet's dreaming eyes the cure was simple and sure. Destruction implied for him an automatic reconstruction, a miraculous survival and rebirth. Uncrown the king, and some noble prophet or philosopher will guide — not rule — the people. Unfrock the priest, and the erstwhile congregation will perfect itself in the practice of virtue. Take the arms from the soldier, the badge from the policeman, the cap and gown from the college president, authority from the judge, and control from the father. The nations will then be peaceful, the mobs orderly, the students studious, the criminals virtuous, the children

well-behaved. An indifferent acquaintance with sociology,
and a comprehensive ignorance of biology, made possible
these pleasing illusions. Nor did it occur to Shelley that
many men, his equals in disinterestedness and his supe-
riors in self-restraint, would have found his reconstructed
world an eminently undesirable dwelling-place.

Two counsels to content stand bravely out from the mass
of contradictory admonitions with which the world's
teachers have bewildered us. Saint Paul, writing to the
Philippians, says simply: 'I have learned, in whatsoever
state I am, therewith to be content'; and Marcus Aurelius,
contemplating the mighty spectacle of life and death,
bids us pass serenely through our little space of time, and
end our journey in content. It is the meeting-point of
objective and subjective consciousness. The Apostle was
having a hard time of it. The things he disciplined himself to accept with content were tangible things, of an
admittedly disagreeable character — hunger and thirst,
imprisonment, and the violence of mobs. They were not
happening to somebody else; they were happening to *him*.
The Emperor, seeking refuge from action in thought,
steeled himself against the nobleness of pity no less than
against the weakness of complaint. John Stuart Mill,
who did not suffer from enervating softness of heart, pronounced the wholesale killing of Christians in the reign
of Marcus Aurelius to be one of the world's great tragedies. It was the outcome, not only of imperial policy, but
of sincere conviction. Therefore historians have agreed to
pass it lightly by. How can a man do better than follow
the dictates of his own conscience, or of his own judgment,
or of whatever directs the mighty ones of earth who make
laws instead of obeying them? But the immensity of

pain, the long-drawn agony involved in this protracted persecution might have disturbed even a Stoic philosopher passing serenely — though not harmlessly — through his little space of time.

This brings me to the consideration of one prolific source of discontent, the habit we have acquired — and cannot let go — of distressing ourselves over the daily progress of events. The classic world, 'innocent of any essential defeat,' was a pitiless world, too clear-eyed for illusions, too intelligent for sedatives. The Greeks built the structure of their lives upon an almost perfect understanding of all that it offered and denied. The Romans, running an empire and ruling a world, had much less time for thinking; yet Horace, observant and acquiescent, undeceived and undisturbed, is the friend of all the ages. It is not from him, or from any classic author, that we learn to talk about the fret and fever of living. He would have held such a phrase to be eminently ill-bred, and unworthy of man's estate.

The Middle Ages, immersed in heaving seas of trouble, and lifted Heavenward by great spiritual emotions, had scant breathing-space for the cultivation of nerves. Men endured life and enjoyed it. Their endurance and their enjoyment were unimpaired by the violence of their fellow men, or by the vision of an angry God. Cruelty, which we cannot bear to read about, and a Hell, which we will not bear to think about, failed signally to curb the zest with which they lived their days. There is no reason to suppose that Dante, whose fervid faith compassed the redemption of mankind, disliked his dream of Hell, or that it irked him to consign to it so many eminent and agreeable people.

The Renaissance gave itself unreservedly to all the pleasures that could be extracted from the business of living, though there was no lack of trouble to damp its zeal. It is interesting and instructive to read the history of a great Italian lady, typical of her day, Isabella d'Este, Marchioness of Mantua. She was learned, adroit, able, estimable, and mistress of herself though duchies fell. She danced serenely at the ball given by the French King at Milan, after he had ousted her brother-in-law, the Duke Ludovico, and sent him to die a prisoner at Loches. When Caesar Borgia snatched Urbino, she improved the occasion by promptly begging from him two beautiful statues which she had always coveted, and which had been the most treasured possessions of Duke Guidobaldo, her relative and the husband of her dearest friend. A chilly heart had Isabella when others came to grief, but a stout one when disaster faced her way. If the men and women who lived through those highly coloured, harshly governed days had fretted too persistently over the misfortunes of others, or had spent their time questioning the moral intelligibility of life, the Renaissance would have failed of its fruition, and the world would be a less engaging place for us to live in now.

There is a discontent which is profoundly stimulating, and there is a discontent which is more wearisome than complacency. Both spring from a consciousness that the time is out of joint, and both have a modern background of nerves. 'The Education of Henry Adams' and the 'Diaries' of Wilfrid Scawen Blunt are cases in point. Blunt's quarrel was with his country, his world, his fellow creatures and his God — a broad field of dissatisfaction, which was yet too narrow to embrace himself. Nowhere does he give any token of even a moderate self-distrust. Britain is an 'engine of evil,' because his party is out of power. 'Americans' (in 1900) 'are spending fifty millions a year in slaughtering the Filipinos' — a crude estimate of work and cost. 'The Press is the most complete engine ever invented for the concealment of historic truth.' 'Patriotism is the virtue of nations in decay.' 'The whole white race is revelling openly in violence, as though it had never pretended to be Christian. God's equal curse be on them all.'

'The whole white race,' be it observed. For a time Blunt dreamed fond dreams of yellow and brown and black supremacy. Europe's civilization he esteemed a failure. Christianity had not come up to his expectations. There remained the civilization of the East, and Mohammedanism — an amended Mohammedanism, innocent of sensuality and averse to bloodshed. Filled with this happy hope, the Englishman set off from Cairo to seek religion in the desert.

Siwah gave him a rude reception. Ragged tribes, ardent but unregenerate followers of the Prophet, pulled down his tents, pillaged his luggage, robbed his servants, and knocked him rudely about. Blunt's rage at this treatment was like the rage of *Punch's* vegetarian who is chased by a bull. 'There is no hope to be found in Islam, and I shall go no further,' is his conclusion. 'The less religion in the world, perhaps the better.'

Humanity and its creeds being thus disposed of, there remained only the animals to contemplate with satisfaction. 'Three quarters of man's misery,' says the diary, 'comes from pretending to be what he is not, a separate creation, superior to that of the beasts and birds, when in reality they are wiser than we are, and infinitely happier.'

This is the kind of thing Walt Whitman used now and then to say, though neither he nor Sir Wilfrid knew any more about the happiness of beasts and birds than do the rest of us. But Whitman would have laughed his loudest over Blunt's final analysis of the situation: 'All the world would be a paradise in twenty years if man could be shut out.' A paradise already imaged by Lord Holland and the poet Gray:

> 'Owls would have hooted in Saint Peter's choir,
> And foxes stunk and littered in Saint Paul's.'

To turn from these pages of pettish and puerile complaint to the deep-seated discontent of Henry Adams is to re-enter the world of the intellect. Mark Pattison confessed that he could not take a train without thinking how much better the time-table might have been planned. It was an unhappy twist of mind; but the Rector of Lincoln utilized his obtrusive critical faculties by applying them to his own labours, and scourging himself to greater effort. So did Henry Adams, though even the greater effort left him profoundly dissatisfied. He was unelated by success, and he could not reconcile himself to that degree of failure which is the common portion of mankind. His criticisms are lucid, balanced, enlightening, and occasionally prophetic, as when he comments on the Irishman's political passion for obstructing even himself, and on the perilous race-inertia of Russia. 'Could inertia on such a scale be broken up, or take new scale?' he asks dismayed; and we read the answer today. A minority ruling with iron hand; a majority accepting what comes to them, as they accept day and night and the seasons.

If there is not an understatement in the five hundred

pages of the 'Education,' which thereby loses the power
of persuasion, there is everywhere an appeal to man's
austere equity and disciplined reason. Adams was not in
love with reason. He said that the mind resorted to it for
want of training, and he admitted that he had never met
a perfectly trained mind. But it was the very essence of
reason which made him see that friends were good to him,
and the world not unkind; that the loveliness of the country about Washington gave him pleasure, even when he
found 'a personal grief in every tree'; and that a self-
respecting man refrains from finding wordy fault with the
conditions under which he lives. He did not believe, with
Wordsworth, that nature is a holy and beneficent thing,
or with Blake, that nature is a wicked and malevolent
thing; but he knew better than to put up a quarrel with
an invincible antagonist. He erred in supposing that
other thoughtful men were as discontented as he was, or
that disgust with the methods of Congress corroded their
hours of leisure; but he expressed clearly and with moderation his unwillingness to cherish 'complete and archaic de-
ceits,' or to live, as we are now expected to live, in a world
of illusions. His summing-up is the summing-up of another austere and uncompromising thinker, Santayana,
when confronted by the same problem: 'A spirit with any
honour is not willing to live except in its own way; a spirit
with any wisdom is not over-eager to live at all.'

As our eagerness and our reluctance are not controlling
factors in the situation, it is unwise to stress them too
heavily. Yet we must think, at least some of us must;
and it is well to think out as clearly as we can, not the
relative advantages of content and discontent — a question which briskly answers itself — but the relative right-

ness. Emerson believed in the essential goodness of life, in the admirable law of compensation. Santayana believes that life has evil for its condition, and is for that reason profoundly sad and equivocal. He sees in the sensuous enjoyment of the Greek, the industrial optimism of the American, only a 'thin disguise for despair.' Yet Emerson and Santayana reach the same general conclusion. The first says that hours of sanity and consideration come to communities as to individuals, 'when the truth is seen, and the martyrs are justified'; the second that 'people in all ages sometimes achieve what they have set their hearts on,' and that, if our will and conduct were better disciplined, 'contentment would be more frequent and more massive.'

It is hard to think of these years of grace as a chosen period of sanity and consideration. The orderly processes of civilization have been so wrenched and shattered that readjustment is blocked at some point in every land, in our own no less than in others. There are those who say that the World War went beyond the bounds of human endurance; and that the peculiar horror engendered by indecent methods of attack has dimmed the faith and broken the spirit of men. But Attila managed to turn a fair proportion of the civilized world into wasteland, with only man-power as a destructive force. Europe today is by comparison unscathed, and there are kinsfolk dwelling upon peaceful continents to whom she may legitimately call for aid.

Legitimately, unless our content is like the content extolled by Little Ann's mother; unless our shoes and stockings are indicative of God's meaningless partiality, and unless the contemplation of our neighbour's bleeding feet

enhances our pious satisfaction. 'I doubt,' says Mr.
Wells sourly, 'if it would make any very serious difference
for some time in the ordinary daily life of Kansas City,
if all Europe were reduced to a desert in the next five years.'
Why Kansas City should have been chosen as the symbol
of unconcern, I do not know; but space has a deadening
influence on pity as on fear. The farther we travel from
the Atlantic coast, the more tepid is the sympathy for
injured France. The farther we travel from the Pacific
coast, the fainter is the prejudice against Japan.

It may be possible to construct a state in which men will
be content with their own lot, if they be reasonable, and
with their neighbours' lot, if they be generous. It is manifestly impossible to construct a world on this principle.
Therefore there will always be a latent grief in the nobler
part of man's soul. Therefore there will always be a content as impious as the discontent from which Pope prayed
to be absolved.

The unbroken cheerfulness, no less than the personal
neatness, of the British prisoners in the World War
astounded the more temperamental Germans. Long, long
ago it was said of England: 'Even our condemned persons
doe goe cheerfullie to their deths, for our nature is free,
stout, hautie, prodigal of life and blood.' This heroic
strain, tempered to an endurance which is free from the
waste of emotionalism, produces the outward semblance
and the inward self-respect of a content which circumstances render impossible. It keeps the soul of man immune from whatever degradation his body may be suffering. It saves the land that bred him from the stigma of
defeat. It is remotely and humanly akin to the tranquillity of the great Apostle in a Roman prison. It is

wholly alien to the sin of smugness which has crept in among the domestic virtues, and rendered them more distasteful than ever to austere thinkers, and to those lonely, generous souls who starve in the midst of plenty.

There is a curious and suggestive paragraph in Mr. Chesterton's volume of loose ends, entitled 'What I Saw in America.' It arrests our attention because, for once, the writer seems to be groping for a thought instead of juggling with one. He recognizes a keen and charming quality in American women, and he is disturbed because he also recognizes a recoil from it in his own spirit. This is manifestly perplexing. 'To complain of people for being brave and bright and kind and intelligent may not unreasonably appear unreasonable. And yet there is something in the background that can be expressed only by a symbol; something that is not shallowness, but a neglect of the subconscious, and the vaguer and slower impulses; something that can be missed amid all that laughter and light, under those starry candelabra of the ideals of the happy virtues. Sometimes it came over me in a wordless wave that I should like to see a sulky woman. How she would walk in beauty like the night, and reveal more silent spaces full of older stars! These things cannot be conveyed in their delicate proportion, even in the most large and elusive terms.'

Baudelaire has conveyed them measurably in four words:

'Sois belle! Sois triste!'

Yet neither 'sulky' nor 'triste' is an adjective suggesting with perfect felicity the undercurrent of discontent which lends worth to courage and charm to intelligence. Back of all our lives is the sombre setting of a world ill at ease, and beset by perils. Darkening all our days is the gathering cloud of ill-will, the ugly hatred of man for man, which is the perpetual threat to progress. We Americans may not be so invincibly optimistic as our critics think us, and we may not yet be 'speeding' down the road to destruction, as our critics painfully foretell; but we are part of an endangered civilization, and cannot hold up our end, unsupported by Europe. An American woman, cautiously investing her money in government bonds, said to her man of business: 'These at least are perfectly secure?' 'I should not say that,' was the guarded reply; 'but they will be the last things to go.'

A few years ago there was a period that saw the workingmen and workingwomen of the United States engaged in three hundred and sixty-five strikes — one for every day of the year — and all of them at once. Something seems lacking in the equity of our industrial life. The *Current History* of the *New York Times* is responsible for the statement that eighty-five thousand men and women met their deaths by violence in the United States during the past decade. Something seems lacking in our programme of peace. We have begun to fear, not vaguely but definitely. 'The fact that fear is rational,' says Mr. Brownell, 'is what makes fortitude divine.'

THE HEADSMAN

THE
HEADSMAN

Et cependant, toute grandeur, toute puissance, toute subordination
repose sur l'exécuteur: il est l'horreur et le lien de l'association humaine.
Otez du monde cet agent incompréhensible; dans l'instant même l'ordre
fait place au chaos, les trônes s'abîment, et la société disparait.

JOSEPH DE MAISTRE

WHAT a sombre and striking figure in the deeply coloured
background of history is the headsman, that passive agent
of strange tyrannies, that masked executor of laws which
were often but the expression of man's violence! He stands
aloof from the brilliant web of life, yet, turn where we will,
his shadow falls across the scene. In the little walled
towns of mediaeval Europe, in the splendid cities, in the
broad lands held by feudal lord or stately monastery,
wherever the struggle for freedom and power was sharpest
and sternest, the headsman played his part. An unreasoning and richly imaginative fear wrapped him in a mantle
of romance, as deeply stained as the scarlet cloak which
was his badge of office. Banished from the cheerful
society of men (de Maistre tells us that if other houses
surrounded his abode, they were deserted, and left to
crumble and decay), he enjoyed privileges that compen-
sated him for his isolation. His tithes were exacted as
ruthlessly as were those of prince or baron; and if his wife
chattered little on summer days with friendly gossips, she
was sought in secret after nightfall for hideous amulets
that blessed — or cursed — the wearer. From father to

son, from son to grandson, the right was handed down;
and the young boy was taught to lift and swing the heavy
sword, that his hand might be as sure as his eye, his
muscles as hard as his heart.

Much of life's brilliant panorama was seen from the
elevation of the scaffold in the days when men had no
chance nor leisure to die lingeringly in their beds. They
fell fighting, or by the assassin's hand, or by the help of
what was then termed law; and the headsman, standing
ever ready for his rôle, beheld human nature in its worst
and noblest aspects, in moments of stern endurance and
supreme emotion, of heroic ecstasy and blank despair.
Had he a turn for the marvellous, it was gratified. He
saw Saint Denis arise and carry his severed head from
Montmartre to the site of the church which bears his
name today. He saw Saint Felix and Saint Alban repeat
the miracle. He heard Lucretia of Ancona pronounce the
sacred name three times after decapitation. Ordericus
Vitalis, that most engaging of historians, tells us the story
of the fair Lucretia; and also of the Count de Galles, who
asked upon the scaffold for time in which to say his Pater
Noster. When he reached the words, '*Et ne nos inducas in
tentationem,*' the headsman — all unworthy of his office —
grew impatient, and brought down his shining sword.
The Count's head rolled on the ground, but from his open
lips came with terrible distinctness the final supplication,
'*Sed libera nos a malo.*'

These were not trivial experiences. What a tale to tell
o' nights was that of Théodoric Schawembourg, whose
headless trunk arose and walked thirty paces from the
block! Auberive, who has preserved this famous legend,
embroiders it with so many fantastic details that the sa-

lient point of the narrative is well-nigh lost; but the dead
and forgotten headsman beheld the deed in all its crude
simplicity. Had he, on the other hand, a taste for experi-
mental science, it was given him to watch the surgeons
of Prague, who in 1679 replaced a severed head upon a
young criminal's shoulders, and kept the lad alive for
half an hour. Panurge, it will be remembered, was permanently successful in a similar operation; but Panurge
was a man of genius. We should hardly expect to find his
like among the doctors of Prague.

Strange and unreasonable laws guaranteed to the headsman his full share of emoluments. He was well paid for
his work, and never suffered from a dull season. From the
towns he received poultry and fodder, from the monasteries, fish and game. The Abbaye de Saint-Germain gave
him every year a pig's head; the Abbaye de Saint-Martin,
five loaves of bread and five bottles of wine. Cakes were
baked for him on the eve of Epiphany. From each leper
in the community he exacted — Heaven knows why! —
a tax at Christmas-time. *Les filles de joie* were his vassals,
and paid him tribute. He had the power to save from
death any woman on her way to the scaffold, provided
he were able and willing to marry her. He was the first
official summoned to the body of a suicide; and standing
on the dead man's breast, he claimed as his own everything he could touch with the point of his long sword.
He might, if he chose, arrest the little pigs that strayed
in freedom through the streets of Paris — like the happy
Plantagenet pigs of London — and carry them as prisoners
to the Hôtel Dieu. Here, unless it could be shown that
they belonged to the monks of Saint Anthony, and so,
for the sake of the good pig that loved the blessed hermit,

were free from molestation, their captor demanded their
heads, or a fine of five sous for every ransomed innocent.
It was his privilege to snatch in the market-place as much
corn as he could carry away in his hands, and the peasants
thus freely robbed submitted without a murmur, crossing
themselves with fervour as he passed. The representative
of law and order was not unlike a licensed libertine in the
easy days of old.

The element of picturesqueness entered into this life,
sombre traditions enriched it, terror steeped it in gloom,
the power for which it stood lent to it dignity and weight.
In Spain the headsman wore a distinctive dress, and his
house was painted a deep and ominous red. In France
the ancient title *'Exécuteur de la haute justice'* had a
full-blown majesty of sound. In Germany superstition
grew like a fungus beneath the scaffold's shade, until even
the sword was believed to be a sentient thing with strange
powers of its own. Who can forget the story of the child,
Annerl, whose mother took her to the headsman's house,
whereupon the great weapon stirred uneasily in its cup-
board, thirsting for her blood. Then the headsman be-
sought the mother to allow him to cut the little girl very
lightly, that the sword might be appeased; but she shud-
deringly refused, and Annerl, abandoned to her destiny,
was led thirty years later to the block. Executions at night
were long in favour, and by the flare of torches the scaffold stood revealed to a great and gaping crowd. For
centuries *la place de Grève* was the theatre for this ghastly
drama, until every foot of the soil was saturated with
blood. Only in 1633 were these torchlight decapitations
forbidden throughout France. They had grown too tur-
bulently entertaining.

The headsman's office was hereditary, and if there were no sons, a son-in-law succeeded to the post. Henri Sanson, the last of his dread name, claimed that he was of good blood, and that the far-off ancestor who handed down his sword to nine generations had been betrayed by love to this dark destiny. He had married a headsman's daughter, and could not escape the terrible dowry she brought him. It is not possible to attach much weight to the Sanson memoirs — they are so plainly apocryphal; but we know that the family plied its craft for nearly two hundred years, and that one woman of the race bore seven sons, who all became executioners. In 1726 Charles Sanson died, leaving a little boy, Jean Baptiste, only seven years old. Upon him devolved his father's office; but, in view of his tender infancy, an assistant was appointed to do the work until he came of age. It was required, however, that the child should stand upon the scaffold at every execution, sanctioning it with his presence.

The pride of the headsman lay in his dexterity. The sword was heavy, the stroke was sure. Capeluche, who during the furious struggle between the Armagnacs and the Burgundians severed many a noble head, was a true enthusiast, practising his art *con amore*, and with incredible delicacy and skill. When the fortunes of war brought him in turn upon the scaffold, he proved no craven, but took a lively and intelligent interest in his own decapitation. His last moments were spent in giving a practical lesson to the executioner; showing him where to stand, where to place the block, and how best to handle his weapon.

The vast audience that assembled so often to witness a drama never staled by repetition was wont to be exceed-

ingly critical. Bungling work drew down upon the headsman the execrations of the mob, and not infrequently
placed his own life in danger. De Thou's head fell only at
the eleventh stroke, the Duke of Monmouth was mangled
piteously, and in both these instances the fury of the mob
rose to murder point. It was ostensibly to save such
sufferings and such scenes that the guillotine was adopted
in France; but for the guillotine it is impossible to cherish
any sentiment save abhorrence. Vile, vulgar, and brutal-
izing, its only merit was the hideous speed with which it
did its work; a speed which the despots of the Terror never
found fast enough. In October, 1792, twenty-one Giron-
dists were beheaded in thirty-one minutes; but as practice
made perfect, these figures were soon outdistanced. The
highest record reached was sixty-two decapitations in
forty-five minutes, which sounds like the work of the
shambles.

Charles Henri Sanson, the presiding genius of the guillotine, has been lifted to notoriety by the torrents of
blood he shed; but his is a contemptible figure, without
any of the dark distinction that marked his predecessors.
His pages of the family memoirs are probably mendacious,
and certainly, as Monsieur Loye pathetically laments,
'insipid.' He poses as a physiologist, and tells strange
tales of the condemned who long survived beheading,
as though sixty-two executions in forty-five minutes left
leisure for the study of such phenomena. He also affects
the tone of a philanthropist, commiserates the king who
died by his hands, and is careful to assure us that it was
an assistant named Legros who, holding up the severed
head of Charlotte Corday, struck the fair cheek which
blushed beneath the blow. We are even asked to believe

that he (Sanson) whispered to Marie Antoinette as she descended from the cart, 'Have courage, Madame!' — counsel of which that daughter of the Caesars stood in little need.

The contrast is sharp between this businesslike butchery where the condemned were begrudged the time it took to die, and the earlier executions, so full of dignity and composure. The vilest criminals felt intuitively that the fulness of their atonement consecrated those last sad moments, and behaved often with unexpected propriety and grace. Madame de Brinvilliers was a full half-hour upon the scaffold. The headsman prepared her for death, untying her capstrings, cutting off her hair, baring her shoulders, and binding her hands. She was composed without bravado, contrite without sanctimoniousness. 'I doubt,' wrote her confessor, Abbé Piron, 'whether in all her life she had ever been so patient under the hands of her maid.' Some natural scorn she expressed at sight of the crowd straining with curiosity to see her die: '*Un beauspectacle, Mesdames et Messieurs!*' — but this was all. The executioner swept off her head with one swift stroke; then, hastily opening a flask, took a deep draught of wine. 'That was a good blow,' he said to the Abbé. 'At these times I always recommend myself to God, and He has never failed me. This lady has been on my mind for a week past. I will have six Masses said for her soul.' Surely such a headsman ennobled in some degree the direful post he bore.

If a murderess, inconceivably callous and cruel, could die with dignity, what of the countless scenes where innocence was sacrificed to ambition, and where the best and noblest blood of Europe was shed upon the block?

What of the death of Conradin on a Neapolitan scaffold?
In the thirteenth century, boys grew quickly into manhood,
and Conradin was seventeen. He had embarked early
upon that desperate game of which the prize was a throne,
and the forfeit, life. He had missed his throw, and earned
his penalty. But he was the grandson of an emperor, the
heir of an imperial crown, and the last of a proud race.
There was a pathetic boyishness in the sudden defiance
with which he hurled his glove into the throng, and in the
low murmur of his mother's name. The headsman had a
bitter part to play that day, for Conradin's death is one of
the world's tragedies; but there are other scaffolds upon
which we still glance back with a pity fresh enough for
pain. When Count Egmont and Admiral Horn were beheaded in the great square of Brussels, the executioner
wisely hid beneath the black draperies until it was time
for him to do his work. He had no wish to parade himself
as part of that sad show.

In England the rules of etiquette were never more binding than upon those who were about to be beheaded.
When the Duke of Hamilton, the Earl of Holland, and
Lord Capel went to the block together, they were told
they must die in the order of their rank, as though they
were going in to dinner; and upon Lord Capel's offering to
address the crowd without removing his hat, it was explained to him that this was incorrect. The scaffold was
not the House of Parliament, and those who graced it were
expected to uncover. On a later and very memorable occasion, the Earl of Kilmarnock, 'with a most just mixture of
dignity and submission,' offered the melancholy precedence to Lord Balmerino. That gallant soldier — 'a natural, brave old gentleman,' says Horace Walpole, though

he was but fifty-eight — would have mounted first, but the headsman interfered. Even upon the scaffold, a belted earl enjoyed the privileges of his rank.

All this formality must have damped the spirits of the condemned; but it seems to have been borne with admirable gaiety and good temper. Lord Balmerino, 'decently unmoved,' was ready to die first or last, and he gave the punctilious executioner three guineas, to prove that he was not impatient. 'He looked quite unconcerned,' says an eye-witness, 'and like some one going on a party of pleasure, or upon some business of little or no importance.' Lord Lovat, beheaded at eighty for his active share in the Jacobite rising of forty-five, derived much amusement from the vast concourse of people assembled to witness his execution — an amusement agreeably intensified by the giving way of some scaffolding, which occasioned the unexpected death of several eager sight-seers. 'The more mischief, the better sport,' said the old lord grimly, and proceeded to quote Ovid and Horace with fine scholarly zest. If the executioner were seldom a person of education, it was from no lack of opportunity. He might, had he chosen, have learned at his post much law and more theology. When Archbishop Laud stood waiting by the block, Sir John Clotworthy conceived it to be a seasonable occasion for propounding some knotty points of doctrine. The prelate courteously answered one or two questions, but time pressed, and controversy had lost its charm. Even so good a churchman may be pardoned for turning wearily away from polemics when his life's span had narrowed down to minutes, and the headsman waited by his side.

In the burial registry of Whitechapel, under the year 1649, is the following entry:

June 21st, Richard Brandon, a man out of Rosemary Lane. This Brandon is held to be the man who beheaded Charles the First.

'Held to be' only, for the mystery of the king's executioner was one which long excited and baffled curiosity. Wild whispers credited the deed to men of rank and station, among them Viscount Stair, the type of strategist to whom all manner of odium naturally and reasonably clung. A less distinguished candidate for the infamy was one William Howlett, actually condemned to death after the Restoration for a part he never played, and saved from the gallows only by the urgent efforts of a few citizens who swore that Brandon did the deed. Brandon was not available for retribution. He had died in his bed five months after Charles was beheaded, and had been hurried ignominiously into his grave in Whitechapel churchyard. As public executioner of London, he could hardly escape his destiny; but it is said that remorse and horror shortened his life. In his supposed 'Confession,' a tract widely circulated at the time, he claimed that he was 'fetched out of bed by a troup of horse,' and carried against his will to the scaffold. Also that he was paid thirty pounds, all in half-crowns, for the work; and had 'an orange stuck full of cloves, and a handkerchief out of the King's pocket.' The orange he sold for ten shillings in Rosemary Lane.

The shadow that falls across the headsman's path deepens in horror when we contemplate the scaffolds of Charles, of Louis, of Marie Antoinette, and of Mary Stuart. The hand that has shed royal blood is stained forever, yet the very magnitude of the offence lends to it a painful and terrible distinction. It is the zenith as well as the nadir of the headsman's history; it is the corner-stone of the impassable barrier which divides the axe and the sword from the hangman's noose, the death of Strafford from the death of Jonathan Wild.

If we turn the page, and look for a moment at the 'gallows tree,' we find that it has its romantic and its comic side, but the comedy is boisterous, the romance savours of melodrama. For centuries one of the recognized amusements of the English people was to see men hanged, and the leading features of the entertainment were modified from time to time to please the popular taste. Doctor Johnson, the sanest as well as the best man of his day, highly commended these public executions as 'satisfactory to all parties. The public is gratified by a procession, the criminal is supported by it.' That the enjoyment was often mutual, it is impossible to deny. There was a world of meaning in the gentle custom, supported for years by a very ancient benefaction, of giving a nosegay to the condemned man on his way to Tyburn. Before the cart climbed Holborn Hill — 'the heavy hill' as it was called, with a touch of poetry rivalling the 'Bridge of Sighs' — it stopped at Saint Sepulchre's church, and on the church steps stood one bearing in his hands the flowers that were to yield their fresh fragrance to the dying. Nor were the candidates without their modest pride. When the noted chimney-sweep, Sam Hall, achieved the honour of a hanging, he was rudely jostled and bidden to stand off by a highwayman, stepping haughtily into the cart, and annoyed at finding himself in such low company. 'Stand off, yourself!' was the indignant answer of the young sweep. 'I have as good a right to be here as you have.'

'Nothing,' says Voltaire, 'is so disagreeable as to be obscurely hanged,' and the loneliness which in this moral age encompasses the felon's last hours should be as salutary as it is depressing. Mr. Housman, who got closer to the plain thoughts of plain men than any poet of modern times, gave stern expression to the awful aloofness of the condemned criminal from his fellow creatures, an aloofness unknown in the cheerful, brutal days of old.

> 'They hang us now in Shrewsbury jail:
> The whistles blow forlorn,
> And trains all night groan on the rail
> To men who die at morn.'

The sociability of Tyburn, if somewhat vehement in character, was a jocund thing by the side of such solitude as this.

Parish registers make curious reading. They tell so much in words so scant and bald that they set us wondering on our own accounts over the unknown details of tragedies which even in their day won no wide hearing, and which have been wholly forgotten for centuries. Mr. Lang quotes two entries that are briefly comprehensive; the first from the register of Saint Nicholas, Durham, August 8, 1592: 'Simson, Arington, Featherston, Fenwick, and Lancaster, were hanged for being Egyptians.'

Featherston and Fenwick might have been hanged on the evidence of their names, good gypsy names both of them, and famous for years in the dark annals of the race; but were these men guilty of no other crime, no indiscretion even, that has escaped recording? Five stalwart rogues might have served the queen in better fashion than by dangling idly on a gallows. The second entry, from the parish church of Richmond in Yorkshire, 1558, is still shorter, a model of conciseness: 'Richard Snell b'rnt, bur. 9 Sept.'

Was Snell a martyr, unglorified by Fox, or a particularly desperate sinner; and if a sinner, what was the nature of his sin? Warlocks were commonly hanged in the sixteenth century, even when their sister witches were burned. '*C'est la loi de l'homme.*' In fact, burning was an unusual, and — save in Queen Mary's mind — an unpopular mode of punishment. 'You are burnt for heresy,' said Mr. Birrell with great good humour. 'That is right enough. No one would complain of that. Hanging is a different matter. It is very easy to get hung; but to be burnt requires a combination of circumstances not always forthcoming.'

Yet Richard Snell, yeoman of Yorkshire, mastered these circumstances; and a single line in a parish register is his meagre share of fame.

WHEN LALLA ROOKH WAS YOUNG

WHEN LALLA ROOKH WAS YOUNG

And give you, mixed with western sentimentalism,
Some glimpses of the finest orientalism.

'STICK to the East,' wrote Byron to Moore, in 1813. 'The oracle, Staël, told me it was the only poetic policy. The North, South, and West have all been exhausted; but from the East we have nothing but Southey's unsaleables, and these he has contrived to spoil by adopting only their most outrageous fictions. His personages don't interest us, and yours will. You will have no competitors; and, if you had, you ought to be glad of it. The little I have done in that way is merely a "voice in the wilderness" for you; and if it has had any success, that also will prove that the public is orientalizing, and pave the way for you.'

There is something admirably businesslike in this advice. Byron, who four months before had sold the 'Giaour' and the 'Bride of Abydos' to Murray for a thousand guineas, was beginning to realize the commercial value of poetry; and, like a true man of affairs, knew what it meant to corner a poetic market. He was generous enough to give Moore the tip, and to hold out a helping hand as well; for he sent him six volumes of Castellan's 'Mœurs des Ottomans,' and three volumes of Toderini's 'De la Littérature des Turcs.' The orientalism afforded by textbooks was the kind that England loved.

From the publication of 'Lalla Rookh' in 1817 to the publication of Thackeray's 'Our Street' in 1847, Byron's far-sighted policy continued to bear golden fruit. For thirty years Caliphs and Deevs, Brahmins and Circassians, rioted through English verse; mosques and seraglios were the stage properties of English fiction; the bowers of Rochnabed, the Lake of Cashmere, became as familiar as Richmond and the Thames to English readers. Some feeble washings of this great tidal wave crossed the estranging sea, to tint the pages of the New York *Mirror*, and kindred journals in the United States. Harems and slave-markets, with beautiful Georgians and sad, slender Arab girls, thrilled our grandmothers' kind hearts. Tales of Moorish Lochinvars, who snatch away the fair daughters — or perhaps the fair wives — of powerful rajahs, captivated their imaginations. Gazelles trot like poodles through these stories, and lend colour to their robust Saxon atmosphere. In one, a neglected 'favourite' wins back her lord's affection by the help of a slave-girl's amulet; and the inconstant Moslem, entering the harem, exclaims, 'Beshrew me that I ever thought another fair!' — which sounds like a penitent Tudor.

'A Persian's Heaven is easily made,
'Tis but black eyes and lemonade;'

and our oriental literature was compounded of the same simple ingredients. When the New York *Mirror*, under the guidance of the versatile Mr. Willis, tried to be impassioned and sensuous, it dropped into such wanton lines as these to a 'Sultana':

'She came — soft leaning on her favourite's arm,
She came, warm panting from the sultry hours,
To rove mid fragrant shades of orange bowers,
A veil light shadowing each voluptuous charm.'

And for this must Lord Byron stand responsible.

The happy experiment of grafting Turkish roses upon English boxwood led up to some curious complications, not the least of which was the necessity of stiffening the moral fibre of the Orient — which was esteemed to be but lax — until it could bear itself in seemly fashion before English eyes. The England of 1817 was not, like the England of 1937, prepared to give critical attention to the decadent. It presented a solid front of denial to habits and ideas which had not received the sanction of British custom; which had not, through national adoption, become part of the established order of the universe. The line of demarcation between Providence and common law was lightly drawn. Jeffrey, a self-constituted arbiter of tastes and morals, assured his nervous countrymen that, although Moore's verse was glowing, his principles were sound.

'The characters and sentiments of "Lalla Rookh" belong to the poetry of rational, honourable, considerate, and humane Europe; and not to the childishness, cruelty, and profligacy of Asia. So far as we have yet seen, there is no sound sense, firmness of purpose, or principled goodness, except among the natives of Europe and their genuine descendants.'

Starting with this magnificent assumption, it became a delicate and a difficult task to unite the customs of the East with the 'principled goodness' of the West; the 'sound sense' of the Briton with the fervour and fanaticism of the Turk. Jeffrey held that Moore had effected this alliance in the most tactful manner, and had thereby 're- deemed the character of oriental poetry'; just as Mr. Thomas Haynes Bayly, ten years later, 'reclaimed festive song from vulgarity.' More carping critics, however, wor- ried their readers a good deal on this point; and the non- conformist conscience cherished uneasy doubts as to Hafed's irregular courtship and Nourmahal's marriage lines. From across the sea came the accusing voice of young Mr. Channing in the *North American*, proclaiming that 'harlotry has found in Moore a bard to smooth her coarseness and veil her effrontery, to give her languor for modesty, and affectation for virtue.' The English *Monthly Review*, less open to alarm, confessed with a sigh 'a de- pressing regret that, with the exception of "Paradise and the Peri," no great moral effect is either attained or at- tempted by "Lalla Rookh." To what purpose all this sweetness and delicacy of thought and language, all this labour and profusion of Oriental learning? What head is set right in one erroneous notion, what heart is softened in one obdurate feeling, by this luxurious quarto?'

It is a lamentable truth that Anacreon exhibits none of Dante's spiritual depth, and that la reine Margot fell short of Queen Victoria's fireside qualities. Nothing could make a moralist of Moore. The light-hearted creature was a model of kindness, of courage, of conjugal fidelity; but — reversing the common rule of life — he preached none of the virtues that he practised. His pathetic attempts to adjust his tales to the established conventions of society failed signally of their purpose. Even Byron wrote him that little Allegra (as yet unfamiliar with her alphabet) should not be permitted to read 'Lalla Rookh'; partly because it wasn't proper, and partly — which was prettily said — lest she should discover 'that there was a better poet than Papa.' It was reserved for Moore's followers to present their verses and stories in the chastened form acceptable to English drawing-rooms, and permitted to English youth. *La Belle Assemblée* published in 1819 an Eastern tale called 'Jahia and Meimoune,' in which the lovers converse like the virtuous characters in 'Camilla.' Jahia becomes the guest of an infamous sheik, who intoxicates him with a sherbet composed of 'sugar, musk, and amber,' and presents him with five thousand sequins and a beautiful Circassian slave. When he is left alone with this damsel, she addresses him thus: 'I feel interested in you, and present circumstances will save me from the charge of immodesty, when I say that I also love you. This love inspires me with fresh horror at the crimes that are here committed.'

Jahia protests that he respectfully returns her passion, and that his intentions are of an honourable character, whereupon the circumspect maiden rejoins: 'Since such are your sentiments, I will perish with you if I fail in delivering you'; and conducts him, through a tangle of adventures, to safety. Jahia then places Meimoune under the chaperonage of his mother until their wedding day; after which we are happy to know that 'they passed their lives in the enjoyment of every comfort attendant on domestic felicity. If their lot was not splendid or magnificent, they were rich in mutual affection; and they experienced that fortunate medium which, far removed from indigence, aspires not to the accumulation of immense wealth, and laughs at the unenvied load of pomp and splendour which it neither seeks, nor desires to obtain.'

It is to be hoped that many obdurate hearts were softened, and many erroneous notions were set right by the influence of a story like this. In the *Monthly Museum* an endless narrative poem, 'Abdallah,' stretched its slow length along from number to number, blooming with fresh moral sentiments on every page; while from an arid wilderness of Moorish love songs, and Persian love songs, and Circassian love songs, and Hindu love songs, I quote this 'Arabian' love song, peerless amid its peers:

> 'Thy hair is black as the starless sky,
>   And clasps thy neck as it loved its home;
> Yet it moves at the sound of thy faintest sigh,
>   Like the snake that lies on the white sea-foam.

> 'I love thee, Ibla. Thou art bright
>   As the white snow on the hills afar;
> Thy face is sweet as the moon by night,
>   And thine eye like the clear and rolling star.

> 'But the snow is poor and withers soon,
>   While thou art firm and rich in hope;
> And never (like thine) from the face of the moon
>   Flamed the dark eye of the antelope.'

The truth and accuracy of this last observation should commend the poem to all lovers of nature.

It is the custom in these days of morbid accuracy to laugh at the second-hand knowledge which Moore so proudly and so innocently displayed. Even Mr. Saintsbury says some unkind things about the notes to 'Lalla Rookh' — scraps of twentieth-hand knowledge, *he* calls them — while pleasantly recording his affection for the poem itself, an affection based upon the reasonable grounds of childish recollections. In the well-ordered home of his infancy, none but 'Sunday books' might be read on Sundays in nursery or schoolroom. 'But this severity was tempered by one of those easements often occurring in a world, which, if not the best, is certainly not the worst of all possible worlds. For the convenience of servants, or for some other reason, the children were much more in the drawing-room on Sundays than on any other day; and it was an unwritten rule that any book that lived in the drawing-room was fit Sunday reading. The consequence was that from the time I could read until childish things were put away, I used to spend a considerable part of the first day of the week in reading and re-reading a collection of books, four of which were Scott's poems, "Lalla Rookh," "The Essays of Elia," and Southey's "Doctor." Therefore it may be that I rank "Lalla Rookh" too high.'

Blessed memories, and thrice blessed influences of childhood! But if 'Lalla Rookh,' like 'Vathek,' was written to be the joy of imaginative little boys and girls (alas for those who now replace it with 'Allan in Alaska,' and 'Little Cora on the Continent'), the notes to 'Lalla Rookh' were, to my infant mind, even more enthralling than the poem. There was a sketchiness about them, a detachment from time and circumstance — I always hated being told the whole of everything — which led me day after day into fresh fields of conjecture. The nymph who was encircled by a rainbow, and bore a radiant son; the scimitars that were so dazzling they made the warriors wink; the sacred well which reflected the moon at midday; and the great embassy that was sent 'from some port of the Indies' — a welcome vagueness of geography — to recover a monkey's tooth, snatched away by an equally nameless conqueror; what child could fail to love such floating stars of erudition?

Our great-grandfathers were profoundly impressed by Moore's textbook acquirements. The *Monthly Review* quoted a solid page of the notes to dazzle British readers, who confessed themselves amazed to find a fellow countryman so much 'at home' in Persia and Arabia. Blackwood authoritatively announced that Moore was familiar, not only 'with the grandest regions of the human soul' — which is expected of a poet — but also with the remotest boundaries of the East; and that in every tone and hue and form he was 'purely and intensely Asiatic.' 'The carping criticism of paltry tastes and limited understandings faded before that burst of admiration with which all enlightened spirits hailed the beauty and magnificence of "Lalla Rookh."'

Few people care to confess to 'paltry tastes' and 'limited understandings.' They would rather join in any general acclamation. 'Browning's poetry obscure!' I once heard a lecturer say with scorn. 'Let us ask ourselves, "Obscure to whom?" No doubt a great many things are obscure to long-tailed Brazilian apes.' After which his audience, with one accord, admitted that it understood 'Sordello.' So when Jeffrey — great umpire of games whose rules he never knew — informed the British public that there was not in 'Lalla Rookh' 'a simile, a description, a name, a trait of history, or allusion to romance that does not indicate entire familiarity with the life, nature, and learning of the East,' the public contentedly took his word for it. When he remarked that 'the dazzling splendours, the breathing odours' of Araby were without doubt Moore's 'native element,' the public, whose native element was neither splendid nor sweet-smelling, envied the Irishman his softer joys. 'Lalla Rookh' might be 'voluptuous' (a word we find in every review of the period), but its orientalism was beyond dispute. Did not Mrs. Skinner tell Moore that she had, when in India, translated the prose interludes into Bengali, for the benefit of her moonshee, and that the man was amazed at the accuracy of the costumes? Did not the nephew of the Persian ambassador in Paris tell Mr. Stretch, who told Moore, that 'Lalla Rookh' had been translated into Persian; that the songs — particularly 'Bendemeer's Stream' — were sung 'everywhere'; and that the happy natives could hardly believe the whole work had not been taken originally from a Persian manuscript?

> 'I'm told, dear Moore, your lays are sung
> (Can it be true, you lucky man?)
> By moonlight, in the Persian tongue,
> Along the streets of Ispahan.'

And not of Ispahan only; for in the winter of 1821 the Berlin court presented 'Lalla Rookh' with such splendour, such wealth of detail, and such titled actors, that Moore's heart was melted and his head was turned (as any other heart would have been melted, and any other head would have been turned) by the reports thereof. A Grand Duchess of Russia took the part of Lalla Rookh; the Duke of Cumberland was Aurungzebe; and a beautiful young sister of Prince Radzivil enchanted all beholders as the Peri. 'Nothing else was talked about in Berlin'; the King of Prussia had a set of engravings made of the noble actors in their costumes; and the Crown Prince sent word to Moore that he slept always with a copy of 'Lalla Rookh' under his pillow, which was foolish, but flattering. Hardly had the echoes of this royal fête died away, when Spontini brought out in Berlin his opera 'The Feast of Roses,' and

Moore's triumph in Prussia was complete. Byron, infinitely amused at the success of his own good advice, wrote to the happy poet: 'Your Berlin drama is an honour unknown since the days of Elkanah Settle, whose "Empress of Morocco" was presented by the court ladies, which was, as Johnson remarked, "the last blast of inflammation to poor Dryden."'

Who shall say that this comparison is without its dash of malice? There is a natural limit to the success we wish our friends, even when we have spurred them on their way.

If the English court did not lend itself with much gaiety or grace to dramatic entertainments, English society was quick to respond to the delights of a modified orientalism. That is to say, it sang melting songs about bulbuls and Shiraz wine; wore ravishing Turkish costumes whenever it had a chance (like the beautiful Mrs. Winkworth in the charades at Gaunt House); and covered its locks — if they were feminine locks — with turbans of portentous size and splendour. When Mrs. Fitzherbert, aged seventy-three, gave a fancy dress ball, so many of her guests appeared as Turks, and Georgians, and sultanas that it was hard to believe that Brighton, and not Stamboul, was the scene of the festivity. At an earlier entertainment, 'a rural breakfast and promenade,' given by Mrs. Hobart at her villa near Fulham, and 'graced by the presence of royalty,' the leading attraction was Mrs. Bristow, who represented Queen Nourjahad in the 'Garden of Roses.' 'Draped in all the magnificence of Eastern grandeur, Mrs. Bristow was seated in the larger drawing-room (which was very beautifully fitted up with cushions in the Indian style), smoking her hookah amidst all sorts of the choicest perfumes. Mrs. Bristow was very profuse with otto of roses, drops of which were thrown about the ladies' dresses. The whole house was scented with the delicious fragrance.'

The *European Magazine*, the *Monthly Museum*, all the dim old periodicals published in the early part of the last century for feminine readers, teem with such 'society notes.' From them, too, we learn that by 1823 turbans of 'rainbow striped gauze frosted with gold' were in universal demand; while 'black velvet turbans, enormously large, and worn very much on one side,' must have given a rakish appearance to stout British matrons. *La Belle Assemblée* describes for us with tender enthusiasm a ravishing turban, 'in the Turkish style,' worn in the winter of 1823 at the theatre and at evening parties. This masterpiece was of 'pink oriental crêpe, beautifully folded in front, and richly ornamented with pearls. The folds are fastened on the left side, just above the ear, with a Turkish scimitar of pearls; and on the right side are tassels of pearls, surmounted by a crescent and a star.'

Here we have Lady Jane or Lady Amelia transformed at once into young Nourmahal; and, to aid the illusion, a 'Circassian corset' was devised, free from encroaching steel or whalebone, and warranted to give its English wearers the 'flowing and luxurious lines' admired in the overfed inmates of the harem. When the passion for orientalism began to subside in London, remote rural districts caught and prolonged the infection. I have sympathized all my life with the innocent ambition of Miss Matty Jenkyns to possess a sea-green turban, like the one worn by Queen Adelaide; and have never been able to forgive that ruthlessly sensible Mary Smith — the chronicler of 'Cranford' — for taking her a 'neat middle-aged cap' instead. 'I was most particularly anxious to prevent

her from disfiguring her small gentle mousy face with a
great Saracen's head turban,' says the judicious Miss
Smith with a smirk of self-commendation; and poor Miss
Matty — the cap being bought — has to bow to this
arbiter of fate. How much we all suffer in life from the
discretion of our families and friends!

Thackeray laughed the dim ghost of 'Lalla Rookh' out
of England. He mocked at the turbans, and at the old
ladies who wore them; at the vapid love songs, and at the
young ladies who sang them.

> I am a little brown bulbul. Come and listen in the moon-
> light. Praise be to Allah! I am a merry bard.

He derided the 'breathing odours of Araby,' and the Eastern travellers who imported this exotic atmosphere into
Grosvenor Square. Young Bedwin Sands, who has 'lived
under tents,' who has published a quarto ornamented with
his own portrait in various oriental costumes, and who
goes about accompanied by a black servant of most un-
prepossessing appearance, 'just like another Brian de
Bois Guilbert,' is only a degree less ridiculous than
Clarence Bulbul, who gives Miss Tokely a piece of the
sack in which an indiscreet Zuleika had been drowned,
and whose servant says to callers: 'Mon maître est au
divan,' or 'Monsieur trouvera Monsieur dans son sérail.
. . . He has coffee and pipes for everybody. I should like
you to have seen the face of old Bowly, his college tutor,
called upon to sit cross-legged on a divan, a little cup of
bitter black mocha put into his hand, and a large amber-
muzzled pipe stuck into his mouth before he could say
it was a fine day. Bowly almost thought he had com-
promised his principles by consenting so far to this Turkish

manner.' Bulbul's sure and simple method of commending himself to young ladies is by telling them they remind him of a girl he knew in Circassia — Ameena, the sister of Schamyle Bey. 'Do you know, Miss Pim,' he thoughtfully observes, 'that you would fetch twenty thousand piastres in the market at Constantinople?' Whereupon Miss Pim is filled with embarrassed elation. An English girl, conscious of being in no great demand at home, was naturally flattered as well as fluttered by the thought of having a market value elsewhere. And perhaps this feminine instinct was at the root of 'Lalla Rookh's' long popularity in England.

ALLEGRA

ALLEGRA

A lovelier toy sweet Nature never made;
A serious, subtle, wild, yet gentle being;
Graceful without design, and unforeseeing;
With eyes — Oh! speak not of her eyes! which seem
Two mirrors of Italian heaven.

IN THESE Wordsworthian lines Shelley describes Lord Byron's little daughter, Allegra, then under two years of age; and the word 'toy' — so keenly suggestive of both the poetic and the masculine point of view — has in this case an unconscious and bitter significance. Allegra was a toy at which rude hands plucked violently, until death lifted her from their clutches, and hid her away in the safety and dignity of the tomb. 'She is more fortunate than we are,' said her father, with a noble and rare lapse into simplicity, and the words were sadly true. Never did a little child make a happier escape from the troublesome burden of life.

In the winter of 1816 a handsome, vivacious, dark-eyed girl sought the acquaintance of Lord Byron, and begged him to use his influence in obtaining for her an engagement at Drury Lane. She was the type of young woman who aspires to a career on the stage, or in any other field, without regard to qualifications, and without the burden of study. She wrote in her first letter (it had many successors): ' The theatre presents an easy method of independence.' She objected vehemently to 'the intolerable drudgery of provincial boards.' She wanted to appear at once in London. And she signed her name, 'Clara Clairmont,' which was prettily alliterative, and suited her better than Jane.

It was an inauspicious beginning of an unhappy intimacy, destined to bring nothing but disaster in its train. Miss Clairmont's stepfather, William Godwin, had confessed, not without reason, 'a feeling of incompetence for the education of daughters.' His own child, Mary, had fled to Europe eighteen months before with the poet Shelley. Miss Clairmont accompanied their flight; and their inexplicable folly in taking her with them was punished — as folly always is — with a relentless severity seldom accorded to sin. To the close of Shelley's life, his sister-in-law continued to be a source of endless irritation and anxiety.

No engagement at Drury Lane was procurable. Indeed, Miss Clairmont soon ceased to desire one. Her infatuation for Lord Byron drove all other thoughts and hopes and ambitions from her heart. She wrote to him repeatedly — clever, foolish, half-mad, and cruelly long letters. She praised the 'wild originality of his countenance.' She sent him her manuscripts to read. There is something pathetic in Byron's unheeded entreaty that she should 'write short.' There is something immeasurably painful in his unconcealed indifference, in his undisguised contempt. The glamour of his fame as a poet gave a compelling power to that fatal beauty which was his undoing. When we read what *men* have written about Byron's head; when we recall the rhapsodies of Moore, the reluctant praise of Trelawny, the eloquence of Coleridge; when we remember that Scott — the sanest man in Great Britain — confessed ruefully that Byron's face was a thing to dream of, we are the less surprised that women should have flung them-

selves at his feet in a frenzy of self-surrender, which a
cold legacy of busts and portraits does little to explain.
Miss Clairmont — to use one of Professor Dowden's
flowers of speech — 'was lightly whirled out of her regular
orbit.' In the spring she travelled with Shelley and Mary
Godwin to Switzerland, and at Sécheron, a little suburb
of Geneva, they met Lord Byron, who was then writing
the splendid third canto of 'Childe Harold.' His letter to
his sister, the Honourable Augusta Leigh, bears witness to
his annoyance at the encounter; but the two poets became
for a season daily companions, and, in some sort, friends.
Shelley thought Byron 'as mad as the winds' (an opinion
which was returned with interest), and deeply regretted
his slavery 'to the vilest and most vulgar prejudices' —
among them a prejudice in favour of Christianity, for
which ancient institution Byron always entertained a profound though unfruitful reverence. Indeed, despite the
revolutionary impetus of his verse, and despite the fact
that he died for revolting Greece, the settled order of
things appealed with force to his eminently practical
nature. 'Sanity and balance,' says Lord Morley, 'mark
the foundations of his character. An angel of reasonableness seems to watch over him, even when he comes
most dangerously near to an extravagance.'

Miss Clairmont did not confide to her guardians the
secret of her intimacy with Lord Byron until after the
meeting at Geneva. When her relations with him were
understood, neither Shelley nor Mary Godwin saw at first
any occasion for distress. They cared nothing for the
broken marriage bond, and they believed, or hoped, that
some true affection had been — as in their own case —
the impelling and upholding power. It was the swift

withering of this hope which filled their hearts with apprehension. They carried Miss Clairmont back to England in the autumn ('I have had all the plague possible to persuade her to go back,' wrote Byron to his sister); and in Bath, the following January, her little daughter was born.

It was a blue-eyed baby of exceptional loveliness. Mrs. Shelley (Mary Godwin had been married to the poet on the death of his wife, two months earlier) filled her letters with praises of its beauty. Miss Clairmont wrote to Byron in 1820 that her health had been injured by her 'attentions' to her child during its first year; but she found time to study Italian, and to write a book, for which Shelley tried in vain to find a publisher, and the very title of which is now forgotten. The little household at Great Marlow was not a tranquil one. Mrs. Shelley had grown weary of her step-sister's society. Her diary — all these young people kept diaries with uncommendable industry — abounds in notes, illustrative of Claire's ill-temper, and of her own chronic irritation. 'Clara imagines that I treat her unkindly.' 'Clara in an ill-humour.' 'Jane [1] gloomy.' 'Jane for some reason refuses to walk.' 'Jane is not well, and does not speak the whole day.'

This was bad enough, but there were other moods more trying than mere sulkiness. Miss Clairmont possessed nerves. She had 'the horrors' when 'King Lear' was read aloud. She was, or professed to be, afraid of ghosts. She would come downstairs in the middle of the night to tell Shelley that an invisible hand had lifted her pillow from her bed, and dumped it on a chair. To such thrilling recitals the poet lent serious attention. 'Her manner,' he

[1] Clara Mary Jane Clairmont was 'Claire's' full name.

wrote in his journal, 'convinced me that she was not deceived. We continued to sit by the fire, at intervals engaged in awful conversation, relative to the nature of these mysteries' — that is, to the migrations of the pillow. As a result of sympathetic treatment, Claire would wind up the night with hysterics, writhing in convulsions on the floor, and shrieking dismally, until poor Mrs. Shelley would be summoned from a sick-bed to soothe her to slumber. 'Give me a garden, and *absentia* Claire, and I will thank my love for many favours,' is the weary comment of the wife, after months of inextinguishable agitation.

There was no loophole of escape, however, from a burden so rashly shouldered. Miss Clairmont made one or two ineffectual efforts at self-support; but found them little to her liking. She could not and she would not live with her mother, Mrs. Godwin — 'a very disgusting woman, and wears green spectacles,' is Charles Lamb's description of this lady, whom, in common with most of her acquaintances, he cordially disliked. When Byron wrote offering to receive and provide for his little daughter, Shelley vehemently opposed the plan, thinking it best that so young an infant should remain under its mother's care. But his wife, who was at heart a singularly sagacious woman, never ceased to urge the advisability of the step. Claire, though reluctant to part from her baby, yielded to these persuasions; and the journey to Italy in the spring was undertaken mainly as a sure though expensive method of conveying Allegra to her father.

That Byron wanted the child, there is no doubt, nor that he had been from the first deeply concerned for her uncertain future. Three months after her birth he wrote to his sister that he had resolved to send for her, and place her in a convent, 'to become a good Catholic, and (it may be) a nun — being a character somewhat needed in our family.' 'They tell me,' he adds, 'that she is very pretty, with blue eyes and dark hair; and although I never was attached, nor pretended attachment to the mother, still, in case of the eternal war and alienation which I foresee about my legitimate daughter, Ada, it may be as well to have something to repose a hope upon. I must love something in my old age; and circumstances may render this poor little creature a great, and perhaps my only, comfort.'

It is not often that Byron's letters reveal this grace of sentiment. Never, after Allegra's arrival, does he allude to any affection he bears her, and he once assured Moore that he did not bear any — a statement which that partial biographer thought fit to disregard. On the other hand, he dwells over and over again, both in his correspondence and in his journal, upon plans for her education and future settlement. He was at all times sternly practical, and pitilessly clear-sighted. He never regarded his daughter as a 'lovely toy,' but as a very serious and troublesome responsibility. The poetic view of childhood failed to appeal to him. 'Any other father,' wrote Claire bitterly, 'would have made of her infancy a sweet idyl of flowers and innocent joy.' Byron was not idyllic. He dosed Allegra with quinine when she had a fever. He abandoned a meditated journey because she was ill. He dismissed a servant who had let her fall. He added a codicil to his will bequeathing her five thousand pounds. These things do not indicate any stress of emotion, but they have their place in the ordinary calendar of parental cares.

A delicate baby, not yet sixteen months old, was a formidable and inharmonious addition to the poet's Venetian household. The Swiss nurse, Elise, who had been sent by the Shelleys from Milan, proved to be a most incapable and unworthy woman, who later on made infinite mischief by telling the foulest of lies. Byron was sorely perplexed by the situation; and when Mrs. Hoppner, the Genevan wife of the English consul-general, offered to take temporary charge of the child, he gladly and gratefully consented. One difficulty in his path he had not failed to foresee — that Claire, having relinquished Allegra of her own free will, would quickly want her back again. In fact, before the end of the summer Miss Clairmont insisted upon going to Venice, and poor Shelley very ruefully and reluctantly accompanied her. Byron received him with genuine delight, and, in an access of good humour, proposed lending the party his villa at Este. There Mrs. Shelley, who had lost her infant daughter, might recover from sorrow and fatigue, and there Allegra might spend some weeks under her mother's care. The offer was frankly accepted, and the two men came once more to an amicable understanding. They were not fitted to be friends — the gods had ruled a severance wide and deep — but when unpricked by the contentiousness of other people, they passed pleasant and profitable hours together.

Meanwhile, the poor little apple of discord was ripening every day into a fairer bloom. 'Allegra has been with me these three months,' writes Byron to his sister in August. 'She is very pretty, remarkably intelligent, and a great favourite with everybody .... She has very blue eyes, a singular forehead, fair curly hair, and a devil of a Spirit — but that is Papa's.' 'I have here my natural daughter, by name Allegra,' he tells Moore six weeks later. 'She is a pretty little girl enough, and reckoned like Papa.' To Murray he writes in the same paternal strain. 'My daughter Allegra is well, and growing pretty; her hair is growing darker, and her eyes are blue. Her temper and her ways, Mr. Hoppner says, are like mine, as well as her features. She will make, in that case, a manageable young lady.'

Other pens bear ready witness to Allegra's temper. Mr. Jeaffreson, who has written a very offensive book about Lord Byron, takes pains to tell us that the poor child was 'greedy, passionate, and, in her fifth year, precocious, vain, and saucy.' Mr. Hoppner, after the publication of the Countess Guiccioli's 'Recollections,' wrote an agitated letter to the *Athenaeum*, assuring an indifferent public that he had no acquaintance with the lady, and that his own respectability was untarnished by any intimacy with the poet, of whose morals he disapproved, and whose companionship he eschewed, save when they rode together — on Byron's horses. 'Allegra was not by any means an amiable child,' he added sourly, 'nor was Mrs. Hoppner nor I particularly fond of her.'

It could hardly have been expected that the daughter of Byron and Claire Clairmont would have been 'amiable'; nor can we wonder that Mr. Hoppner, who had a seven-months-old baby of his own, should have failed to wax enthusiastic over another infant. But his warm-hearted wife did love her little charge, and grieved sincerely when the child's quick temper subsided into listlessness under the fierce Italian heat. 'Mon petit brille, et il est toujours gai et sautillant,' she wrote prettily to the Shelleys, after their departure from Venice; 'et Allegra, par contre, est devenue tranquille et sérieuse, comme une petite vieille, ce que nous peine beaucoup.'

Byron was frankly grateful to Mrs. Hoppner for her kindness to his daughter; and after he had carried the child to Ravenna, where the colder, purer air brought back her gaiety and bloom, he wrote again and again to her former guardians, now thanking them for 'a whole treasure of toys' which they had sent, now assuring them that 'Allegrina is flourishing like a pomegranate blossom,' and now reiterating the fact which seemed to make most impression upon his mind — that she was growing prettier and more obstinate every day. He added many little details about her childish ailments, her drives with the Countess Guiccioli, and her popularity in his household. It was to the overindulgence of his servants, as well as to heredity, that he traced her high temper and imperious will. He consulted Mrs. Hoppner more than once about Allegra's education; and he poured into her husband's ears his bitter resentment at Miss Clairmont's pardonable but exasperating interference.

For Claire, clever about most things, was an adept in the art of provocation. She wrote him letters calculated to try the patience of a saint, and he retaliated by a cruel and contemptuous silence. In vain Shelley attempted to play the difficult part of peacemaker. 'I wonder,' he pleaded, 'at your being provoked by what Claire writes, though that she should write what is provoking is very probable. You are conscious of performing your duty to Allegra, and your refusal to allow her to visit Claire at this distance you conceive to be part of that duty. That Claire should have wished to see her is natural. That her disappointment should vex her, and her vexation make her write absurdly, is all in the natural order of things. But, poor thing, she is very unhappy and in bad health, and she ought to be treated with as much indulgence as possible. The weak and the foolish are in this respect the kings — they can do no wrong.'

Byron was less generous. The weak and the foolish — especially when their weakness and folly took the form of hysteria — irritated him beyond endurance. The penalty that an hysterical woman pays for her self-indulgence is that no one believes in the depth or sincerity of her emotions. Byron had no pity for the pain that Claire was suffering. She was to him simply a young woman who never lost an opportunity to make a scene, and he hated scenes. On one point he was determined. Allegra should never again be sent to her mother, nor to the Shelleys. He had views of his own upon the education of little girls, which by no means corresponded with theirs.

'About Allegra,' he writes to Mr. Hoppner in 1820, 'I can only say to Claire that I so totally disapprove of the mode of Children's treatment in their family, that I should look upon the Child as going into a hospital. Is it not so? Have they reared one? Her health has hitherto been excellent, and her temper not bad. She is sometimes vain and obstinate, but always clean and cheerful; and as, in a year or two, I shall either send her to England, or put her in a Convent for education, these defects will be remedied as far as they can be in human nature. But the Child shall not quit me again to perish of Starvation and green fruit, or be taught to believe that there is no Deity. Whenever there is convenience of vicinity and access, her Mother can always have her with her; otherwise no. It was so stipulated from the beginning.'

Five months later, he reiterates these painfully prosaic
views. He has taken a house in the country, because the
air agrees better with Allegra. He has two maids to attend
her. He is doing his best, and he is very angry at Claire's
last batch of letters. 'Were it not for the poor little child's
sake,' he writes, 'I am almost tempted to send her back
to her atheistical mother, but that would be too bad. . . .
If Claire thinks that she shall ever interfere with the child's
morals or education, she mistakes; she never shall. The
girl shall be a Christian, and a married woman, if possible.'

On these two points Byron had set his heart. The
Countess Guiccioli — kindly creature — assures us that
'his dearest paternal care was the religious training to be
given to his natural daughter, Allegra'; and while the
words of this sweet advocate weigh little in the scale,
they are in some degree confirmed by the poet's conduct
and correspondence. When he felt the growing insecurity
of his position in Ravenna, he determined to place the
child at a convent school twelve miles away, and he explained very clearly and concisely to all whom it might
concern his reasons for the step. 'Allegra is now four
years old complete,' he wrote to Mr. Hoppner in April,
1821; 'and as she is quite above the control of the servants,
and as a man living without any woman at the head of
his house cannot much attend to a nursery, I had no
resource but to place her for a time (at a high pension too)
in the convent of Bagnacavallo (twelve miles off), where
the air is good, and where she will, at least, have her
learning advanced, and her morals and religion inculcated.
I had also another motive. Things were and are in such
a state here, that I have no reason to look upon my own

personal safety as insurable, and thought the infant best
out of harm's way for the present.

'It is also fit that I should add that I by no means
intended nor intend to give a natural child an English
education, because, with the disadvantages of her birth,
her after settlement would be doubly difficult. Abroad,
with a fair foreign education, and a portion of five or six
thousand pounds, she might and may marry very respect-
ably. In England, such a dowry would be a pittance,
while elsewhere it is a fortune. It is, besides, my wish
that she should be a Roman Catholic, a religion which I
look upon as the best, as it is assuredly the oldest, of the
various branches of Christianity. I have now explained
my notions as to the place where she is. It is the best
I could find for the present, but I have no prejudices in
its favour.'

Both Mr. and Mrs. Hoppner were strongly in favour of a
Swiss, rather than an Italian school; and Byron, who never
doubted the sincerity of their affection for his child, lent
a ready ear to their suggestions. 'If I had but known your
ideas about Switzerland before,' he wrote to Mr. Hoppner
in May; 'I should have adopted them at once. As it is,
I shall let Allegra remain in her convent, where she seems
healthy and happy, for the present. But I shall feel much
obliged if you will inquire, when you are in the cantons,
about the usual and better modes of education there for
females, and let me know the result of your inquiries. It
is some consolation that both Mr. and Mrs. Shelley have
written to approve entirely of my placing the child with
the nuns for the present. I can refer to my whole conduct,
as having spared no trouble, nor kindness, nor expense,
since she was sent to me. People may say what they

please. I must content myself with not deserving (in this case) that they should speak ill.

'The place is a country town, in a good air, where there is a large establishment for education, and many children, some of considerable rank, placed in it. As a country town, it is less liable to objections of every kind. It has always appeared to me that the moral defect in Italy does not proceed from a conventual training — because, to my certain knowledge, girls come out of their convents innocent, even to ignorance, of moral evil — but to the society into which they are plunged directly on coming out of it. It is like educating an infant on a mountain top, and then taking him to the sea, and throwing him into it, and desiring him to swim.'

Other letters to Mr. Hoppner, to Shelley, and to Moore are equally practical and explicit. Byron writes that he has regular reports of Allegra's health; that she has mastered her alphabet; that he is having her reared a Catholic, 'so that she may have her hands full'; that he meditates increasing her dowry, 'if I live, and she is correct in her conduct'; that he thinks a Swiss gentleman might make her a better husband than an Italian. Pamela the virtuous was not more set upon her own 'marriage lines' than was Lord Byron upon his daughter's. Respectability was the golden boon he coveted for the poor little pledge of an illicit and unhappy passion. No one knew better than he how well it is to walk a safe and sheltered road; and no correct church-going father in England was ever more concerned for the decent settlement of his child.

There were others who took a more impassioned view of the situation. Miss Clairmont was spending her Carnival merrily in Florence, when word came that Allegra had been sent to school. It was a blow, says Professor Dowden, 'under which she staggered and reeled.' In vain Shelley and his wife represented to her the wisdom of the step. In vain Byron wrote that the air of the Romagna was exceptionally good, and that he paid double fees for his little daughter, to ensure her every care and attention. Claire, piteously unreasonable, answered only with frenzied reproaches and appeals. She taunted the poet with his unhappy married life — which was applying vitriol to a raw wound; she inveighed against the 'ignorance and degradation' of convent-reared women, she implored permission to carry her child to England. 'I propose,' she wrote with maddening perversity, 'to place her at my own expense in one of the very best English boarding-schools, where, if she is deprived of the happiness of a home and paternal care, she at least would receive an English education, which would enable her, after many years of painful and unprotected childhood, to be benefited by the kindness and affection of her parents' friends. . . . By adopting this plan, you will save yourself credit and also the expense; and the anxiety for her safety and well-being need never trouble you. You will become as free as if you had no such tie.'

As an example of the purely exasperating, this letter has few peers in recorded correspondence. 'At my own expense,' meant at Shelley's expense; and Byron, loving or unloving, had never sought to shirk his paternal responsibilities. The alluring prospect of freedom from all concern offered little temptation to a father who had his child's future very seriously at heart. Miss Clairmont was surrounded at this time by a group of eminently foolish counsellors, the most prominent of whom were Lady

Mountcashell, Mr. Tighe, and Miss Elizabeth Parker. Lady Mountcashell had a venerable husband in England, but preferred living in Italy with Mr. Tighe. There she employed her leisure in writing a book upon the training of children — a work which her friends highly esteemed, and which they held to be an ample compensation to society for any irregularities in her own life. The couple were known as Mr. and Mrs. Mason. Miss Parker was an orphan girl, sent from England by Mrs. Godwin to be a companion to Lady Mountcashell, and profit by her example. These people kept alive in Claire's heart the flame of resentment and unrest. Mr. Tighe dwelt mournfully upon the austerity, as well as upon the degradation of convent life, until the mother's grief grew so excessive that in August, 1821, the long-suffering Shelley made a pilgrimage to Ravenna and to Bagnacavallo, to see how Allegra was placed, and to assure himself of her health and happiness. His charming letter — too long to be quoted in full — gives us the prettiest imaginable picture of a little school-girl, not yet five years old.

I went the other day to see Allegra at her convent, and stayed with her about three hours. She is grown tall and slight for her age, and her face is somewhat altered. She yet retains the beauty of her deep blue eyes and of her mouth; but she has a contemplative seriousness, which, mixed with her excessive vivacity which has not yet deserted her, has a very peculiar effect in a child. She is under strict discipline, as may be observed from the immediate obedience she accords to the will of her attendants. This seems contrary to her nature; but I do not think it has been obtained at the expense of much severity. Her hair, scarcely darker than it was, is beautifully profuse, and hangs in large curls on her neck. She was prettily dressed in white muslin, and an apron of black silk, with trousers. Her light and airy figure and her graceful motions were a striking contrast to the other children there. She seemed a thing of a finer and a higher order. At first she was very shy; but after a little caressing, and especially after I had given her a gold chain which I had bought for her at Ravenna, she grew more familiar, and led me all over the garden and all over the convent, running and skipping so fast that I could hardly keep up with her. She showed me her little bed, and the chair where she sat at dinner, and the carozzina in which she and her favourite companions drew each other along a walk in the garden. I had brought her a basket of sweetmeats, and, before eating any of them, she gave her friends and each of the nuns a portion. This is not like the old Allegra.... Her intellect is not much cultivated. She knows certain *orazioni* by heart, and talks and dreams of *Paradiso* and all sorts of things, and has a prodigious list of saints, and is always talking of the Bambino. This will do her no harm; but the idea of bringing up so sweet a creature in the midst of such trash till sixteen.

Shelley's content with Allegra's situation (the little tempest-tossed bark had at last sailed into quiet waters) failed to bring comfort to Claire. The convent walls rose — a hopeless barrier — between mother and child; and the finality of the separation weighed cruelly upon her spirits. One of her most bitter grievances was the fear that her daughter was being educated with the children of tradespeople — an unfounded alarm, as we see from the list compiled by Signor Biondi of the little *marchesas* and *contessas* who were Allegra's playmates. Another, and a reasonable anxiety, came with the approach of winter. Miss Clairmont then thinks less about the ignorance and immorality of Italian women, and more about the undoubted cold of Italian convents. She is afraid, and

naturally afraid, that her child is not warm enough.
There is one piteous letter in which she says that she cannot look at a glowing fire without a sorrowful remem-
brance of her little daughter in the chilly convent halls.

All these sources of disquietude were strengthened the
following year by a new and unreasoning terror. Miss
Clairmont appears to have actually persuaded herself
that Lord Byron meant to leave Allegra at Bagnacavallo,
in the event of his own departure from Italy. We know
now from his letters that it was his settled purpose to
take her with him, wherever he went. Even when he
meditated — briefly — an exile to South America, the
child was to accompany his flight. But his persistent
silence, his maddening refusal to answer Claire's appeals
or remonstrances, left her in painful ignorance, and a prey
to consuming fears. She conceived the mad design of
stealing Allegra from the convent — a scheme which was
warmly supported by those discreet monitors, Lady
Mountcashell and Mr. Tighe. Together they discussed
ways and means. Mr. Tighe was of the opinion that the
time had come for extreme measures; and the ardent Miss
Parker assured Miss Clairmont that, were she Allegra's
mother, she would not hesitate to stab Lord Byron to the
heart, and so free his unhappy offspring from captivity.

In the midst of this melodramatic turmoil we hear Mrs.
Shelley's voice, pleading vainly for patience and common
sense. She points out in an earnest letter to Claire that
Lady Noel's death will probably compel Byron to go to
England, and may even lead to a reconciliation with his
wife. In that event he will be more willing to give back
Allegra to her mother; and for the present there is no
cause for apprehension. 'Your anxiety about the child's

health,' she writes reassuringly, 'is to a great extent unfounded. You ought to know, and any one will tell you, that the towns of Romagna situated where Bagnacavallo is, enjoy the best air in Italy. Imola and the neighbouring *paese* are famous. Bagnacavallo especially, being fifteen miles from the sea, and situated on an eminence, is peculiarly salutary. Considering the affair reasonably, Allegra is well taken care of there. She is in good health, and in all probability will continue so.'

One fact she strives to make clear. Her husband has no money for the furtherance of any plots that Miss Clairmont and Mr. Tighe may devise. On this score, Shelley himself is equally explicit. He had never wanted Allegra to go to her father, and he cannot resist the temptation of saying, 'I told you so,' though he says it with grave kindness. But he was even less willing that, having been given up, she should be stolen back again. His letter of remonstrance proves both the anxiety he felt, and his sense of shame at the part he was expected to play.

My Dear Clare — I know not what to think of the state of your mind, nor what to fear for you. Your plan about Allegra seems to me, in its present form, pregnant with irremediable infamy to all the actors in it except yourself; — in any form wherein I must actively coöperate, with inevitable destruction. I *could not* refuse Lord Byron's challenge; though that, however to be deprecated, would be the least in the series of mischiefs consequent upon my intervention in such a plan. I am shocked at the thoughtless violence of your designs, and I wish to put my sense of their madness in the strongest light. I may console myself, however, with the reflection that the attempt even is impossible, as I have no money. So far from being ready to lend me three or four hundred pounds, Horace Smith has lately declined to ad-

vance six or seven napoleons for a musical instrument which
I wished to buy for Jane Williams in Paris. Nor have I any
other friends to whom I could apply.

There was no need of heroics on the one side, nor of
apprehension on the other. While Miss Clairmont was
fretting and scheming in Florence, fever was scourging the
Romagna, so seldom visited by infection, and the little
English-born girl fell one of its earliest victims. Allegra
died at her convent school in the spring of 1822. Byron
admitted that death was kind. 'Her position in the
world would scarcely have allowed her to be happy,' he
said, pitying remorsefully the 'sinless child of sin,' so
harshly handicapped in life. But he felt his loss, and
bitterly, though silently, mourned it. The Countess
Guiccioli was with him when the tidings came. In her
eyes, he had always been a fond and solicitous father;
yet the violence of his distress amazed and frightened her.
He sent her away, and faced his grief, and his remorse —
if he felt remorse — alone. The next day, when she
sought him, he said very simply, 'It is God's will. She is
more fortunate than we are'; and never spoke of the child
again. 'From that time' she adds, 'he became more anxious about his daughter Ada; — so much so as to disquiet
himself when the usual accounts sent him were for a post
or two delayed.'

Byron's letters to Shelley, to Murray, and to Scott,
bear witness to the sincerity of his grief, and also to his
sense of compunction. He was still ready to defend his
conduct; but to Shelley, at least, he admitted: 'It is a
moment when we are apt to think that, if this or that
had been done, such an event might have been prevented.'
Indeed, of the four actors so deeply concerned in this

brief tragedy of life, Shelley alone could hold himself free
from blame. From first to last he had been generous,
reasonable, and kind. It was his painful part to comfort
Miss Clairmont, to restrain her frenzy of anger and wretch-
edness, to make what shadow of peace he could between
the parents of the dead child. In all this he endured more
than his share of worry and vexation. Two weeks after
Allegra's death, he wrote to Lord Byron:

> I have succeeded in dissuading Clare from the melancholy
> design of visiting the coffin at Leghorn, much to the profit
> of my own shattered health and spirits, which would have
> suffered greatly in accompanying her on such a journey.
> She is much better. She has, indeed, altogether suffered in
> a manner less terrible than I expected, after the first shock,
> during which, of course, she wrote the letter you enclose. I
> had no idea that her letter was written in that temper; and
> I think I need not assure you that, whatever mine or Mary's
> ideas might have been respecting the system of education
> you intended to adopt, we sympathize too much in your
> loss, and appreciate too well your feelings, to have allowed
> such a letter to be sent to you, had we suspected its con-
> tents.

A dead grief is easier to bear than a live trouble. By
early summer, Shelley was able to report Miss Clairmont
as once more 'talkative and vivacious.' It was he who
befriended her to the end, and who bequeathed her a
large share of his estate. It was he who saw — or deemed
he saw — the image of Allegra rise smiling and beckoning
from the sea.

According to the Countess Guiccioli, Byron bore the
'profound sorrow' occasioned by his little daughter's
death 'with all the fortitude belonging to his great soul.'
In reality his sense of loss was tempered by relief. Allegra's

future had always been to him a subject of anxiety, and it was not without an emotion of joy that he realized the child's escape from a world which he had found bad, and which he had done little to make better. Two days after she died, he wrote to Murray: 'You will regret to hear that I have received intelligence of the death of my daughter, Allegra, of a fever, in the convent of Bagnacavallo, where she was placed for the last year to commence her education. It is a heavy blow for many reasons, but must be borne — with time.'

A fortnight later he wrote to Scott: 'I have just lost my natural daughter, Allegra, by a fever. The only consolation, save time, is the reflection that she is either at rest or happy; for her few years (only five) prevented her from having incurred any sin, except what we inherit from Adam.

'"Whom the gods love die young."'

In a third letter, published by Mr. Prothero, Byron repeats these sentiments with even greater emphasis, and with a keener appreciation of their value. 'Death has done his work, and I am resigned. . . . Even at my age I have become so much worn and harassed by the trials of the world, that I cannot refrain from looking upon that early rest which is at times granted to the young, as a blessing. There is a purity and holiness in the apotheosis of those who leave us in their brightness and their beauty, which instinctively lead us to a persuasion of their beatitude.'

It was the irony of fate that, after being an innocent object of contention all her life, Allegra should, even in death, have been made the theme of an angry and bitter dispute. Her body was sent to England, and Byron begged Murray to make all the necessary arrangements for her burial. His directions were exceedingly minute. He indicated the precise spot in Harrow Church where he wished the child interred, and he wrote the inscription to be engraved upon her tablet.

IN MEMORY OF

ALLEGRA,

DAUGHTER OF G. G. LORD BYRON,

WHO DIED AT BAGNACAVALLO,

IN ITALY, APRIL 20th, 1822,

AGED FIVE YEARS AND THREE MONTHS.

I shall go to her, but she shall not return to me.

2 Samuel, XII, 23.

The funeral he desired to be 'as private as is consistent with decency'; and he expressed a hope that his friend, the Reverend Henry Drury, would read the church service.

Murray found himself beset by unexpected difficulties. The vicar of Harrow, the Reverend J. W. Cunningham, objected strenuously to the erection of Allegra's tablet, and stated his objections at length — not to Lord Byron (which was prudent), but to the unhappy publisher, who all his life had everybody's business to attend to. Mr. Cunningham declared that the proposed inscription 'would be felt by every man of refined taste, to say nothing of sound morals, to be an offence against taste and propriety.' He explained cautiously that, as he did not dare to say this to Byron, he expected Murray to do so. 'My correspondence with his Lordship has been so small that I can scarcely venture myself to urge these objections. You, perhaps, will feel no such scruple. I have seen no

person who did not concur in the propriety of stating them.
I would intreat, however, that, should you think it right
to introduce my name into any statement made to Lord
Byron' (as if it could well have been left out), 'you will
not do so without assuring him of my unwillingness to
oppose the smallest obstacle to his wishes, or give the
slightest pain to his mind. The injury which, in my judgment, he is from day to day inflicting upon society is no
justification for measures of retaliation and unkindness.'

Even the expansive generosity of this last sentiment
failed to soften Byron's wrath, when the vicar's scruples
were communicated to him. He anathematized the reverend gentleman in language too vigorous for repetition,
and he demanded of Murray, 'what was the matter with
the inscription' — apparently under the impression that
he had mistaken his dates or misquoted his text. His
anger deepened into fury when he was subsequently informed that Allegra's interment in Harrow Church was
held to be a deliberate insult to Lady Byron, who occasionally attended the services there. He wrote passionately
that of his wife's church-goings he knew nothing; but that,
had he known, no power would have induced him to bury
his poor infant where her foot might tread upon its grave.
Meanwhile, Mr. Cunningham had marshalled his church-
wardens, who obediently withheld their consent to the
erection of the tablet; so that matter was settled forever.
Two years later, Doctor Ireland, Dean of Westminster,
refused to permit Lord Byron's body to be buried in
Westminster Abbey. Even Thorwaldsen's statue of the
poet, now in Trinity College, Cambridge, was rejected by
this conscientious dignitary. 'I do indeed greatly wish
for a figure by Thorwaldsen here,' he wrote piously to

Murray; 'but no taste ought to be indulged to the prejudice of a duty.' The statue lay unheeded for months in a shed on the Thames wharf, and was finally transferred to the library of Trinity College. Comment is superfluous. Byron was denied a grave in Westminster Abbey; but Gifford, through Doctor Ireland's especial insistence, was buried within its walls.

Allegra lies in Harrow Church, with no tablet to mark her resting-place, or to preserve her memory. Visitors searching sentimentally for 'Byron's tomb' — by which they mean a stone in the churchyard, 'on the brow of the hill, looking towards Windsor,' where, as a boy, he was wont to sit and dream for hours — seldom know the spot where his little daughter sleeps.

CRUELTY AND HUMOUR

CRUELTY AND HUMOUR

THE unhallowed alliance between the cruelty that we hate and the humour that we prize is a psychological problem which frets the candid mind. Hazlitt analyzed it pitilessly, but without concern, because humanity was not his playing card. No writer of the nineteenth century dared to be so clearly and consciously inhumane as was Hazlitt. Shakespeare and Scott recognized this alliance, and were equally unconcerned, because they accepted life on its own terms, and were neither the sport of illusions nor the prey of realities. It took the public — always more or less kind-hearted — two hundred years to sympathize with the wrongs of Shylock, and three hundred years to wince at the misery of Malvolio.

It was with something akin to regret that Andrew Lang watched the shrivelling of that 'full-blown comic sense' which accompanied the cruel sports of an earlier generation, the bull-baiting and badger-drawing and cock-fights and prize-fights which Englishmen loved, and which taught them to value courage and look unmoved on pain. In 1699 the old East India Company lost its claim against the New Company by two parliamentary votes; and this measure was passed in the absence of friendly members who had been seduced from their posts by the unwonted spectacle of a tiger-baiting. In 1818 Christopher North

(black be his memory!) described graphically and with
smothered glee the ignoble game of cat-worrying, which
ran counter to British sporting instincts, to the roughly
interpreted fair play which severed brutality from baseness. There was never a time when some English voice
was not raised to protest against that combination of
cruelty and cowardice which pitted strength against
weakness, or overwhelming odds against pure gallantry of
spirit. The first Englishman to assert that animals had a
right to legal protection was John Evelyn. He grasped
this novel point of view through sheer horror and disgust
because a stallion had been baited with dogs in London,
and had fought so bravely that the dogs could not fasten
on him until the men in charge ran him through with
their swords. Evelyn asked, and asked in vain, that the
law should intervene to punish such barbarity.

A century later we hear the same cry of indignation,
the same appeal for pity and redress. This time it comes
from Horace Walpole, who is beside himself with fury because some scoundrels at Dover had roasted a fox alive,
to mark — with apt symbolism — their disapproval of
Charles Fox. Walpole, whom Lord Minto characterized
as 'a prim, precise, pretending, conceited savage, but a
most un-English one,' demonstrated on this occasion the
alien nature of his sympathies by an outbreak of rage
against the cruelty which he was powerless to punish. It
is interesting to note that he denounced the deed as 'a
savage meanness which an Iroquois would have scorned';
showing that he and Lord Minto regarded savagery from
different angles. So, it will be remembered, did Lord
Byron and Izaak Walton. When the former dared to
call the latter 'a sentimental savage,' he brought down

upon his own head, 'bloody but unbowed,' the wrath of British sportsmen, of British churchmen, of British sensibility. Even in far-off America an outraged editor protested shrilly against this *monde bestorné*, this sudden onslaught of vice upon virtue, this reversal of outlawry and order.

The effrontery of the attack startled a decorous world. Lord Byron had so flaunted his immoralities that he had become the scapegoat of society. He had been driven forth from a pure, or at least respectable, island, to dally with sin under less austere skies. The household virtues shuddered at his name. Izaak Walton, on the contrary, had been recognized in his day as a model of domestic sobriety. He had lived happily with two wives (one at a time), and had spent much of his life 'in the families of the eminent clergymen of England, by whom he was greatly beloved.' He was buried in Winchester Cathedral, where English fishermen erected a statue to commemorate his pastime. His bust adorns the church of Saint Mary, Stafford, where he was baptized. His second wife sleeps under a monument in Worcester Cathedral. Doctor Johnson and Wordsworth — great sponsors of morality — united in his praise. Mr. Lang (an enthusiastic angler) pronounced him to be 'a kind, humorous, and pious soul.' Charles Lamb, who thought angling a cruel sport, wrote to Wordsworth, 'Izaak Walton hallows any page in which his reverend name appears.'

This admirable Crichton, this honoured guest of 'eminent clergymen,' was the man whom Byron — who had never so much as supped with a curate — selected to attack in his most scandalously indecent poem. His lilting lines,

'The quaint, old, cruel coxcomb in his gullet
Should have a hook, and a small trout to pull it,'

were ribald enough in all conscience; but, by way of super-defiance, he added a perfectly serious note in which he pointed out the deliberate character of Walton's inhumanity. The famous passage in 'The Compleat Angler,' which counsels fishermen to use the impaled frog as though they loved him — 'that is, harm him as little as you may possibly, that he may live the longer' — and the less famous, but equally explicit, passages which deal with the tender treatment of dace and snails, sickened Byron's soul, especially when topped off by the most famous passage of all: 'God never did make a more calm, quiet, innocent recreation than fishing.' The picture of the Almighty smiling down on the pangs of his irrational creatures, in sportsmanlike sympathy with his rational creature (who could recite poetry and quote the Scriptures) was more than Byron could bear. He was keenly aware that he offered no shining example to the world; but he had never conceived of God as a genial spectator of cruelty or of vice.

Therefore this open-eyed sinner called the devout and decent Walton a sentimental savage. Therefore he wrote disrespectful words about the 'cruel, cold, and stupid sport of angling.' Therefore he said, 'No angler can be a good man'; which comprehensive remark caused the public to ask tartly — and not unreasonably — who appointed Lord Byron to be its monitor? The fantastic love of animals, which was one of the poet's most engaging traits, may have been deepened by his resentment against men. Nevertheless, we recognize it as a genuine and generous sentiment, ennobling and also amusing, as most genuine and generous sentiments are apt to be. The eaglet that he shot on the shore of Lepanto, and whose life he vainly tried to save, was the last bird to die by his hand. He had an embarrassing habit of becoming attached to wild animals and to barnyard fowls. An ungrateful civet-cat, having bitten a footman, escaped from bondage. A goose, bought to be fattened for Michaelmas, never achieved its destiny; but was raised to the dignity and emoluments of a household pet, and carried about in a basket, swung securely under the poet's travelling carriage. These amiable eccentricities won neither respect nor esteem. Byron could not in cold blood have hurt anything that breathed; but there was a general impression that a man who was living with another man's wife had no business to be so kind to animals, and certainly no business to censure respectable and church-going citizens who were cruel to them.

Nevertheless, the battle so inauspiciously begun has been waged ever since, and has found more impeccable champions. It was possible for Charles Lamb to sigh with one breath over the 'intolerable pangs' inflicted by 'meek' anglers, and to rejoice with the next over the page hallowed by the angler's reverend name. Happily for himself and for his readers, he had that kind of a mind. But Huxley, whose mind was singularly inflexible and unaccommodating, refused such graceful concessions. All forms of cruelty were hateful to him. Of one distinguished and callous vivisector he said plainly that he would like to send him to the treadmill. But he would hear no word against vivisection from gentlemen who angled with live bait, and he expressed this unsportsmanlike view in his 'Elementary Lessons in Physiology.' Mr. Arthur Christopher Benson's piteous lines on a little dace, whose hard fate it is to furnish an hour's 'innocent recreation' for an angler, had not then been written; but Huxley needed no such incentive to pity. No man in England reverenced the gospel of

amusement less than he did. No man was less swayed by
sentiment, or daunted by ridicule.

When Hazlitt wrote, 'One rich source of the ludicrous
is distress with which we cannot sympathize from its ab-
surdity or insignificance,' he touched the keynote of unconcern. Insignificant distress makes merry a humane
world. 'La malignité naturelle aux hommes est le principe
de la comédie.' Distress which could be forced to appear
absurd made merry a world that had not been taught the
elements of humanity. The elaborate jests which enlivened the Roman games were designed to show that terror
and pain might, under rightly conceived circumstances,
be infinitely amusing. When the criminal appointed to
play the part of Icarus lost his wings at the critical moment
which precipitated him into a cage of hungry bears, the
audience appreciated the humour of the situation. It was
a good practical joke, and the possible distaste of Icarus
for his rôle lent pungency to the cleverly contrived performance. 'By making suffering ridiculous,' said Mr.
Pater, 'you enlist against the sufferer much real and all
would-be manliness, and do much to stifle any false sentiment of compassion.'

Scott, who had a clear perception of emotions he did not
share, gives us in 'Quentin Durward' an apt illustration
of human suffering rendered absurd by its circumstances,
and made serviceable by the pleasure which it gives. Louis
the Eleventh and Charles of Burgundy are fairly healed of
rancorous fear and hatred by their mutual enjoyment of a
man-hunt. The sight of the mock herald doubling and
turning in mad terror with the great boar-hounds at his
heels so delights the royal spectators that the king, reeling
with laughter, catches hold of the duke's ermine mantle

for support; the duke flings his arm over the king's shoulder; and these mortal enemies are converted, through sympathy with each other's amusement, into something akin to friendship. When Charles, wiping his streaming eyes, says poignantly, 'Ah, Louis, Louis, would to God thou wert as faithful a monarch as thou art a merry companion!' we recognize the touch of nature — of fallen nature — which makes the whole world kin. Ambroise Paré tells us that at the siege of Metz, in 1552, the French soldiers fastened live cats to their pikes, and hung them over the walls, crying, 'Miaut, Miaut'; while the Spanish soldiers shot at the animals as though they had been popinjays, and both besiegers and besieged enjoyed the sport in a spirit of frank derision.

This simple, undisguised barbarity lacks one element, intensely displeasing to the modern mind — the element of bad taste. Imperial Rome had no conception of a slave or a criminal as a being whose sensations counted, save as they affected others, save as they afforded, or failed to afford, a pleasurable experience to Romans. Human rights were as remote from its cognizance as animal rights were remote from the cognizance of the Middle Ages. The survival of savagery in man's heart is terrifying rather than repellent; it humiliates more than it affronts. Whatever is natural is likely to be bad; but it is also likely to come within the scope, if not of our sympathy, at least of our understanding. Where there is no introspection there is no incongruity, nothing innately and sickeningly inhuman and ill-bred.

The most unpleasant record which has been preserved for us is the long Latin poem written by Robert Grove, afterwards Bishop of Chichester, and printed in 1685. It is dedicated to the memory of William Harvey, and describes with unshrinking serenity the vivisection of a dog to demonstrate Harvey's discovery of the circulation of the blood. Such experiments, made before the day of anaesthetics, involved the prolonged agony of the animal used for experimentation. Harvey appears to have been a man as remote from pity as from cruelty. He desired to reach and to prove a supremely valuable scientific truth. He succeeded, and there are few who question his methods. But that a man should write in detail — and in verse — about such dreadful work, that he should dwell composedly upon the dog's excruciating pain, and compliment the poor beast on the useful part he plays, goes beyond endurance. Grove, who had that pretty taste for classicism so prevalent among English clerics, calls on Apollo and Minerva to lend Harvey their assistance, and promises the dog that (if Apollo and Minerva play their parts) he will become a second Lycisca, and will join Procyon and Sirius in the heavens.

Here is an instance in which a rudimentary sense of propriety would have saved a gentleman and a scholar from insulting the principles of good taste. It is more agreeable to contemplate the brutal crowd surrounding a baited bear than to contemplate this clergyman writing in the seclusion of his library. Religion and scholarship have their responsibilities. The German soldiers who ravaged Belgium outraged the sentiments of humanity; but the German professors who sat at their desks, alternately defending and denying these ravages, outraged, not merely humanity, but the taste and intelligence of the world. Theirs was the unpardonable sin.

Cruelty is as old as life, and will cease only when life

ceases. It has passed its candid stage long, long ago. It must now be condoned for its utility, or laughed at for its fun. Our comic sense, if less full-blown than of yore, still relishes its measure of brutality. To write gaily about the infliction of pain is to win for it forgiveness. Douglas Jerrold found something infinitely amusing in the sensations of the lobster put into a pot of cold water, and boiled. His description of the perspiring crustacean, unable to understand the cause of its rapidly increasing discomfort, was thought so laughable that it was reprinted, as a happy example of the writer's humour, in a volume on Jerrold's connection with *Punch*. The same genial spirit animated an American Senator who opposed the sentimental exclusion of egrets from commerce. It was the opinion of this gallant gentleman that the Lord created white herons to supply ornaments 'for the hats of our beautiful ladies'; and, having expressed his sympathy with the designs of Providence, he proposed in merry mood that we should establish foundling asylums for the nestlings deprived of their over-decorated parents — as waggish a witticism as one would want to hear.

When an eminently respectable American newspaper can be convulsively funny, or at least can try to be convulsively funny, over the sale of a horse, twenty-seven years old, blind, rheumatic, and misshapen, to a Chicago huckster for fifteen cents, we have no need to sigh over our waning sense of humour. The happy thought of calling the horse Algernon gave a rich twang to this comic episode, and saved the cheerful reader from any intrusive sentiment of pity. When a pious periodical, published in the interests of a Christian church, can tell us in a rollicking Irish story how a farmer, speeding through the frozen night, empties

a bag of kittens into the snow, and whips up his horse, pretending playfully that the 'craitures' are overtaking him,
we make comfortably sure that religion lends itself as
deftly as journalism to the light-hearted drolleries of the
cruel.

Novelists, who understand how easy a thing it is to
gratify our humorous susceptibilities, venture upon doubtful jests. Mr. Tarkington knows very well that the spectacle of a boy dismembering an insect calls for reprobation;
but that if the boy's experiments can be described as 'in-
fringing upon the domain of Doctor Carrell,' they make a
bid for laughter. 'Penrod's efforts — with the aid of a pin
— to effect a transference of living organism were unsuc-
cessful; but he convinced himself forever that a spider
cannot walk with a beetle's legs.' It is funny to those who
relish the fun. If it does not, as Mr. Pater hints, make
suffering ridiculous, it makes sympathy ridiculous, as being a thing more serious than the occasion warrants. The
reader who is not amused tries to forget the incident, and
hurries cheerfully on.

A more finished example of callous gaiety, and one
which in its day was widely appreciated, may be found in
a story called 'Crocker's Hole,' by Blackmore. It tells
how a young man named Pike, whom 'Providence' had
created for angling (the author is comfortably sure on this
point), caught an old and wary trout by the help of a new
and seductive bait. The overwrought, overcoloured beauty
of Blackmore's style is in accord with his highly sophisti-
cated sense of humour:

> The lover of the rose knows well a gay, voluptuous beetle,
> whose pleasure it is to lie embedded in a fount of beauty.
> Deep among the incurving petals of the blushing fragrance

he loses himself in his joys till a breezy waft reveals him.
And when the sunlight breaks upon his luscious dissipation,
few would have the heart to oust such a gem from such a
setting. All his back is emerald sparkles; all his front, red
Indian gold, and here and there he grows white spots to save
the eye from aching. Pike slipped in his finger, fetched him
out, and gave him a little change of joys by putting a Limerick
hook through his thorax, and bringing it out between his
elytra. *Cetonia aurata* liked it not, but pawed the air very
naturally, fluttered his wings, and trod prettily upon the
water under a lively vibration. He looked quite as happy,
and considerably more active than when he had been cra-
dled in the anthers of a rose.

The story is an angling story, and it would be unreasonable to spoil it by sympathizing with the bait. But there
is something in the painting of the little beetle's beauty,
and in the amused description of its pain, which would
sicken a donkey-beating costermonger, if he were cultivated enough to know what the author was driving at. It
takes education and an unswerving reverence for sport to
save us from the costermonger's point of view.

There are times when it is easier to mock than to pity;
there are occasions when we may be seduced from blame,
even if we are not won all the way to approval. Mrs.
Pennell tells us in her very interesting and very candid life
of Whistler that the artist gratified a grudge against his
Venetian landlady by angling for her goldfish (placed
temptingly on a ledge beneath his window-sill); that he
caught them, fried them, and dropped them dexterously
back into their bowl. It is a highly illustrative anecdote,
and we are more amused than we have any business to be.
Mr. Whistler's method of revenge was the method of the
Irish tenants who hocked their landlord's cattle; but the

adroitness of his malice, and the whimsical picture it presents, disarms sober criticism. A sympathetic setting for such an episode would have been a comedy played in the streets of Mantua, under the gay rule of Francesco Gonzaga, and before the eyes of that fair Isabella d'Este who bore tranquilly the misfortunes of others.

We hear so much about the sanitary qualities of laughter, we have been taught so seriously the gospel of amusement, that any writer, preacher, or lecturer, whose smile is broad enough to be infectious, finds himself a prophet in the market-place. Laughter, we are told, freshens our exhausted spirits and disposes us to good-will — which is true. It is also true that laughter quiets our uneasy scruples and disposes us to simple savagery. Whatever we laugh at, we condone, and the echo of man's malicious merriment rings pitilessly through the centuries. Humour which has no scorn, wit which has no sting, jests which have no victim, these are not the pleasantries which have provoked mirth, or fed the comic sense of a conventionalized rather than a civilized world. 'Our being,' says Montaigne, 'is cemented with sickly qualities; and whoever should divest man of the seeds of those qualities would destroy the fundamental conditions of life.'

WHAT IS MORAL SUPPORT?

WHAT IS
MORAL
SUPPORT?

IN THE 'News of the Day,' as presented ten years ago in a moving-picture hall, there was shown to the audience a photograph of President Coolidge speaking in Cambridge, Massachusetts, on the one hundred and fiftieth anniversary of Washington's taking command of the Colonial forces. The caption read: 'President holds out helping hand to Europe.'

Naturally the photographer did not know what was in Mr. Coolidge's outstretched hand; but the reporters for the press were better informed. The headlines of one newspaper ran thus: 'Coolidge Bids Europe Frame Security Pacts. Pledges Moral Support of United States, But Specifically Excepts Political Participation.' An editorial in another newspaper of the same date emphasized the President's approval of 'mutual covenants for mutual security,' and quoted to this effect from his speech: 'While our country should refrain from making political commitments where it does not have political interests, such covenants would always have the moral support of our Government.'

Words have a meaning. It is all that gives them value. Therefore the two words 'moral support' must have a tangible significance in the minds of those who use them. Henry Adams, who hated mental confusion, and had the prevailing discontent of the clear-sighted, said that morality was a private and costly luxury. 'Masses of men invariably follow interests in deciding morals.' Yet, while Americans are frankly and reasonably determined to let their own interests dictate their policies, they retain morality as a political weapon, or at least as a political slogan. They offer the approbation of the American conscience as something which is directly or indirectly an asset to the nations of Europe. If they are acute, as was President Coolidge, they admit that the financing of foreign enterprise is a matter of policy. If they are blatant, as is the occasional habit of politicians, they intimate that moral support is a species of largesse in the gift of moral leadership, and that moral leadership is a recognized attribute of size and numbers, as exemplified by the United States. Like the little girl who was so good that she knew how good she was, we are too well-informed not to be aware of our pre-eminence in this field.

In the spring of 1925 the American Ambassador at the Court of Saint James's delivered himself of a speech before the Pilgrims' Dinner in London. In it he defined with great precision the attitude of the United States toward her former allies. His remarks, as reported, read like a sermon preached in a reformatory; but it is possible that they had a more gracious sound when delivered urbanely over the wine glasses, and that the emphasis laid upon 'the position of the plain people of America toward the reconstruction of Europe' was less contemptuous than it appeared in print.

'The full measure of American helpfulness,' said our

representative, 'can be obtained only when the American people are assured that the time for destructive methods and policies has passed, and that the time for peaceful up-building has come. They are asking themselves today if that time has, in fact, arrived, and they cannot answer the question. The reply must come from the people of Europe, who alone can make the decision. If it be peace, then you may be sure that America will help to her generous ut-most. But if the issue shall continue to be confused and doubtful, I fear the helpful processes which are now in motion must inevitably cease. We are not, as a people, interested in making speculative advances. We can under-take to help only those who help themselves.'

I try to imagine these words addressed to an American audience by a British official (presuming conditions were reversed), and I hear the deep-mouthed profanity rising from the heart to the lips of every American who listened to them. Yet our press in general expressed no distaste for such lofty hectoring. Editors reminded us that it 'did no more than state the feeling of the nation'; that it sounded a 'timely warning' to Europeans who counted on our aid; and that it was 'in the nature of an ultimatum from one hundred and ten millions of Americans.'

The passion for counting heads is occasionally mislead-ing. If one hundred and ten millions of Americans acqui-esced seemingly in this 'timely warning' to our creditors, it was because one hundred million knew little, and cared less, about the matter. The comments of the foreign press were naturally of an ironic order, though the London *Times* took the wind out of our sails by acquiescing cor-dially in our Ambassador's views, and congratulating the United States on its 'co-operation with Great Britain in the task of reconstructing Europe'; thus robbing us of the lead with a graceful and friendly gesture, and a reminder that England had yet to be paid the debts her allies owed her. The Paris *Temps*, on the other hand, offered with exaggerated courtesy the suggestion that France was endeavouring to follow America's advice to help herself, and was at that very moment engaged in repairing the devastations wrought by an invading army purposed to destroy. She was 'peacefully upbuilding' her shattered towns. As for the Berlin newspapers, they seemed unanimously disposed to consider both the speech and the ensuing discussion as personal affronts to von Hindenburg.

The interesting criticisms from my point of view were contributed by the *Cleveland Press*, the *New York Evening Post*, and the *New York Times*. The *Cleveland Press* generously regretted that 'our highly desired and much sought moral helpfulness had been conspicuously withheld from Europe.' The *Post* said with severity: 'The aid we are now giving, whether monetary or moral, will come to an end unless good faith and mutual trust drive out hatred and mistrust.' The *Times*, with the habitual restraint of a vastly influential newspaper, contented itself with observing that 'the Administration seems to believe the time has come for a showdown, and that Europe must display more earnestness in settling her own affairs if she is to keep on asking for America's moral and monetary support.'

Here were three clear-cut recognitions of moral, as apart from financial or political support, and three clear-cut intimations that moral support is in itself a thing of value which the nations of Europe would be loath to lose. Yet I cannot think that any one of those three journals seriously considered that England and France covet our esteem any more than they covet the esteem of the rest of the world. Why should they? Every nation must respect itself, and make that self-respect the goal and guerdon of all effort. 'Great tranquillity of heart hath he who careth neither for praise nor blame,' wrote à Kempis; and the single-mindedness of the man who has some better purpose than to please is but a reflex of the single-mindedness of the nation which reveres its own traditions and ideals too deeply to make them interchangeable with the traditions and ideals of other nations.

Suppose Italy were to threaten the United States with the withdrawal of her moral support. How droll the idea would be! Yet Italy is a country civilized to the core. Her ignorance is often less crude than is information elsewhere; her methods of approach have in them the charm of im- memorial amenities. She is as seriously religious as we are; and her people are more law-abiding than ours, perhaps because they are given less choice in the matter. There is every reason why Rome and Washington should respect each other, and be as morally helpful to each other as they know how to be; but there is no reason on earth why the moral support of one should be of more value than the moral support of the other, unless we translate morality into terms of strength and wealth.

As there is nothing new under the sun, history supplies us with more than one instance of moral support offered in place of material assistance, and always by a nation strong enough to give weight to such an unsubstantial commodity. The great Elizabeth dealt largely in it because it cost her nothing, won the approval of her subjects, indicated her authority, nourished her sense of omnipotence, and gave opportunity for the noble wording (she was a past

mistress of words) of purposes never destined to be fulfilled.

How superbly, yet how economically, the Queen placed
England on record as the champion of the oppressed,
when, after the Massacre of Saint Bartholomew, she
draped herself and her court in mourning before consenting to receive the importunate French Ambassador! What
a magnificent gesture of grief and stern repudiation! It is
probable that the unlucky Frenchman felt himself as embarrassed as he was meant to be, though he knew perfectly
well that Elizabeth had never kept her 'fair promises' to
Coligny, and that she had no mind to discontinue her
international flirtation with the Duke d'Alençon, merely
because his royal mother stood responsible for the murder
of a few thousand French Protestants. He accepted the
rebuff to his country as disagreeable but not dangerous,
and created a diversion by producing a letter from d'Alençon — one of the many amorous epistles which passed
between these make-believe lovers — which was very
graciously received. Notwithstanding the fact that England was filled with 'an extreme indignation and a marvellous hatred,' the Ambassador was able, six weeks after his
humiliating reception, to write to Catherine that the English Queen would stand firmly by her alliance with France.

The relations between Elizabeth and Catherine de'
Medici form an engaging page of history. Their correspondence is to be recommended as a complete course in
duplicity. Both were accomplished liars, and each politely
professed to believe the other's lies. Catherine cherished
the preposterous hope that the English Queen would
marry one of her sons. Elizabeth had no such intention;
but she liked — Heaven knows why! — to pretend that

she would. Her only bond with Catherine was their mutual fear and hatred of Spain. It was a heavy cross to her that she could not weaken France without strengthening Spain. Providence was hard on her in this matter. Providence was hard on her in the matter of the rebellious Netherlands, and in the matter of John Knox. She never wanted to give more than moral support to any cause, and she was constantly being pushed to the fore by virtue of the power she held.

The Protestant insurgents in the Netherlands had the sympathy of England. William of Nassau was a hero in English eyes, and Burghley stoutly advocated his cause. The London merchants, always practical, raised a force at their own expense, and shipped it to Rotterdam, with Sir Humphrey Gilbert at its head. But Elizabeth held back her hand. It was not only that she hated to spend the money, and not only that she was by nature incapable of committing herself generously to any principle. It was that in her heart of hearts this daughter of the Tudors disapproved of subjects opposing their sovereigns. She was a sovereign herself, and she knew that fomenting rebellion is like throwing a boomerang. Being at odds with the Pope, she would lend moral support to the French Protestants; and, being at odds with Spain, she would lend moral support to the Dutch insurgents. This was in accord with her own conscience and with the conscience of England. But, like conscientious America a few centuries later, she would 'refrain from making political commitments where she did not have political interests.'

With the same caution, and the same characteristic understanding of her own position, Elizabeth was content that John Knox should harass the Queen Regent, Mary of

Guise, and, later on, the young Queen of Scots. Such harassments were commendable, as being a species of warfare against the Church of Rome. But as for permitting this firebrand, this arrogant defamer of feminine sovereignty, to set foot on English soil, she would as soon have thought of raising John Stubbs to the peerage. Her cold and vigorous understanding set at naught the protestations of a man who had presumed unwisely on her indulgence. So did the great Tsaritsa, Catherine, regard the Lutheran and Calvinistic clergymen to whom she had lent her moral support when they were conveniently remote; and who, confiding in her goodwill, actually sought to enter Holy Russia, and build their chapels at her doors.

The interest felt by France in the rebellious American Colonies was called sympathy, an intelligible word with a modest and a friendly sound. The cause of the Colonists was extolled as the sacred cause of liberty. Franklin, like Mrs. Jarley, was 'the delight of the nobility and gentry.' If the French Government delayed sending money and men until the American arms showed some reasonable chance of success, it stood ready to turn that chance into a certainty. Louis the Sixteenth cherished a sentimental regard for principles which eventually conducted him to the scaffold. He gave Franklin six million francs out of his own deplenished purse; and the citizens of Franklin's town repaid him by hailing with indecent glee the news of his execution. It is to be noted that the logical French mind never disregarded America's real needs. France took no great risks; but neither did she offer her esteem as an actual asset to the colonies.

Seven years ago a writer in the World's Work intimated that the United States, being congested with money, stood in especial need of Europe's 'moral support.' This was turning the tables on us with a vengeance, because we had always considered that our admonitions derived authority from our wealth. Now that we are limitlessly in debt, and financial security is a thing of the past, we have an altered outlook. Russia has never esteemed us highly, and she can afford foreign propaganda on a scale of well-considered lavishness. We had hoped to mend the world in our fashion. Russia is now keen to mend it in hers. And the beautiful dangerous world, which cannot be drydocked for repairs, is patched here and there with amazing ingenuity as it spins on its unresting way.

THE ESTRANGING SEA

THE
ESTRANGING
SEA

'God bless the narrow sea which keeps her off,
And keeps our Britain whole within herself.'

So SPEAKS 'the Tory member's elder son,' in 'The Prin-
cess':

'... God bless the narrow seas!
I wish they were a whole Atlantic broad';

and the trans-Atlantic reader, pausing to digest this conservative sentiment, wonders what difference a thousand
leagues would make. If the little strip of roughened water
which divides Dover from Calais were twice the ocean's
breadth, could the division be any wider and deeper than
it is?

We Americans cross from continent to continent, and
are merged blissfully into the Old-World life. Inured from
infancy to contrasts, we seldom resent the unfamiliar.
Our attitude towards it is, for the most part, frankly receptive, and full of joyous possibilities. We take kindly,
or at least tolerantly, to foreign creeds and customs. We
fail to be affronted by what we do not understand. We are
not without a shadowy conviction that there may be other
points of view than our own, other beliefs than those we
have been taught to cherish. Augustine Birrell, endeav-

ouring to account for Charlotte Brontë's hostility to the
Belgians — who had been uncommonly kind to her —
says that she 'had never any patience' with Catholicism.
The remark invites the reply of the Papal chamberlain to
Prince Herbert Bismarck, when that nobleman, being in
attendance upon the Emperor, pushed rudely — and un-
bidden — into Pope Leo's audience chamber. 'I am
Prince Herbert Bismarck,' shouted the German. 'That,'
said the urbane Italian, 'explains, but does not excuse
your conduct.'

So much has been said and written about England's
'splendid isolation,' the phrase has grown so familiar to
English eyes and ears, that the political and social attitude which it represents is a source of pride to thousands
of Englishmen who are intelligent enough to know what
isolation costs. 'It is of the utmost importance,' says the
Spectator, 'that we should understand that the temper with
which England regards the other states of Europe, and the
temper with which those states regard her, is absolutely
different.' And then, with ill-concealed elation, the writer
adds: 'The English are the most universally disliked nation on the face of the earth.'

Diplomatically, this may be true, though it is hard to
see why. Socially and individually, it is not true at all.
The English possess too many agreeable traits to permit
them to be as much disliked as they think and hope they
are. Even on the Continent, even in that strange tourist
world where hostilities grow apace, where the courtesies of
life are relaxed, and where every nationality presents its
least lovable aspect, the English can never aspire to the
prize of unpopularity. They are too silent, too clean, too
handsome, too fond of fresh air, too schooled in the laws of

justice which compel them to acknowledge — however reluctantly — the rights of other men. They are certainly uncivil, but that is a matter of no great moment. We do not demand that our fellow tourists should be urbane, but that they should evince a sense of propriety in their behaviour, that they should be decently reluctant to annoy. There is distinction in the Englishman's quietude, and in his innate respect for order.

But why should he covet alienation? Why should he dread popularity, lest it imply that he resembles other men? When the tide of fortune turned in the South African war, and the news of the relief of Mafeking drove London mad with joy, there were Englishmen who expressed grave alarm at the fervid demonstrations of the populace. England, they said, was wont to take her defeats without despondency, and her victories without elation. They feared the national character was changing, and becoming more like the character of Frenchmen and Americans.

This apprehension — happily unfounded — was very insular and very English. National traits are, as a matter of fact, as enduring as the mountain-tops. They survive all change of policies, all shifting of boundary lines, all expansion and contraction of dominion. When Froissart tranquilly observed, 'The English are affable to no other nation than themselves,' he spoke for the centuries to come. Sorbières, who visited England in 1663, who loved the English turf, hated and feared the English cooking, and deeply admired his hospitable English hosts, admitted that the nation had 'a propensity to scorn all the rest of the world.' The famous verdict, '*Les Anglais sont justes, mais pas bons*,' crystallizes the judgment of time. Foreign opinion is necessarily an imperfect diagnosis, but

it has its value to the open mind. He is a wise man who
heeds it, and a dull man who holds it in derision. When an
English writer in 'Macmillan' remarks with airy contempt that French criticisms on England have 'all the pi-
quancy of a woman's criticisms on a man,' the American
— standing outside the ring — is amused by this superb
simplicity of self-conceit.

Fear of a French invasion and the carefully nurtured
detestation of the Papacy — these two controlling influences must be held responsible for prejudices too deep to
be fathomed, too strong to be overcome. 'We do naturally
hate the French,' observes Mr. Pepys, with genial candour; and this ordinary, everyday prejudice darkened into
fury when Napoleon's conquests menaced the world. Our
school histories have taught us (it is the happy privilege of
a school history to teach us many things which make no
impression on our minds) that for ten years England ap-
prehended a descent upon her shores; but we cannot realize
what the apprehension meant, how it ate its way into the
hearts of men, until we stumble upon some such paragraph
as this, from a letter of Lord Jeffrey, written to Francis
Horner in the winter of 1808: 'For my honest impression
is that Bonaparte will be in Dublin in about fifteen
months, perhaps. And then, if I survive, I shall try to go
to America.'

'If I survive!' What wonder that Jeffrey, who was a
clear-headed, unimaginative man, cherished all his life a
cold hostility to France? What wonder that the painter
Haydon, who was highly imaginative and not in the least
clear-headed, felt such hostility to be an essential part of
patriotism? 'In *my* day,' he writes in his journal, 'boys
were born, nursed, and grew up, hating and to hate the

name of Frenchman.' He did hate it with all his heart, but then his earliest recollection — when he was but four years old — was seeing his mother lying on her sofa and crying bitterly. He crept up to her, puzzled and frightened, poor baby, and she sobbed out: 'They have cut off the Queen of France's head, my dear.' Such an ineffaceable recollection colours childhood and sets character. It is an education for life.

As for the Papacy — well, years have softened but not destroyed England's hereditary detestation of Rome. The easy tolerance of the American for any religion, or for all religions, or for no religion at all, is the natural outcome of a mixed nationality, and of a tolerably serene background. We have shed very little of our blood, or of our neighbour's blood, for the faith that was in us, or in him; and, during the past half-century, forbearance has broadened into unconcern. Even the occasional refusal of a pastor to allow a cleric of another denomination to preach in his church, can hardly be deemed a violent form of persecution.

What American author, for example, can recall such childish memories as those which Sir Edmund Gosse described with illuminating candour in 'Father and Son'? 'We welcomed any social disorder in any part of Italy, as likely to be annoying to the Papacy. If there was a custom-house officer stabbed in a fracas at Sassari, we gave loud thanks that liberty and light were breaking in upon Sardinia.' What American scientist, taking a holiday in Italy, ever carried around with him such uncomfortable sensations as those described by Professor Huxley in some of his Roman letters? 'I must have a strong strain of Puritan blood in me somewhere,' he wrote to Sir John Donnelly, after a morning spent at Saint Peter's, 'for I am possessed with a desire to arise and slay the whole brood of idolaters, whenever I assist at one of these services.'

Save and except Miss Georgiana Podsnap's faltering fancy for murdering her partners at a ball, this is the most blood-thirsty sentiment on record, and suggests but a limited enjoyment of a really beautiful service. Better the light-hearted unconcern of Mr. John Richard Green, the historian, who, albeit a clergyman of the Church of England, preferred going to the Church of Rome when Catholicism had an organ, and Protestantism, a harmonium. 'The difference in truth between them doesn't seem to me to make up for the difference in instruments.'

Mr. Lowell speaks somewhere of a 'divine provincialism,' which expresses the sturdy sense of a nation, and is but ill replaced by a cosmopolitanism lacking in virtue and distinction. Perhaps this is England's gift, and insures for her a solidarity which Americans lack. Ignoring or misunderstanding the standards of other races, she sets her own so high we needs must raise our eyes to consider them. Yet when Mr. Arnold scandalized his fellow countrymen by the frank confession that he found foreign life 'liberating,' what did he mean but that he refused to

'drag at each remove a lengthening chain'?

His mind leaped gladly to meet new issues and fresh tides of thought; he stood ready to accept the reasonableness of usages which differed materially from his own; and he took delight in the trivial happenings of every day, precisely because they were un-English and unfamiliar. Even the names of strange places, of German castles and French villages, gave him, as they gave Mr. Henry James, a curious satisfaction, a sense of harmony and ordered charm.

In that caustic volume, 'Elizabeth in Rügen,' there is an amusing description of the indignation of the bishop's wife, Mrs. Harvey-Browne, over what she considers the stupidities of German speech.

'What,' she asks with asperity, 'could be more supremely senseless than calling the Baltic the Ostsee?'

'Well, but why shouldn't they, if they want to?' says Elizabeth densely.

'But, dear Frau X, it is so foolish. East sea! Of what is it the east? One is always the east of something, but one doesn't talk about it. The name has no meaning whatever. Now "Baltic" exactly describes it.'

This is fiction, but it is fiction easily surpassed by fact — witness the English tourist in France who said to Sir Leslie Stephen that it was 'unnatural' for soldiers to dress in blue. Then, remembering certain British instances, he added hastily: 'Except, indeed, for the Artillery, or the Blue Horse.' 'The English model,' commented Sir Leslie, 'with all its variations, appeared to him to be ordained by nature.'

The rigid application of one nation's formulas to another nation's manners has its obvious disadvantages. It is praiseworthy in an Englishman to carry his conscience — like his bathtub — wherever he goes, but both articles are sadly in his way. The American who leaves his conscience and his tub at home, and who trusts to being clean and good after a foreign fashion, has an easier time, and is not permanently stained. Being less cock-sure in the start about his standing with Heaven, he is subject to reasonable doubts as to the culpability of other people. The joyous outdoor Sundays of France and Germany please him at least as well as the shut-in Sundays of England and Scotland. He takes kindly to concerts, enlivened, without demoralization, by beer, and wonders why he cannot have them at home. Whatever is distinctive, whatever is national, interests and delights him; and he seldom feels called upon to decide a moral issue which is not submitted to his judgment.

I was once in Valais when a rude play was acted by the peasants of Vissoye. It set forth the conversion of the Huns to Christianity through the medium of a miracle vouchsafed to Zachéo, the legendary apostle of Anniviers. The little stage was erected on a pleasant hillside, the procession bearing the cross wound down from the village church, the priests from all the neighbouring towns were present, and the pious Valaisans — as overjoyed as if the Huns were a matter of yesterday — sang a solemn *Te Deum* in thanksgiving for the conversion of their land. It would be hard to conceive of a drama less profane; indeed, only religious fervour could have breathed life into so much controversy; yet I had English friends, intelligent, cultivated, and deeply interested, who refused to go with me to Vissoye because it was Sunday afternoon. They stood by their guns, and attended their own service in the drawing-room of the deserted little hotel at Zinal; gaining, I trust, the approval of their own consciences, and losing the experience of a lifetime.

Disapprobation has ever been a powerful stimulus to the Saxon mind. The heroic measures which it enforces command our faltering homage, and might incite us to emulation, were we not temperamentally disposed to ask ourselves the fatal question, 'Is it worth while?' When we remember that twenty-five thousand people in Great Britain left off eating sugar, by way of protest against slavery

in the West Indies, we realize how the individual Englishman holds himself morally responsible for wrongs he is
innocent of inflicting, and powerless to redress. Hood and
other light-minded humourists laughed at him for drinking
bitter tea; but he was not to be shaken by ridicule. Miss
Edgeworth voiced the conservative sentiment of her day
when she objected to eating unsweetened custards; but
he was not to be chilled by apathy.

The same strenuous spirit impelled the English to express their sympathy for Captain Alfred Dreyfus by stay-
ing away from the Paris fair of 1900. The London press
loudly boasted that Englishmen would not give the sanction of their presence to any undertaking of the French
Government, and called attention again and again to their
absence from the exhibition. I myself was asked a number
of times in England whether this absence were a noticeable
thing; but truth compelled me to admit that it was not.
With Paris brimming over like a cup filled to the lip, with
streets and fair-grounds thronged, with every hotel
crowded and every cab engaged, and with twenty thousand of my own countrymen clamorously enlivening the
scene, it was not possible to miss anybody anywhere. It
obviously had not occurred to Americans to see any connection between the trial of Captain Dreyfus and their enjoyment of the most beautiful and brilliant thing that
Europe had to give. The pretty adage, '*Tout homme a
deux pays: le sien et puis la France,*' is truer of us than of
any other people in the world. And we may as well pardon
a nation her transgressions, if we cannot keep away from
her shores.

England's public utterances anent the United States
are of the friendliest character. Her newspapers and maga-

zines say flattering things about us. Her poet-laureate —
unlike his great predecessor who unaffectedly detested us —
began his official career by praising us with such fervour
that we felt we ought in common honesty to tell him that
we were nothing like so good as he thought us. An English
textbook, published a few years ago, explained generously
to the school-boys of Great Britain that the United States
should not be looked upon as a foreign nation. 'They are
peopled by men of our blood and faith, enjoy in a great
measure the same laws that we do, read the same Bible,
and acknowledge, like us, the rule of King Shakespeare.'

All this is very pleasant, but the fact remains that Englishmen express surprise and pain at our most innocent
idiosyncrasies. They correct our pronunciation and our
misuse of words. They regret our nomadic habits, our
shrill voices, our troublesome children, our inability to
climb mountains or 'do a little glacier work' (it sounds
like embroidery, but means scrambling perilously over
ice), our taste for unwholesome — or, in other words, sea-
soned — food. When I am reproved by English acquaintances for the 'Americanisms' which disfigure my speech
and proclaim my nationality, I cannot well defend myself
by asserting that I read the same Bible as they do — for
maybe, after all, I don't.

The tenacity with which English residents on the Continent cling to the customs and traditions of their own
country is pathetic in its loyalty and in its misconceptions
Their scheme of life does not permit a single foreign observance, their range of sympathies seldom includes a single
foreign ideal. 'An Englishman's happiness,' says M.
Taine, 'consists in being at home at six in the evening,
with a pleasing, attached wife, four or five children, and

respectful domestics.' This is a very good notion of happiness, no fault can be found with it, and something on the same order, though less perfect in detail, is highly prized and commended in America. But it does not embrace every avenue of delight. The Frenchman who seems never to go home, who seldom has a large family, whose wife is often his business partner and helpmate, and whose servants are friendly allies rather than automatic menials, enjoys life also, and with some degree of intelligence. He may be pardoned for resenting the attitude of English exiles, who, driven from their own country by the harshness of the climate, or the cruel cost of living, never cease to deplore the unaccountable foreignness of foreigners. 'Our social tariff amounts to prohibition,' said a witty Englishman in France. 'Exchange of ideas takes place only at the extreme point of necessity.'

It is not under such conditions that any nation gives its best to strangers. It is not to the affronted soul that the charm of the unfamiliar makes its sweet and powerful appeal. Lord Byron was furious when one of his countrywomen called Chamonix 'rural'; yet, after all, the poor creature was giving the scenery what praise she understood. The Englishman who complained that he could not look out of his window in Rome without seeing the sun, had a legitimate grievance (we all know what it is to sigh for grey skies, and for the unutterable rest they bring); but if we want Rome, we must take her sunshine, along with her fleas and her Church. Accepted philosophically, they need not mar our infinite content.

There is a wonderful sentence in Mrs. Humphry Ward's 'Marriage of William Ashe,' which subtly and strongly protests against the blight of mental isolation. Lady Kitty

Bristol is reciting Corneille in Lady Grosville's drawing-room. 'Her audience,' says Mrs. Ward, 'looked on at first with the embarrassed or hostile air which is the Englishman's natural protection against the great things of art.' To write a sentence at once so caustic and so flawless is to triumph over the limitations of language. The reproach seems a strange one to hurl at a nation which has produced the noblest literature of the world since the light of Greece waned; but we must remember that distinction of mind, as Mrs. Ward understood it, and as it was understood by Mr. Arnold, is necessarily allied with a knowledge of French arts and letters, and with some insight into the qualities which clarify French conversation. 'Divine provincialism' had no halo for the man who wrote 'Friendship's Garland.' He regarded it with an impatience akin to mistrust, and bordering upon fear. Perhaps the final word was spoken long ago by a writer whose place in literature is so high that few aspire to read him. England was severing her sympathies sharply from much which she had held in common with the rest of Europe, when Dryden wrote: 'They who would combat general authority with particular opinion must first establish for themselves a reputation of understanding better than other men.'

THE CHILL OF ENTHUSIASM

THE CHILL
OF
ENTHUSIASM

Surtout, pas de zèle. — TALLEYRAND.

THERE is no aloofness so forlorn as our aloofness from an uncontagious enthusiasm, and there is no hostility so sharp as that aroused by a fervour which fails of response. Charles Lamb's 'D—n him at a hazard,' was the expression of a natural and reasonable frame of mind with which we are all familiar, and which, though admittedly unlovely, is in the nature of a safeguard. If we had no spiritual asbestos to protect our souls, we should be consumed to no purpose by every wanton flame. If our sincere and restful indifference to things which concern us not were shaken by every blast, we should have no available force for things which concern us deeply. If eloquence did not sometimes make us yawn, we should be besotted by oratory. And if we did not approach new acquaintances, new authors, and new points of view with life-saving reluctance, we should never feel that vital regard which, being strong enough to break down our barriers, is strong enough to hold us for life.

The worth of admiration is, after all, in proportion to the value of the thing admired — a circumstance overlooked by the people who talk much pleasant nonsense about sympathy, and the courage of our emotions, and the open and generous mind. We know how Mr. Arnold felt when an American lady wrote to him, in praise of American authors, and said that it rejoiced her heart to think of such excellence as being 'common and abundant.' Mr. Arnold, who considered that excellence of any kind was very uncommon and beyond measure rare, expressed his views on this occasion with more fervour and publicity than the circumstances demanded; but his words are as balm to the irritation which some of us suffer and conceal when drained of our reluctant applause.

It is perhaps because women have been trained to a receptive attitude of mind, because for centuries they have been valued for their sympathy and appreciation rather than for their judgment, that they are so perilously prone to enthusiasm. It has come to all of us of late to hear much feminine eloquence, and to marvel at the nimbleness of woman's wit, at the speed with which she thinks, and the facility with which she expresses her thoughts. A woman who, until fifteen years ago, never addressed a larger audience than that afforded by a reading-club or a dinner-party, will now thrust and parry on a platform, wholly unembarrassed by timidity or by ignorance. Sentiment and satire are hers to command; and while neither is convincing, both are tremendously effective with people already convinced, with the partisans who throng unwearyingly to hear the voicing of their own opinions. The ease with which such a speaker brings forward the great central fact of the universe, maternity, as an argument for or against political activity (it works just as well either way); the glow with which she associates Jeanne d'Arc with federated clubs and social service; and the gay defiance she hurls at customs and prejudices so profoundly obsolete that the lantern of Diogenes could not find them lurking in a village street — these things may chill the unemotional listener into apathy, but they never fail to awaken the sensibilities of an audience. The simple process, so highly commended by debaters, of ignoring all that cannot be denied, makes demonstration easy. 'A crowd,' said Mr. Ruskin, 'thinks by infection.' To be immune from infection is to stand outside the sacred circle of enthusiasts.

Yet if the experience of mankind teaches anything, it is that vital convictions are not at the mercy of eloquence. The 'oratory of conviction,' to borrow a phrase of Mr. Bagehot's, is so rare as to be hardly worth taking into account. Fox used to say that if a speech read well, it was 'a damned bad speech,' which is the final word of cynicism spoken by one who knew. It was the saving sense of England, that solid, prosaic, dependable common sense, the bulwark of every great nation, which, after Sheridan's famous speech, demanding the impeachment of Warren Hastings, made the House adjourn 'to collect its reason' — obviously because its reason had been lost. Sir William Dolden, who moved the adjournment, frankly confessed that it was impossible to give a 'determinate opinion' while under the spell of oratory. So the lawmakers, who had been fired to white heat, retired to cool down again; and when Sheridan — always as deep in difficulties as Micawber — was offered a thousand pounds for the manuscript of the speech, he remembered Fox's verdict, and refused to risk his unballasted eloquence in print.

Enthusiasm is praised because it implies an unselfish concern for something outside our personal interest and advancement. It is reverenced because the great and wise amendments, which from time to time straighten the roads we walk, may always be traced back to somebody's zeal for reform. It is rich in prophetic attributes, banking largely on the unknown, and making up in nobility of design what it lacks in excellence of attainment. Like simplicity, and candour, and other much-commended qualities, enthusiasm is charming until we meet it face to face, and cannot escape from its charm. It is then that we begin to understand the attitude of Goethe, and Talleyrand, and Pitt, and Sir Robert Peel, who saved themselves from being consumed by resolutely refusing to ignite. 'It is folly,' observed Goethe, 'to expect that other men will consent to believe as we do'; and, having reconciled himself to this elemental obstinacy of the human heart, it no longer troubled him that those whom he felt to be wrong should refuse to acknowledge their errors.

There are men and women — not many — who have the happy art of making their most fervent convictions endurable. Their hobbies do not spread desolation over the social world, their prejudices do not insult our intelligence. They may be so 'abreast with the times' that we cannot keep track of them, or they may be basking serenely in some Early Victorian close. They may believe buoyantly in the Baconian cipher, or in thought transference, or in the serious purposes of Mr. George Bernard Shaw, or in anything else which invites credulity. They may even express these views, and still be loved and cherished by their friends.

How illuminating is the contrast which Hazlitt unconsciously draws between the enthusiasms of Lamb which everybody was able to bear, and the enthusiasms of Cole-

ridge which nobody was able to bear. Lamb would parade
his admiration for some favourite author, Donne, for example, whom the rest of the company probably abhorred.
He would select the most crabbed passages to quote and
defend; he would stammer out his piquant and masterful
half sentences, his scalding jests, his controvertible asser-
tions; he would skilfully hint at the defects which no one
else was permitted to see; and if he made no converts
(wanting none), he woke no weary wrath. But we all have
a sneaking sympathy for Holcroft, who, when Coleridge
was expatiating rapturously and oppressively upon the
glories of German transcendental philosophy, and upon his
own supreme command of the field, cried out suddenly and
with exceeding bitterness: 'Mr. Coleridge, you are the most
eloquent man I ever met, and the most unbearable in your
eloquence.'

I am not without a lurking suspicion that George Borrow must have been at times unbearable in his eloquence.
'We cannot refuse to meet a man on the ground that he is
an enthusiast,' observes Mr. George Street, obviously lamenting this circumstance; 'but we should at least like to
make sure that his enthusiasms are under control.' Borrow's enthusiasms were never under control. He stood
ready at a moment's notice to prove the superiority of the
Welsh bards over the paltry poets of England, or to relate
the marvellous Welsh prophecies, so vague as to be always
safe. He was capable of inflicting Armenian verbs upon
Isopel Berners when they sat at night over their gipsy kettle in the dingle (let us hope she fell asleep as sweetly as
does Milton's Eve when Adam grows too garrulous); and
he met the complaints of a poor farmer on the hardness of
the times with jubilant praises of evangelicalism. 'Better

pay three pounds an acre, and live on crusts and water in the present enlightened days,' he told the disheartened husbandman, 'than pay two shillings an acre, and sit down to beef and ale three times a day in the old superstitious ages.' This is *not* the oratory of conviction. There are un-reasoning prejudices in favour of one's own stomach which eloquence cannot gainsay. 'I defy the utmost power of language to disgust me wi' a gude denner,' observes the Ettrick Shepherd; thus putting on record the attitude of the bucolic mind, impassive, immutable, since earth's first harvests were gleaned.

The artificial emotions which expand under provocation, and collapse when the provocation is withdrawn, must be held responsible for much mental confusion. Election ora-tory is an old and cherished institution. It is designed to make candidates show their paces, and to give innocent amusement to the crowd. Properly reinforced by brass bands and bunting, graced by some sufficiently august presence, and enlivened by plenty of cheering and hat-flourishing, it presents a strong appeal. A political party is, moreover, a solid and self-sustaining affair. All sound and alliterative generalities about virile and vigorous man-hood, honest and honourable labour, great and glorious causes, are understood, in this country at least, to refer to the virile and vigorous manhood of Republicans or Dem-ocrats, as the case may be; and to uphold the honest and honourable, great and glorious Republican or Democratic principles, upon which, it is also understood, depends the welfare of the nation.

Yet even this sense of security cannot always save us from the chill of collapsed enthusiasm. I was once at a great mass meeting, held in the interests of municipal re-

form, and at which the principal speaker was a candidate
for office. He was delayed for a full hour after the meeting
had been opened, and this hour was filled with good platform oratory. Speechmaker after speechmaker, all adepts
in their art, laid bare before our eyes the evils which consumed us, and called upon us passionately to support the
candidate who would lift us from our shame. The fervour
of the house rose higher and higher. Martial music stirred
our blood, and made us feel that reform and patriotism
were one. The atmosphere grew tense with expectancy,
when suddenly there came a great shout, and the sound of
cheering from the crowd in the streets, the crowd which
could not force its way into the huge and closely packed
opera house. Now there are few things more profoundly
affecting than cheers heard from a distance, or muffled by
intervening walls. They have a fine dramatic quality unknown to the cheers which rend the air about us. When
the chairman of the meeting announced that the candidate
was outside the doors, speaking to the mob, the excitement
reached fever heat. When some one cried, 'He is here!'
and the orchestra struck the first bars of 'Hail Columbia,'
we rose to our feet, waving multitudinous flags, and shouting out the rapture of our hearts.

And then — and then there stepped upon the stage a
plain, tired, bewildered man, betraying nervous exhaustion in every line. He spoke, and his voice was not the assured voice of a leader. His words were not the happy
words which instantly command attention. It was evident
to the discerning eye that he had been driven for days, perhaps for weeks, beyond his strength and endurance; that
he had resorted to stimulants to help him in this emer-
gency, and that they had failed; that he was striving with

feeble desperation to do the impossible which was expected of him. I wondered even then if a few common words of explanation, a few sober words of promise, would not have satisfied the crowd, already sated with eloquence. I wondered if the unfortunate man could feel the chill settling down upon the house as he spoke his random and undignified sentences, whether he could see the first stragglers slipping down the aisles. What did his decent record, his honest purpose, avail him in an hour like this? He tried to lash himself to vigour, but it was spurring a broken-winded horse. The stragglers increased into a flying squadron, the house was emptying fast, when the chairman in sheer desperation made a sign to the leader of the orchestra, who waved his baton, and 'The Star-Spangled Banner' drowned the candidate's last words, and brought what was left of the audience to its feet. I turned to a friend beside me, the wife of a local politician who had been the most fiery speaker of the evening. 'Will it make any difference?' I asked, and she answered disconsolately: 'The city is lost, but we may save the state.'

Then we went out into the quiet streets, and I bethought me of Voltaire's driving in a blue coach powdered with gilt stars to see the first production of 'Irène,' and of his leaving the theatre to find that enthusiasts had cut the traces of his horses, so that the shouting mob might drag him home in triumph. But the mob, having done its shouting, melted away after the irresponsible fashion of mobs, leaving the blue coach stranded in front of the Tuileries with Voltaire shivering inside of it, until the horses could be brought back, the traces patched up, and the driver recalled to his duty.

That 'popular enthusiasm is but a fire of straw' has been

amply demonstrated by all who have tried to keep it going. It can be lighted to some purpose, as when money is extracted from the enthusiasts before they have had time to cool; but even this process — so skilfully conducted by the initiated — seems unworthy of great and noble charities, or of great and noble causes. It is true also that the agitator — no matter what he may be agitating — is always sure of his market; a circumstance which made that most conservative of chancellors, Lord Eldon, swear with bitter oaths that, if he were to begin life over again, he would begin it as an agitator. Tom Moore tells a pleasant story (one of the many pleasant stories embalmed in his vast sarcophagus of a diary) about a street orator whom he heard address a crowd in Dublin. The man's eloquence was so stirring that Moore was ravished by it, and he expressed to Richard Sheil his admiration for the speaker. 'Ah,' said Sheil carelessly, 'that was a brewer's patriot. Most of the great brewers have in their employ a regular patriot who goes about among the publicans, talking violent politics, which helps to sell the beer.'

Honest enthusiasm, we are often told, is the power which moves the world. Therefore it is perhaps that honest enthusiasts seem to think that if they stopped pushing, the world would stop moving — as though it were a new world which didn't know its way. This belief inclines them to intolerance. The more keen they are, the more contemptuous they become. What Wordsworth admirably called 'the self-applauding sincerity of a heated mind' leaves them no loophole for doubt, and no understanding of the doubter. In their volcanic progress they bowl over the non-partisan — a man and a brother — with splendid unconcern. He, poor soul, stunned but not convinced, clings

desperately to some pettifogging convictions which he
calls truth, and refuses a clearer vision. His habit of remembering what he believed yesterday clogs his mind, and
makes it hard for him to believe something entirely new
today. Much has been said about the inconvenience of
keeping opinions, but much might be said about the serenity of the process. Old opinions are like old friends —
we cease to question their worth because, after years of intimacy and the loss of some valuable illusions, we have
grown to place our slow reliance on them. We know at
least where we stand, and whither we are tending, and we
refuse to bustle feverishly about the circumference of life,
because, as Amiel warns us, we cannot reach its core.

THE CONDESCENSION OF BORROWERS

THE
CONDESCENSION
OF BORROWERS

*Il n'est si riche qui quelquefois ne doibve. Il n'est si pauvre de qui quel-
quefois on ne puisse emprunter. — Pantagruel.*

'I LENT my umbrella,' said my friend, 'to my cousin,
Maria. I was compelled to lend it to her because she could
not, or would not, leave my house in the rain without it.
I had need of that umbrella, and I tried to make it as plain
as the amenities of language permitted that I expected to
have it returned. Maria said superciliously that she hated
to see other people's umbrellas littering the house, which
gave me a gleam of hope. Two months later I found my
property in the hands of her ten-year-old son, who was being marshalled with his brothers and sisters to dancing-
school. In the first joyful flash of recognition I cried, "Os-
wald, that is my umbrella you are carrying!" whereupon
Maria said still more superciliously than before, "Oh, yes,
don't you remember?" (as if reproaching me for my for-
getfulness) — "you gave it to me that Saturday I lunched
with you, and it rained so heavily. The boys carry it to
school. Where there are children, you can't have too many
old umbrellas at hand. They lose them so fast." She
spoke,' continued my friend impressively, 'as if she were
harbouring my umbrella from pure kindness, and because

she did not like to wound my feelings by sending it back to me. She made a virtue of giving it shelter.'

This is the arrogance which places the borrower, as Charles Lamb discovered long ago, among the great ones of the earth, among those whom their brethren serve. Lamb loved to contrast the 'instinctive sovereignty,' the frank and open bearing of the man who borrows with the 'lean and suspicious' aspect of the man who lends. He stood lost in admiration before the great borrowers of the world — Alcibiades, Falstaff, Steele, and Sheridan; an incomparable quartette, to which might be added the shining names of William Godwin and Leigh Hunt. All the characteristic qualities of the class were united, indeed, in Leigh Hunt, as in no other single representative. Sheridan was an unrivalled companion — could talk seven hours without making even Byron yawn. Steele was the most lovable of spendthrifts. Lending to these men was but a form of investment. They paid in a coinage of their own. But Leigh Hunt combined in the happiest manner a readiness to extract favours with a confirmed habit of never acknowledging the smallest obligation for them. He is a perfect example of the condescending borrower, of the man who permits his friends, as a pleasure to themselves, to relieve his necessities, and who knows nothing of gratitude or loyalty.

It would be interesting to calculate the amount of money which Hunt's friends and acquaintances contributed to his support in life. Shelley gave him at one time fourteen hundred pounds, an amount which the poet could ill spare; and, when he had no more to give, wrote in misery of spirit to Byron, begging a loan for his friend, and promising to repay it, as he feels tolerably sure that Hunt never will.

Byron, generous at first, wearied after a time of his position in Hunt's commissariat (it was like pulling a man out of a river, he wrote to Moore, only to see him jump in again), and coldly withdrew. His withdrawal occasioned inconvenience, and has been sharply criticized. Hunt, says Sir Leslie Stephen, loved a cheerful giver, and Byron's obvious reluctance struck him as being in bad taste. His biographers, one and all, have sympathized with this point of view. Even Mr. Frederick Locker, from whom one would have expected a different verdict, has recorded his conviction that Hunt had probably been 'sorely tried' by Byron.

It is characteristic of the preordained borrower, of the man who simply fulfils his destiny in life, that not his obligations only, but his anxieties and mortifications are shouldered by other men. Hunt was care-free and light-hearted; but there is a note akin to anguish in Shelley's petition to Byron, and in his shamefaced admission that he is himself too poor to relieve his friend's necessities. The correspondence of William Godwin's eminent contemporaries teem with projects to alleviate Godwin's needs. His debts were everybody's affair but his own. Sir James Mackintosh wrote to Rogers in the autumn of 1815, suggesting that Byron might be the proper person to pay them. Rogers, enchanted with the idea, wrote to Byron, proposing that the purchase money of 'The Siege of Corinth' be devoted to this good purpose. Byron, with less enthusiasm, but resigned, wrote to Murray, directing him to forward the six hundred pounds to Godwin; and Murray, having always the courage of his convictions, wrote back, flatly refusing to do anything of the kind. In the end, Byron used the money to pay his own debts, thereby disgusting everybody but his creditors.

Six years later, however, we find him contributing to a fund which tireless philanthropists were raising for Godwin's relief. On this occasion all men of letters, poor as well as rich, were pressed into active service. Even Lamb, who had nothing of his own, wrote to the painter, Haydon, who had not a penny in the world, and begged him to beg Mrs. Coutts to pay Godwin's rent. He also confessed that he had sent 'a very respectful letter' — on behalf of the rent — to Sir Walter Scott; and he explained naïvely that Godwin did not concern himself personally in the matter, because he 'left all to his Committee' — a peaceful thing to do.

But how did Godwin come to have a 'committee' to raise money for him, when other poor devils had to raise it for themselves, or do without? He was not well-beloved. On the contrary, he bored all whom he did not affront. He was not grateful. On the contrary, he held gratitude to be a vice, as tending to make men 'grossly partial' to those who have befriended them. His condescension kept pace with his demands. After his daughter's flight with Shelley, he expressed his just resentment by refusing to accept Shelley's cheque for a thousand pounds unless it were made payable to a third party, unless he could have the money without the formality of an acceptance. Like the great lords of Picardy, who had the 'right of credit' from their loyal subjects, Godwin claimed his dues from every chance acquaintance. Crabb Robinson introduced him one evening to a gentleman named Rough. The next day both Godwin and Rough called upon their host, each man expressing his regard for the other, and each asking Robinson if he thought the other would be a likely person to lend him fifty pounds.

There are critics who hold that Haydon excelled all other borrowers known to fame; but his is not a career upon which an admirer of the art can look with pleasure. Haydon's debts hunted him like hounds, and if he pursued borrowing as a means of livelihood — more lucrative than painting pictures which nobody would buy — it was only because no third avocation presented itself as a possibility. He is not to be compared for a moment with a true expert like Sheridan, who borrowed for borrowing's sake, and without any sordid motive connected with rents or butchers' bills. Haydon would, indeed, part with his money as readily as if it belonged to him. He would hear an 'inward voice' in church, urging him to give his last sovereign; and, having obeyed this voice 'with as pure a feeling as ever animated a human heart,' he had no resource but immediately to borrow another. It would have been well for him if he could have followed on such occasions the memorable example of Lady Cook, who was so impressed by a begging sermon that she borrowed a sovereign from Sydney Smith to put into the offertory; and — the gold once between her fingers — found herself equally unable to give it or to return it, so went home, a pound richer for her charitable impulse.

Haydon, too, would rob Peter to pay Paul, and rob Paul without paying Peter; but it was all after an intricate and troubled fashion of his own. On one occasion he borrowed ten pounds from Webb. Seven pounds he used to satisfy another creditor, from whom, on the strength of this payment, he borrowed ten pounds more to meet an impending bill. It sounds like a particularly confusing game; but it was a game played in dead earnest, and without the humorous touch which makes the charm of Lady Cook's, or

of Sheridan's methods. Haydon would have been deeply
grateful to his benefactors, had he not always stood in need
of favours to come. Sheridan might perchance have been
grateful, could he have remembered who his benefactors
were. He laid the world under tribute; and because he had
an aversion to opening his mail — an aversion with which
it is impossible not to sympathize — he frequently made
no use of the tribute when it was paid. Moore tells us that
James Wesley once saw among a pile of papers on Sheridan's desk an unopened letter of his own, containing a ten-
pound note, which he had lent Sheridan some weeks before.
Wesley quietly took possession of the letter and the money,
thereby raising a delicate, and as yet unsettled, question
of morality. Had he a right to those ten pounds because
they had once been his, or were they not rather Sheridan's
property, destined in the natural and proper order of things
never to be returned.

Yet men, even men of letters, have been known to pay
their debts, and to restore borrowed property. Moore paid
Lord Lansdowne every penny of the generous sum advanced by that nobleman after the defalcation of Moore's
deputy in Bermuda. Doctor Johnson paid back ten pounds
after a lapse of twenty years — a pleasant shock to the
lender — and on his death-bed (having fewer sins than most
of us to recall) begged Sir Joshua Reynolds to forgive him
a trifling loan. It was the too honest return of a pair of
borrowed sheets (unwashed) which first chilled Pope's
friendship for Lady Mary Wortley Montagu. That excellent gossip, Miss Letitia Matilda Hawkins, who stands
responsible for this anecdote, lamented all her life that her
father, Sir John Hawkins, could never remember which
of the friends borrowed and which lent the offending sheets;

but it is a point easily settled in our minds. Pope was probably the last man in Christendom to have been guilty of such a misdemeanour, and Lady Mary was certainly the last woman in Christendom to have been affronted by it. Like Doctor Johnson, she had 'no passion for clean linen.'

Coleridge, though he went through life leaning his inert weight on other men's shoulders, did remember in some mysterious fashion to return the books he borrowed, enriched often, as Lamb proudly records, with marginal notes which tripled their value. His conduct in this regard was all the more praiseworthy inasmuch as the cobweb statutes which define books as personal property have never met with literal acceptance. Lamb's theory that books belong with the highest propriety to those who understand them best (a theory often advanced in defence of depredations which Lamb would have scorned to commit), was popular before the lamentable invention of printing. The library of Lucullus was, we are told, 'open to all,' and it would be interesting to know how many precious manuscripts remained ultimately in the great patrician's villa.

Richard Heber, that most princely of collectors, so well understood the perils of his position that he met them bravely by buying three copies of every book — one for show, one for use, and one for the service of his friends. The position of the show-book seems rather melancholy, but perhaps, in time, it replaced the borrowed volume. Heber's generosity has been nobly praised by Scott, who contrasts the hard-heartedness of other bibliophiles, those 'gripple niggards' who preferred holding on to their treasures, with his friend's careless liberality.

'Thy volumes, open as thy heart,
Delight, amusement, science, art,
To every ear and eye impart.
Yet who, of all who thus employ them,
Can, like the owner's self, enjoy them?'

The 'gripple niggards' might have pleaded feebly in
their own behalf that they could not all afford to spend,
like Heber, a hundred thousand pounds in the purchase
of books; and that an occasional reluctance to part with
some hard-earned, hard-won volume might be pardonable
in one who could not hope to replace it. Lamb's books
were the shabbiest in Christendom; yet how keen was his
pang when Charles Kemble carried off the letters of 'that
princely woman, the thrice noble Margaret Newcastle,'
an 'illustrious folio' which he well knew Kemble would
never read. How bitterly he bewailed his rashness in ex-
tolling the beauties of Sir Thomas Browne's 'Urn Burial'
to a guest who was so moved by this eloquence that he
promptly borrowed the volume. 'But so,' sighed Lamb
'have I known a foolish lover to praise his mistress in the
presence of a rival more qualified to carry her off than himself.'

Johnson cherished a dim conviction that because he
read, and Garrick did not, the proper place for Garrick's
books was on his — Johnson's — bookshelves; a point
which could never be settled between the two friends, and
which came near to wrecking their friendship. Garrick
loved books with the chilly yet imperative love of the col-
lector. Johnson loved them as he loved his soul. Garrick
took pride in their sumptuousness, in their immaculate,
virginal splendour. Johnson gathered them to his heart
with scant regard for outward magnificence, for the glories

of calf and vellum. Garrick bought books. Johnson borrowed them. Each considered that he had a prior right to the objects of his legitimate affection. We, looking back with softened hearts, are fain to think that we should have held our volumes doubly dear if they had lain for a time by Johnson's humble hearth, if he had pored over them at three o'clock in the morning, and had left sundry tokens — grease-spots and spatterings of snuff — upon many a spotless page. But it is hardly fair to censure Garrick for not dilating with these emotions.

Johnson's habit of flinging the volumes which displeased him into remote and dusty corners of the room was ill calculated to inspire confidence, and his powers of procrastination were never more marked than in the matter of restoring borrowed books. We know from Cradock's 'Memoirs' how that gentleman, having induced Lord Harborough to lend him a superb volume of manuscripts, containing poems of James the First, proceeded to re-lend this priceless treasure to Johnson. When it was not returned — as of course it was not — he wrote an urgent letter, and heard to his dismay that Johnson was not only unable to find the book, but that he could not remember having ever received it. The despairing Cradock applied to all his friends for help; and George Steevens, who had a useful habit of looking about him, suggested that a sealed packet, which he had several times observed lying under Johnson's ponderous inkstand, might possibly contain the lost manuscripts. Even with this ray of hope for guidance, it never seemed to occur to anyone to storm Johnson's fortress and rescue the imprisoned volume; but after the Doctor's death, two years later, Cradock made a formal application to the executors; and Lord Harborough's property was dis-

covered under the inkstand, unopened, unread, and consequently, as by a happy miracle, uninjured.

Such an incident must needs win pardon for Garrick's
churlishness in defending his possessions. 'The history of
book-collecting,' says a caustic critic, 'is a history relieved
but rarely by acts of pure and undiluted unselfishness.'
This is true, but are there not virtues so heroic that plain
human nature can ill aspire to compass them?

There is something piteous in the futile efforts of reluctant lenders to save their property from depredation.
They place their reliance upon artless devices which never
yet were known to stay the marauder's hand. They have
their names and addresses engraved on foolish little plates,
which, riveted to their umbrellas, will, they think, suffice
to insure the safety of these useful articles. As well might
the border farmer have engraved his name and address on
the collars of his grazing herds, in the hope that the riever
would respect this symbol of authority. The history of
book-plates is largely the history of borrower versus lender.
The orderly mind is wont to believe that a distinctive
mark, irrevocably attached to every volume, will insure
permanent possession. Sir Edmund Gosse, for example,
expressed a touching faith in the efficacy of the book-
plate. He had but to explain that he 'made it a rule'
never to lend a volume thus decorated, and the would-be
borrower bowed to this rule as to a decree of fate. 'To
have a book-plate,' he joyfully observed, 'gives a col-
lector great serenity and confidence.'

Is it possible that the world has grown virtuous without our observing it? Can it be that the old stalwart race
of book-borrowers, those 'spoilers of the symmetry of
shelves,' are foiled by so childish an expedient? Imagine

Doctor Johnson daunted by a scrap of pasted paper! Or Coleridge, who seldom went through the formality of asking leave, but borrowed armfuls of books in the absence of their legitimate owners! How are we to account for the presence of book-plates — quite a pretty collection at times — on the shelves of men who possess no such toys of their own? When I was a girl I had access to a small and well-chosen library (not greatly exceeding Montaigne's fourscore volumes), each book enriched with an appropriate device of scaly dragon guarding the apples of Hesperides. Beneath the dragon was the motto (Johnsonian in form if not in substance), 'Honour and Obligation demand the prompt return of borrowed Books.' These words ate into my innocent soul, and lent a pang to the sweetness of possession. Doubts as to the exact nature of 'prompt return' made me painfully uncertain as to whether a month, a week, or a day were the limit which Honour and Obligation had set for me. But other and older borrowers were less sensitive, and I have reason to believe that — books being a rarity in that little Southern town — most of the volumes were eventually absorbed by the gaping shelves of neighbours. Perhaps even now (their generous owner long since dead) these worn copies of Boswell, of Elia, of Herrick, and Moore, may still stand forgotten in dark and dusty corners, like gems that magpies hide.

It is vain to struggle with fate, with the elements, and with the borrower; it is folly to claim immunity from a fundamental law, to boast of our brief exemption from the common lot. 'Lend therefore cheerfully, O man ordained to lend. When thou seest the proper authority coming, meet it smilingly, as it were halfway.' Resistance to an appointed force is but a futile waste of strength.

THE GROCER'S CAT

THE
GROCER'S CAT

Of all animals, the cat alone attains to the Contemplative Life. —
ANDREW LANG.

THE grocer's window is not one of those gay and glittering
enclosures which display only the luxuries of the table,
and which give us the impression that there are favoured
classes subsisting exclusively upon Malaga raisins, French
chocolates, and Nuremberg gingerbread. It is an unassum-
ing window, filled with canned goods and breakfast foods,
wrinkled prunes devoid of succulence, and boxes of starch
and candles. Its only ornament is the cat, and his beauty
is more apparent to the artist than to the fancier. His
splendid stripes, black and grey and tawny, are too wide
for noble lineage. He has a broad benignant brow, like
Benjamin Franklin's; but his brooding eyes, golden, un-
fathomable, deny benignancy. He is large and sleek —
the grocery mice must be many, and of an appetizing fat-
ness — and I presume he devotes his nights to the pleasures of the chase. His days are spent in contemplation,
in a serene and wonderful stillness which isolates him from
the bustling vulgarities of the street.

Past the window streams the fretful crowd; in and out of
the shop step loud-voiced customers. The cat is as remote
as if he were drowsing by the waters of the Nile. Pedes-
trians pause to admire him, and many of them endeavour,
with well-meant but futile familiarity, to win some notice

in return. They tap on the window pane, and say, 'Halloo, Pussy!' He does not turn his head, nor lift his lustrous eyes. They tap harder, and with more ostentatious friendliness. The stone cat of Thebes could not pay less attention. It is difficult for human beings to believe that their regard can be otherwise than flattering to an animal; but I did see one man intelligent enough to receive this impression. He was a decent and a good-tempered young person, and he had beaten a prolonged tattoo on the glass with the handle of his umbrella, murmuring at the same time vague words of cajolery. Then, as the cat remained motionless, absorbed in revery, and seemingly unconscious of his unwarranted attentions, he turned to me, a new light dawning in his eyes. 'Thinks itself some,' he said, and I nodded acquiescence. As well try to patronize the Sphinx as to patronize a grocer's cat.

Now, surely this attitude on the part of a small and helpless beast, dependent upon our bounty for food and shelter, and upon our sense of equity for the right to live, is worthy of note, and, to the generous mind, is worthy of respect. Yet there are people who most ungenerously resent it. They say the cat is treacherous and ungrateful, by which they mean that she does not relish unsolicited fondling, and that, like Mr. Chesterton, she will not recognize imaginary obligations. If we keep a cat because there are mice in our kitchen or rats in our cellar, what claim have we to gratitude? If we keep a cat for the sake of her beauty, and because our hearth is but a poor affair without her, she repays her debt with interest when she dozes by our fire. She is the most decorative creature the domestic world can show. She harmonizes with the kitchen's homely comfort, and with the austere seclusion of the library. She gratifies our sense of fitness and our sense of distinction, if we chance to possess these qualities. Did not Isabella d' Este, Marchioness of Mantua, and the finest exponent of distinction in her lordly age, send far and wide for cats to grace her palace? Did she not instruct her agents to make especial search through the Venetian convents, where might be found the deep-furred pussies of Syria and Thibet? Alas for the poor nuns, whose cherished pets were snatched away to gratify the caprice of a great and grasping lady who habitually coveted all that was beautiful in the world.

The cat seldom invites affection, and still more seldom responds to it. A well-bred tolerance is her nearest approach to demonstration. The dog strives with pathetic insistence to break down the barriers between his intelligence and his master's, to understand and to be understood. The wise cat cherishes her isolation, and permits us to play but a secondary part in her solitary and meditative life. Her intelligence, less facile than the dog's, and far less highly differentiated, owes little to our tutelage; her character has not been moulded by our hands. The changing centuries have left no mark upon her; and, from a past inconceivably remote she has come down to us, a creature self-absorbed and self-communing, undisturbed by our feverish activity, a dreamer of dreams, a lover of the mysteries of night.

And yet a friend. No one who knows anything about the cat will deny her capacity for friendship. Rationally, without enthusiasm, without illusions, she offers us companionship on terms of equality. She will not come when she is summoned — unless the summons be for dinner — but she will come of her own sweet will, and bear us company for hours, sleeping contentedly in her armchair, or watching with half-shut eyes the quiet progress of our work. A lover of routine, she expects to find us in the same place at the same hour every day: and when her expectations are fulfilled (cats have some secret method of their own for telling time), she purrs approval of our punctuality. What she detests are noise, confusion, people who bustle in and out of rooms, and the unpardonable intrusions of the housemaid. On those unhappy days when I am driven from my desk by the iron determination of this maid to 'clean up,' my cat is as comfortless as I am. Companions in exile, we wander aimlessly to and fro, lamenting our lost hours. I cannot explain to Lux that the fault is none of mine, and I am sure that he holds me to blame.

There is something indescribably sweet in the quiet, self-respecting friendliness of my cat, in his marked predilection for my society. The absence of exuberance on his part, and the restraint I put upon myself, lend an element of dignity to our intercourse. Assured that I will not presume too far on his good nature, that I will not indulge in any of those gross familiarities, those boisterous gambols which delight the heart of a dog, Lux yields himself more and more passively to my persuasions. He will permit an occasional caress, and acknowledge it with a perfunctory purr. He will manifest a patronizing interest in my work, stepping sedately among my papers, and now and then putting his paw with infinite deliberation on the page I am writing, as though the smear thus contributed spelt, 'Lux, his mark,' and was a reward of merit. But he never curls himself upon my desk, never usurps the place sacred to the memory of a far dearer cat. Some invisible influence restrains him. When his tour of inspection is ended,

he returns to his chair by my side, stretching himself lux-
uriously on his cushions, and watching with steady, sombre
stare the inhibited spot, and the little grey phantom which
haunts my lonely hours by right of my inalienable love.

Lux is a lazy cat, wedded to a contemplative life. He
cares little for play, and nothing for work — the appointed
work of cats. The notion that he has a duty to perform,
that he owes service to the home which shelters him, that
only those who toil are worthy of their keep, has never entered his head. He is content to drink the cream of idleness, and he does this in a spirit of condescension, wonderful to behold. The dignified distaste with which he surveys
a dinner not wholly to his liking carries confusion to the
hearts of his servitors. It is as though Lucullus, having
ordered Neapolitan peacock, finds himself put off with
nightingales' tongues.

For my own part, I like to think that my beautiful and
urbane companion is not a midnight assassin. His profound and soulless indifference to mice pleases me better
than it pleases my household. From an economic point of
view, Lux is not worth his salt. Huxley's cat, be it remembered, was never known to attack anything larger and
fiercer than a butterfly. 'I doubt whether he has the heart
to kill a mouse,' wrote the proud possessor of this prodigy;
'but I saw him catch and eat the first butterfly of the season, and I trust that the germ of courage thus manifested
may develop with years into efficient mousing.'

Even Huxley was disposed to take a utilitarian view of
cathood. Even Cowper, who owed to the frolics of his kitten a few hours' respite from melancholy, had no conception that his adult cat could do better service than slay
rats. 'I have a kitten, my dear,' he wrote to Lady Hesketh,

'the drollest of all creatures that ever wore a cat's skin. Her gambols are incredible, and not to be described. She tumbles head over heels several times together. She lays her cheek to the ground, and humps her back at you with an air of most supreme disdain. From this posture she rises to dance on her hind feet, an exercise which she performs with all the grace imaginable; and she closes these various exhibitions with a loud smack of her lips, which, for want of greater propriety of expression, we call spitting. But, though all cats spit, no cat ever produced such a sound as she does. In point of size, she is likely to be a kitten always, being extremely small for her age; but time, that spoils all things, will, I suppose, make her also a cat. You will see her, I hope, before that melancholy period shall arrive; for no wisdom that she may gain by experience and reflection hereafter will compensate for the loss of her present hilarity. She is dressed in a tortoise-shell suit, and I know that you will delight in her.'

Had Cowper been permitted to live more with kittens, and less with evangelical clergymen, his hours of gaiety might have outnumbered his hours of gloom. Cats have been known to retain in extreme old age the 'hilarity' which the sad poet prized. Nature has thoughtfully provided them with one permanent plaything; and Mr. Frederick Locker vouches for a light-hearted old Tom who, at the close of a long and ill-spent life, actually squandered his last breath in the pursuit of his own elusive tail. But there are few of us who would care to see the monumental calm of our fireside sphinx degenerate into senile sportiveness. Better far the measured slowness of her pace, the superb immobility of her repose. To watch an ordinary cat move imperceptibly and with a rhythmic waving of her tail through a doorway (while we are patiently holding open the door) is like looking at a procession. With just such deliberate dignity, in just such solemn state, the priests of Ra filed between the endless rows of pillars into the sunlit temple court.

The cat is a freebooter. She draws no nice distinctions between a mouse in the wainscot, and a canary swinging in its gilded cage. Her traducers, indeed, have been wont to intimate that her preference is for the forbidden quarry; but this is one of many libellous accusations. The cat, though she has little sympathy with our vapid sentiment, can be taught that a canary is a privileged nuisance, immune from molestation. The bird's shrill notes jar her sensitive nerves. She abhors noise, and a canary's pipe is the most piercing and persistent of noises, welcome to that large majority of mankind which prefers sound of any kind to silence. Moreover, a cage presents just the degree of hindrance to tempt a cat's agility. That she habitually refrains from ridding the household of canaries is proof of her innate reasonableness, of her readiness to submit her finer judgment and more delicate instincts to the common caprices of humanity.

As for wild birds, the robins and wrens and thrushes which are predestined prey, there is only one way to save them, the way which Archibald Douglas took to save the honour of Scotland — 'bell the cat.' A good-sized sleigh-bell, if she be strong enough to bear it, a bunch of little bells, if she be small and slight — and the pleasures of the chase are over. One little bell is of no avail, for she learns to move with such infinite precaution that it does not ring until she springs, and then it rings too late. There is an element of cruelty in depriving the cat of sport, but from the bird's point of view the scheme works to perfection. Of course rats and mice are as safe as birds from the claws of a belled cat, but if we are really humane, we will not regret their immunity.

The boasted benevolence of man is, however, a purely superficial emotion. What am I to think of a friend who anathematizes the family cat for devouring a nest of young robins, and then tells me exultingly that the same cat has killed twelve moles in a fortnight. To a pitiful heart the life of a little mole is as sacred as the life of a little robin. To an artistic eye the mole in his velvet coat is handsomer than the robin, which is at best a bouncing, bourgeois sort of bird, a true suburbanite, with all the defects of his class. But my friend has no mercy for the mole because he destroys her garden — her garden which she despoils every morning, gathering its fairest blossoms to droop and wither in her crowded rooms. To wax compassionate over a bird, and remain hard as flint to a beast, is possible only to humanity. The cat, following her predatory instincts, is at once more logical and less ruthless, because the question of property does not distort her vision. She has none of the vices of civilization.

> Cats I scorn, who, sleek and fat,
> Shiver at a Norway rat.
> Rough and hardy, bold and free,
> Be the cat that's made for me;
> He whose nervous paw can take
> My lady's lapdog by the neck,
> With furious hiss attack the hen,
> And snatch a chicken from the pen.'

So sang Doctor Erasmus Darwin's intrepid pussy (a better poet than her master) to the cat of Miss Anna Seward, surely the last lady in all England to have encouraged such lawlessness on the part of a — presumably — domestic animal.

For the cat's domesticity is at best only a presumption. It is one of life's ironical adjustments that the creature who fits so harmoniously into the family group should be alien to its influences, and independent of its cramping conditions. She seems made for the fireside she adorns, and where she has played her part for centuries. Lamb, delightedly recording his 'observations on cats,' sees only their homely qualities. 'Put 'em on a rug before the fire, they wink their eyes up, and listen to the kettle, and then purr, which is *their* music.' The hymns which Shelley loved were sung by the roaring wind, the hissing kettle, and the kittens purring by his hearth. Heine's cat, curled close to the glowing embers, purred a soft accompaniment to the rhythms pulsing in his brain; but he at least, being a German, was not deceived by this specious show of impeccability. He knew that when the night called, his cat obeyed the summons, abandoning the warm fire for the hard-frozen snow, and the innocent companionship of a poet for the dancing of witches on the hilltops.

The same grace of understanding — more common in the sixteenth than in the nineteenth century — made the famous Milanese physician, Jerome Cardan, abandon his students at the University of Pavia, in obedience to the decision of his cat. 'In the year 1552,' he writes with becoming gravity, 'having left in the house a little cat of placid and domestic habits, she jumped upon my table, and tore at my public lectures; yet my Book of Fate she touched not, though it was the more exposed to her attacks. I gave up my chair, nor returned to it for eight years.' O wise physician, to discern so clearly that 'placid and domestic habits' were but a cloak for mysteries too deep to fathom, for warnings too pregnant to be disregarded.

The vanity of man revolts from the serene indifference of the cat. He is forever lauding the dog, not only for its fidelity, which is a beautiful thing, but for its attitude of humility and abasement. A distinguished American prelate has written some verses on his dog, in which he assumes that, to the animal's eyes, he is as God — a being whose word is law, and from whose sovereign hand flow all life's countless benefactions. Another complacent enthusiast describes *his* dog as sitting motionless in his presence, 'at once tranquil and attentive, as a saint should be in the presence of God. He is happy with the happiness which we perhaps shall never know, since it springs from the smile and the approval of a life incomparably higher than his own.'

Of course, if we are going to wallow in idolatry like this, we do well to choose the dog, and not the cat, to play the worshipper's part. I am not without a suspicion that the dog is far from feeling the rapture and the reverence which we so delightedly ascribe to him. What is there about any one of us to awaken such sentiments in the breast of an intelligent animal? We have taught him our vices, and he fools us to the top of our bent. The cat, however, is equally free from illusions and from hypocrisy. If we aspire to a petty omnipotence, she, for one, will pay no homage at our shrine. Therefore her greatest defamer, Maeterlinck, branded her as ungrateful and perfidious. The cat of 'The Blue Bird' fawns and flatters, which is something no real cat was ever known to do. When and where did M. Maeterlinck encounter an obsequious cat? That the wise little beast should resent Tyltyl's intrusion into the ancient realms of night is conceivable, and that, unlike the dog, she should see nothing godlike in a masterful human boy is hardly a matter for regret; but the most subtle of dramatists should have better understood the most subtle of animals, and have forborne to rank her as man's enemy because she will not be man's dupe. Rather let us turn back and learn our lesson from Montaigne, serenely playing with his cat as friend to friend, for thus, and thus only, shall we enjoy the sweets of her companionship. If we want an animal to prance on its hind legs, and, with the over-faithful Tylo, cry out 'little god, little god,' at every blundering step we take; if we are so constituted that we feel the need of being worshipped by something or somebody, we must feed our vanity as best we can with the society of dogs and men. The grocer's cat, enthroned on the grocer's starch-box, is no fitting friend for us.

As a matter of fact, all cats and kittens, whether royal Persians or of the lowliest estate, resent patronage, jocoseness (which they rightly hold to be in bad taste), and demonstrative affection — those lavish embraces which lack delicacy and reserve. This last prejudice they carry sometimes to the verge of unkindness, eluding the caresses of their friends, and wounding the spirits of those who love them best. The little eight-year-old English girl who composed the following lines when smarting from unrequited affection, had learned pretty much all there is to know concerning the capricious nature of cats:

> 'Oh, Selima shuns my kisses!
> Oh, Selima hates her missus!
> I never did meet
> With a cat so sweet,
> Or a cat so cruel as this is.'

In such an instance I am disposed to think that Selima's coldness was ill-judged. No discriminating cat would have shunned the kisses of such an enlightened little girl. But I confess to the pleasure with which I have watched other Selimas extricate themselves from well-meant but vulgar familiarities. I once saw a small black-and-white kitten playing with a judge, who, not unnaturally, conceived that he was playing with the kitten. For a while all went well. The kitten pranced and paddled, fixed her gleaming eyes upon the great man's smirking countenance, and pursued his knotted handkerchief so swiftly that she tumbled head over heels, giddy with her own rapid evolutions. Then the judge, being but human, and ignorant of the wide gap which lies between a cat's standard of good taste and the lenient standard of the courtroom, ventured upon one of those doubtful pleasantries which a few cats permit to privileged friends, but which none of the race ever endure from strangers. He lifted the kitten by the tail until only her forepaws touched the rug, which she clutched desperately, uttering a loud protesting mew. She looked so droll in her helplessness and wrath that several members of the household (her own household, which should have known better) laughed outright — a shameful thing to do.

Here was a social crisis. A little cat of manifestly humble origin, with only an innate sense of propriety to oppose to a coarse-minded magistrate, and a circle of mocking friends. The judge, imperturbably obtuse, dropped the kitten on the rug, and prepared to resume their former friendly relations. The kitten did not run away, she did not even walk away; that would have been an admission of defeat. She sat down very slowly, as if first searching for a particular spot in the intricate pattern of the rug, turned her back upon her former playmate, faced her false friends, and tucked her outraged tail carefully out of sight. Her aspect was that of a cat alone in a desert land, brooding over the mystery of her nine lives. In vain the handkerchief was trailed seductively past her little nose, in vain her contrite family spoke words of sweetness and repentance. She appeared as aloof from her surroundings as if she had been wafted to Arabia; and presently began to wash her face conscientiously and methodically, with the air of one who finds solitude better than the companionship of fools. Only when the judge had put his silly handkerchief into his pocket, and had strolled into the library under the pretence of hunting for a book which he had never left there, did the kitten close her eyes, lower her obdurate little head, and purr herself tranquilly to sleep.

A few years afterwards I was permitted to witness another silent combat, another signal victory. This time the cat was, I grieve to say, a member of a troupe of performing animals, exhibited at the Folies-Bergère in Paris. Her fellow actors, poodles and monkeys, played their parts with relish and a sense of fun. The cat, a thing apart, condescended to leap twice through a hoop, and to balance herself very prettily on a large rubber ball. She then retired to the top of a ladder, made a deft and modest toilet, and composed herself for slumber. Twice the trainer spoke to her persuasively, but she paid no heed, and evinced no further interest in him nor in his entertainment. Her time for condescension was past.

The next day I commented on the cat's behaviour to some friends who had also been to the Folies-Bergère on different nights. 'But,' said the first friend, 'the evening I went, that cat did wonderful things; came down the lad-

der on her ball, played the fiddle, and stood on her head.'
'Really,' said the second friend. 'Well, the night *I*
went, she did nothing at all except cuff one of the monkeys
that annoyed her. She just sat on the ladder, and watched
the performance. I presumed she was there by way of de-
coration.'

All honour to the cat, who, when her little body is en-
slaved, can still preserve the freedom of her soul. The dogs
and the monkeys obeyed their master; but the cat, like
Montaigne's happier pussy long ago, had 'her time to begin or to refuse,' and showman and audience waited upon
her will.

THE END